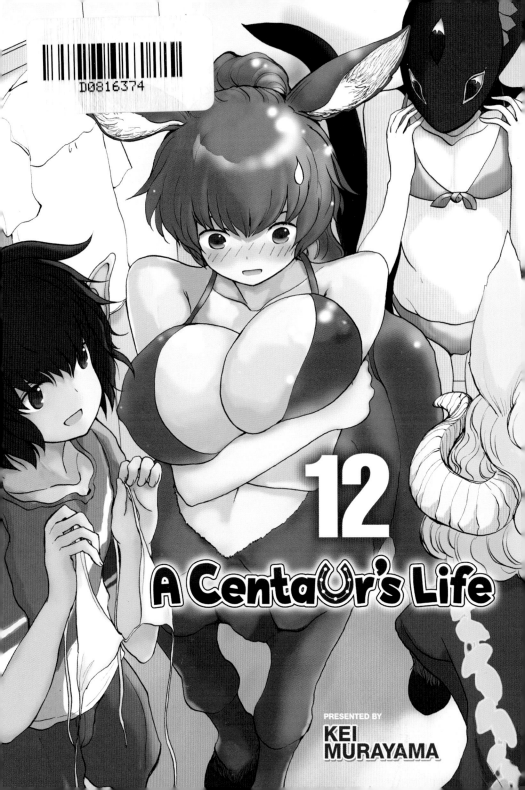

12

A Centaur's Life

PRESENTED BY
KEI MURAYAMA

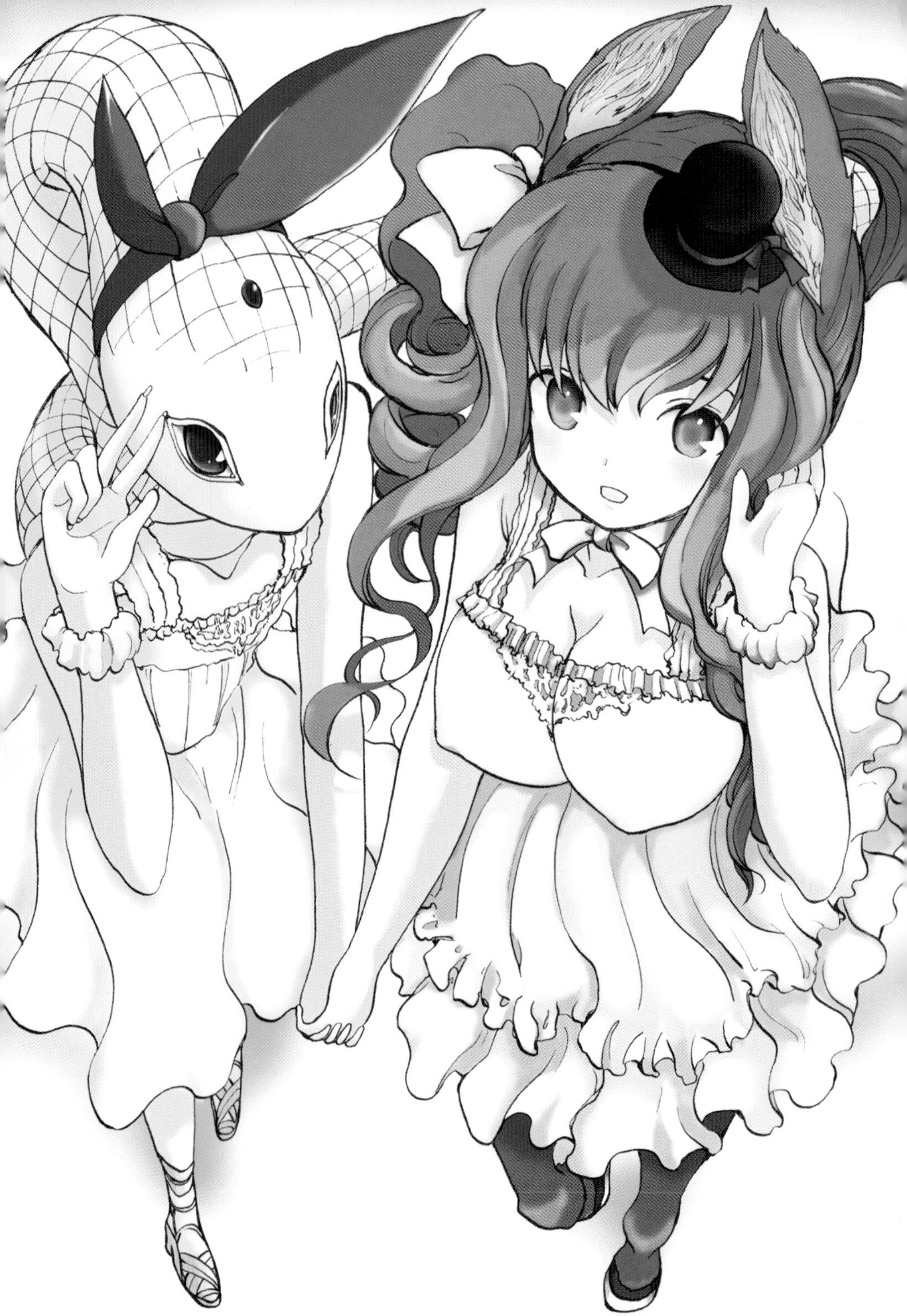

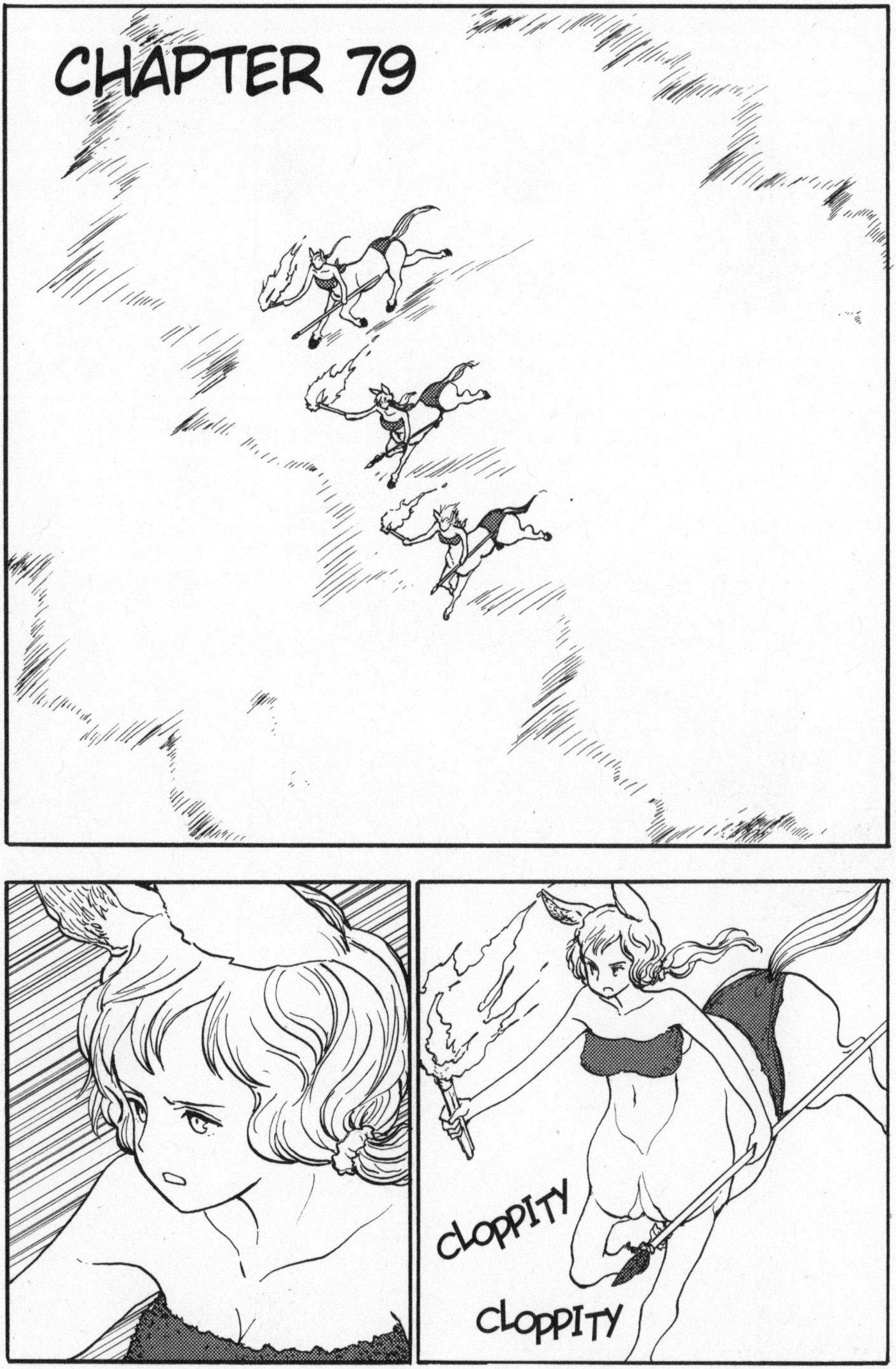
CHAPTER 79
CLOPPITY
CLOPPITY

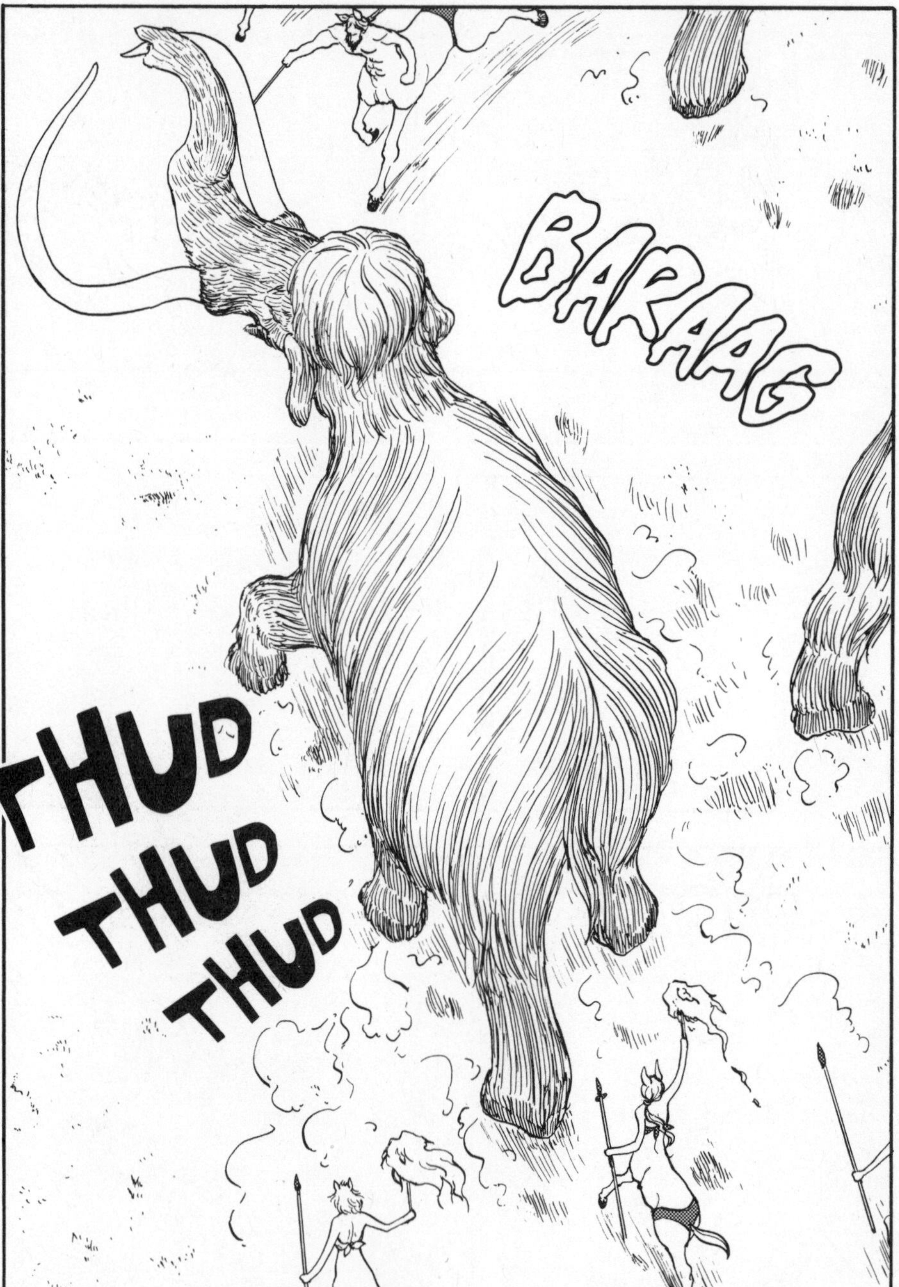
BARAAG
THUD
THUD
THUD

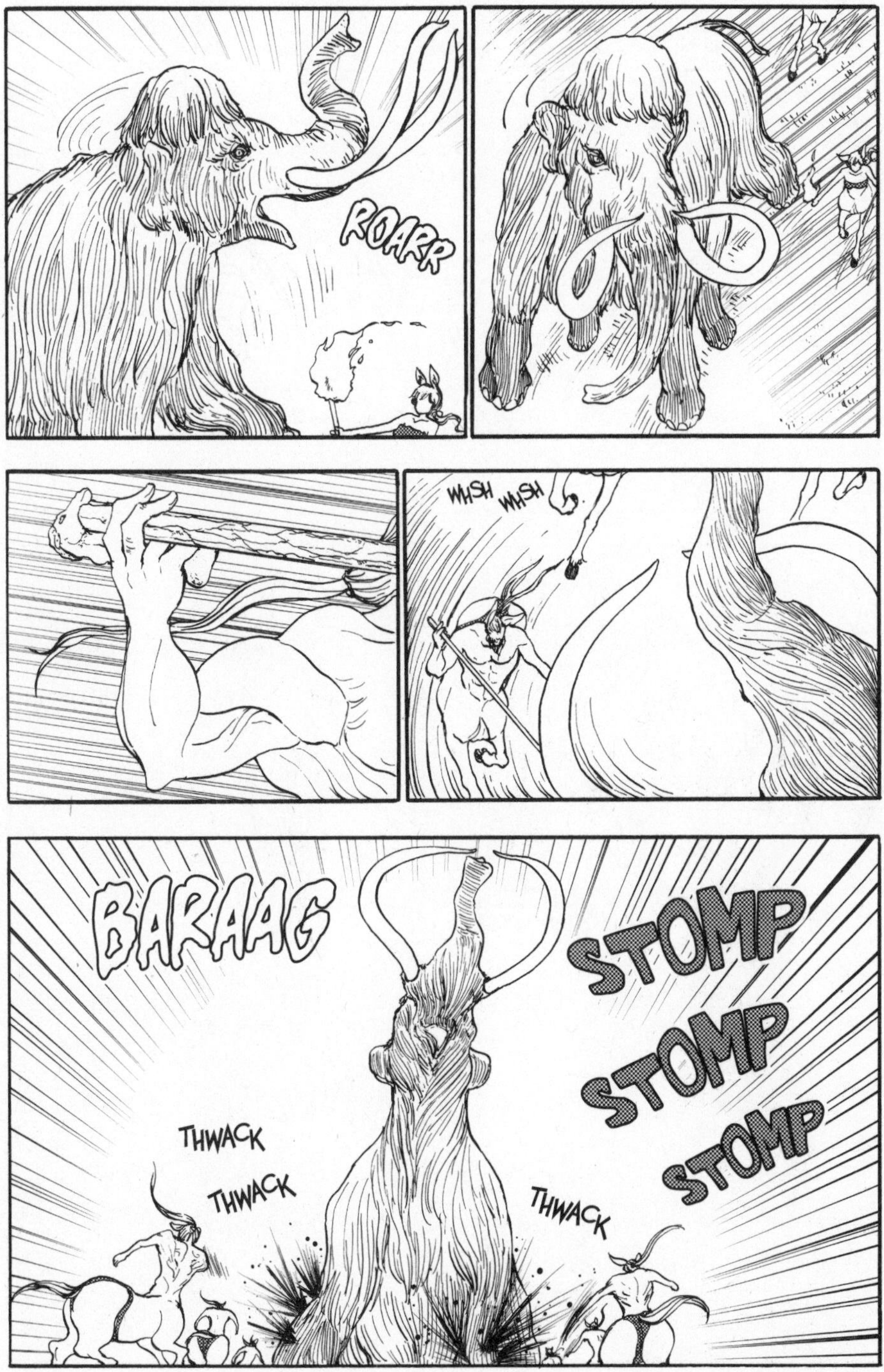
ROARR
WHSH
WHSH
STOMP
STOMP
STOMP
BARAAG
THWACK
THWACK
THWACK

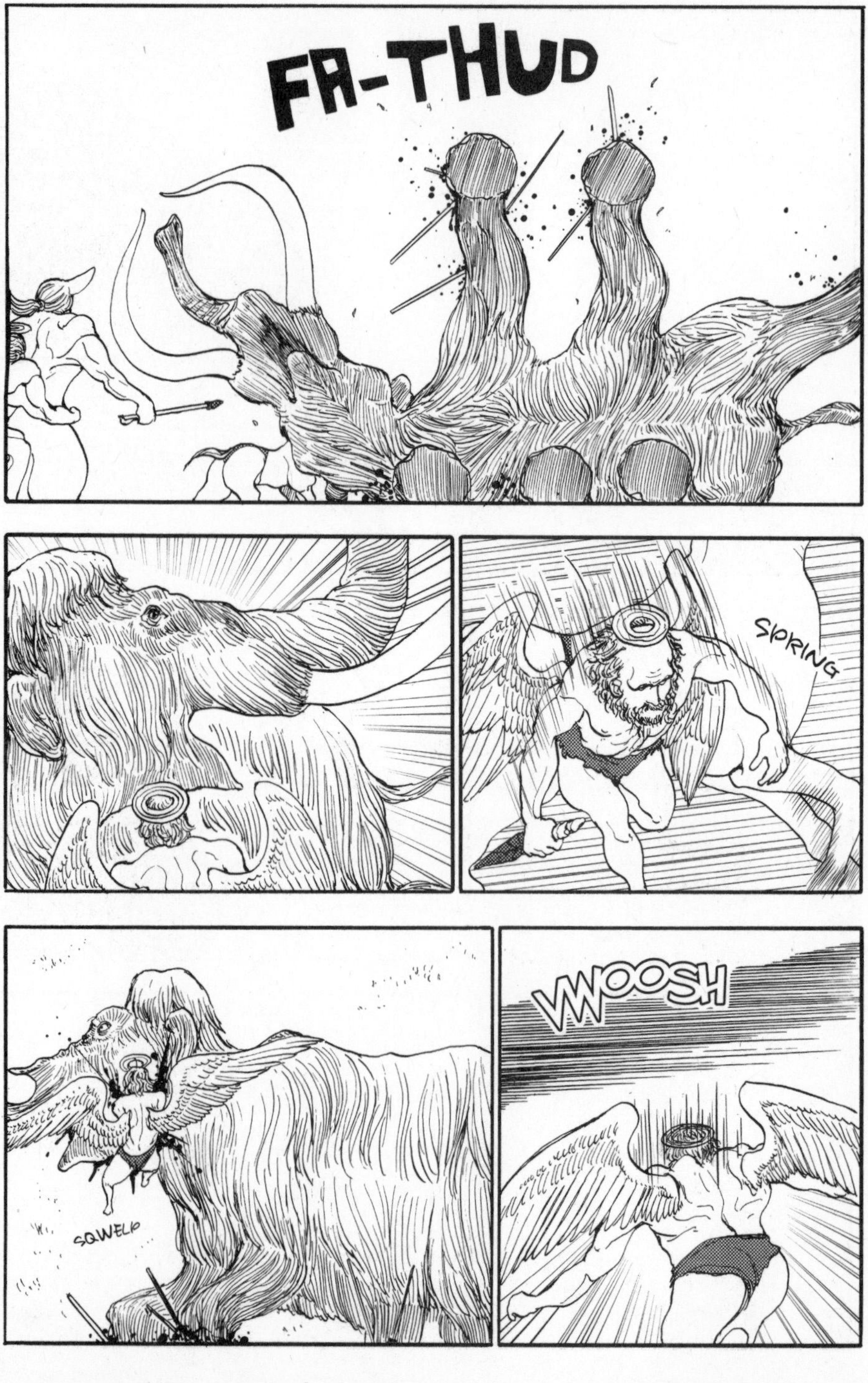
FA-THUD
SPRING
VWOOSH
SQWELK

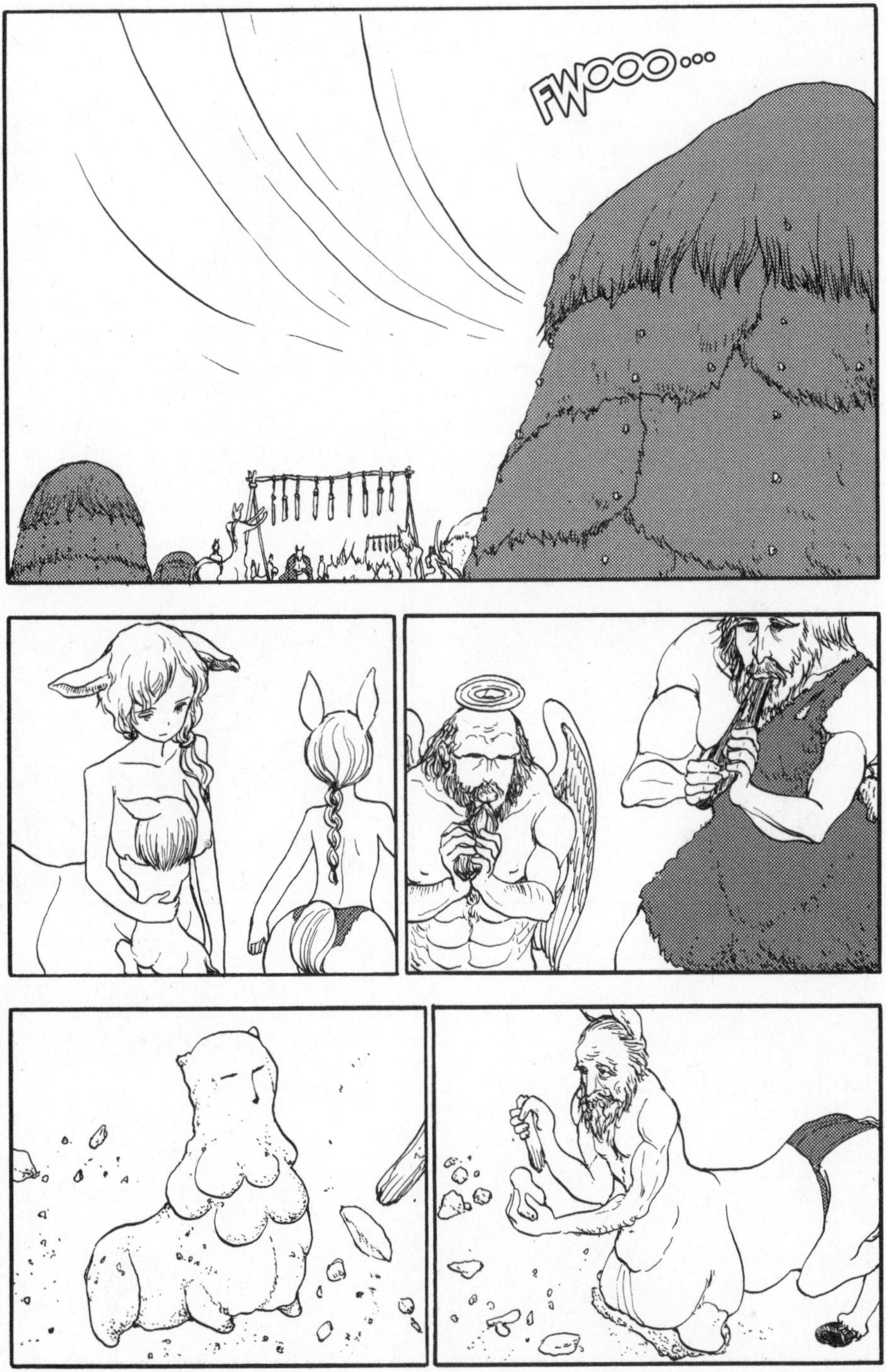
FWOOO...

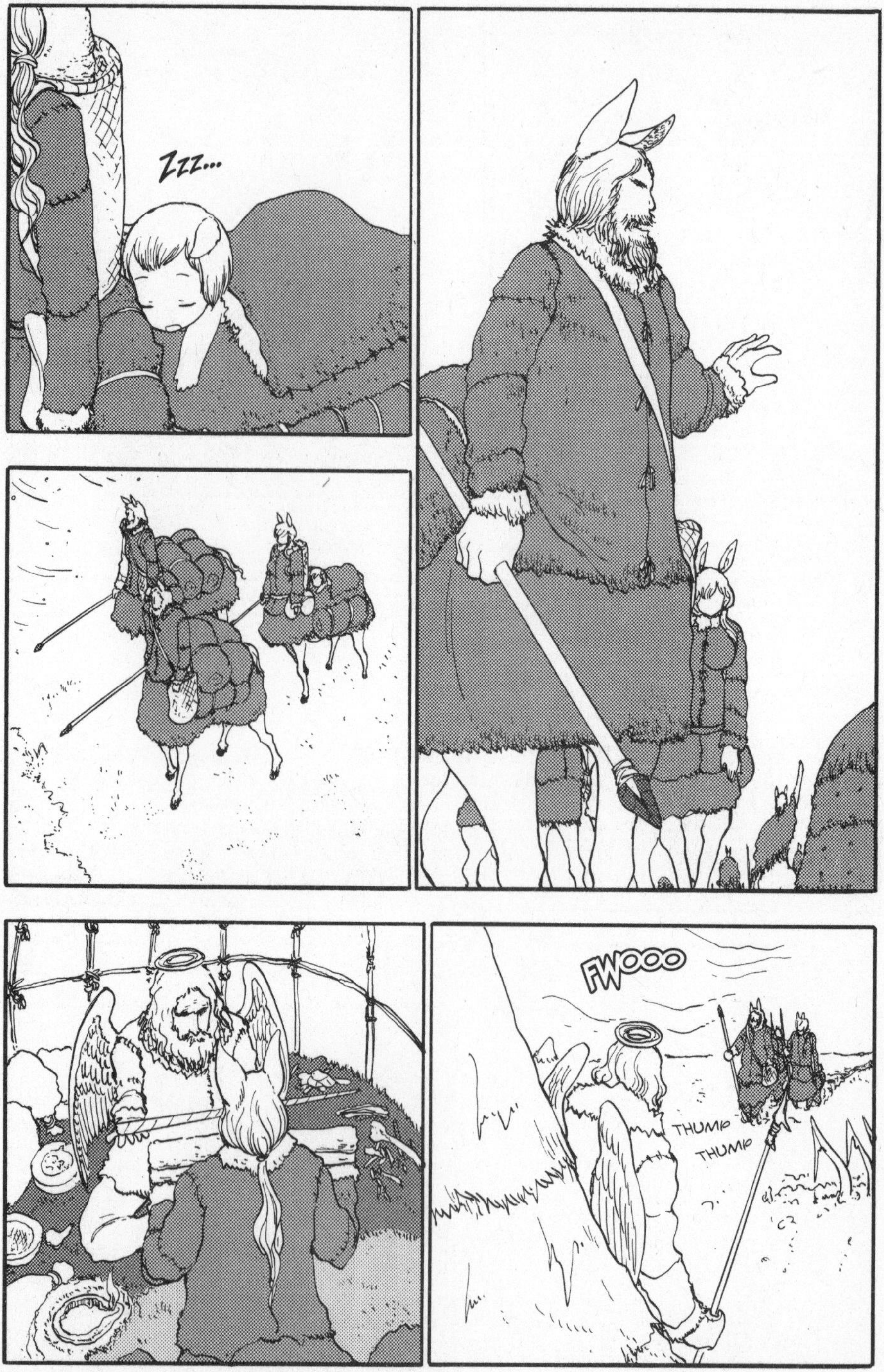
Zzz...
FWOOO
THUMP
THUMP

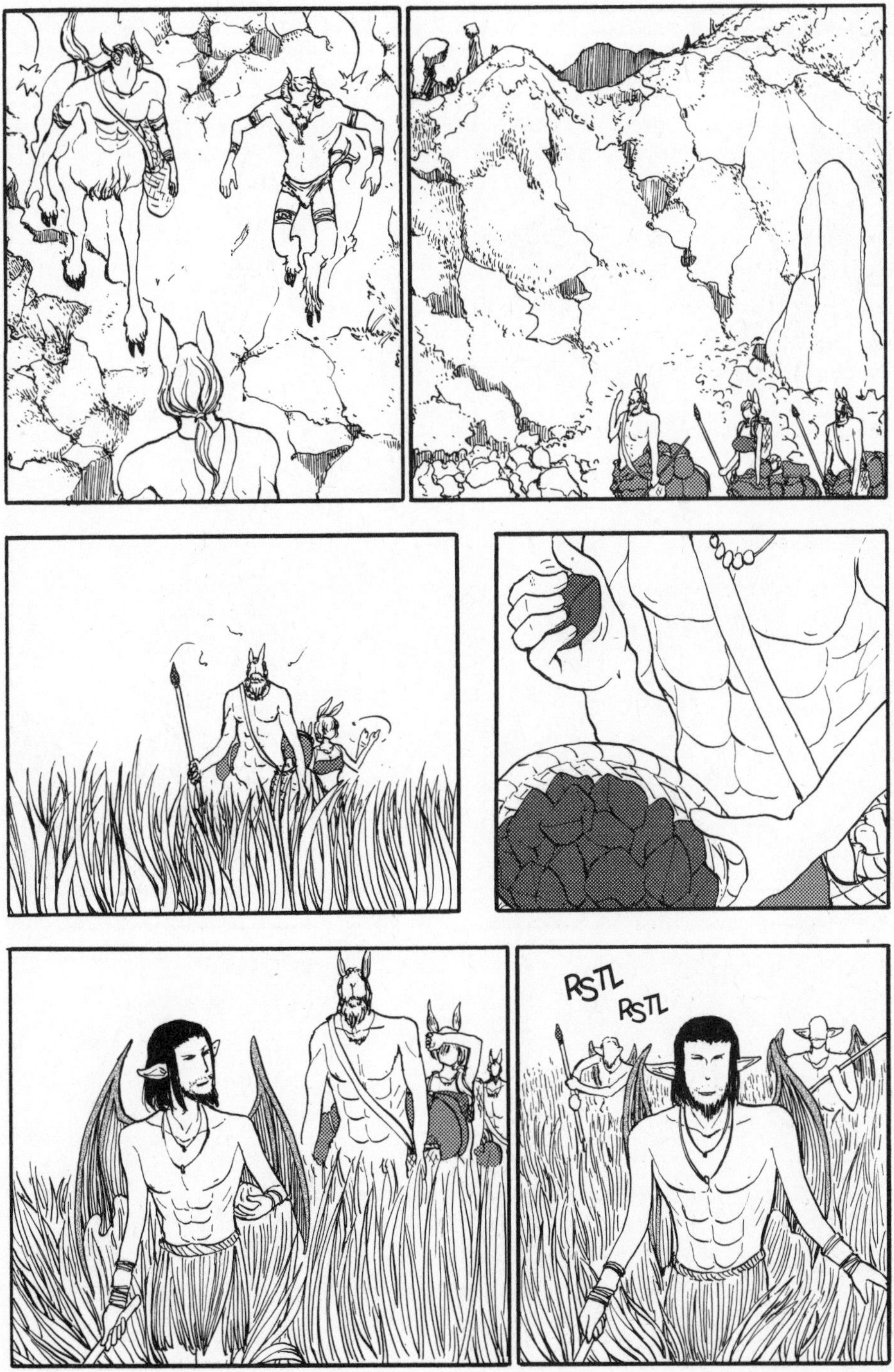
RSTL
RSTL

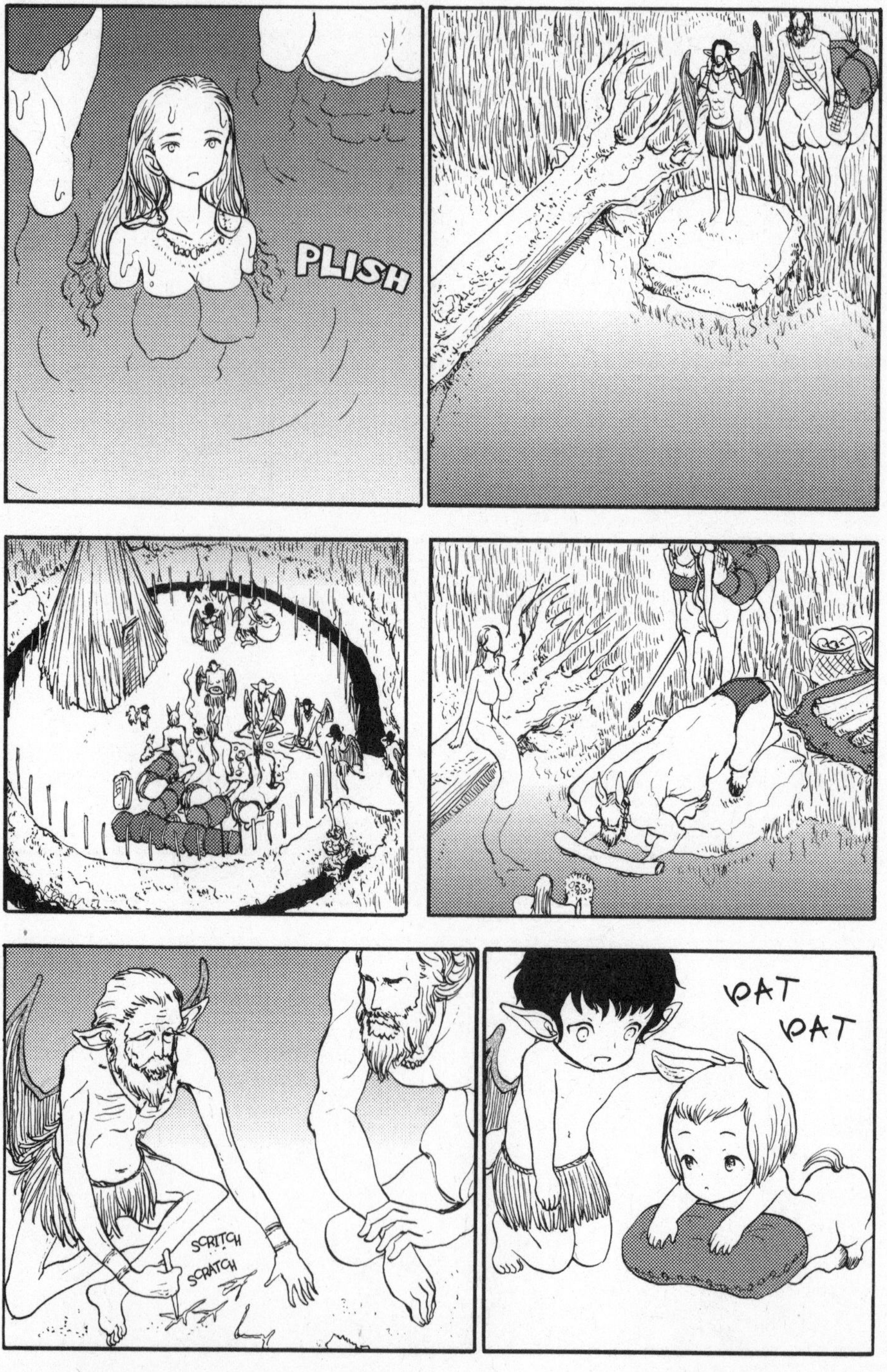
PLISH
PAT PAT
SCRITCH SCRATCH

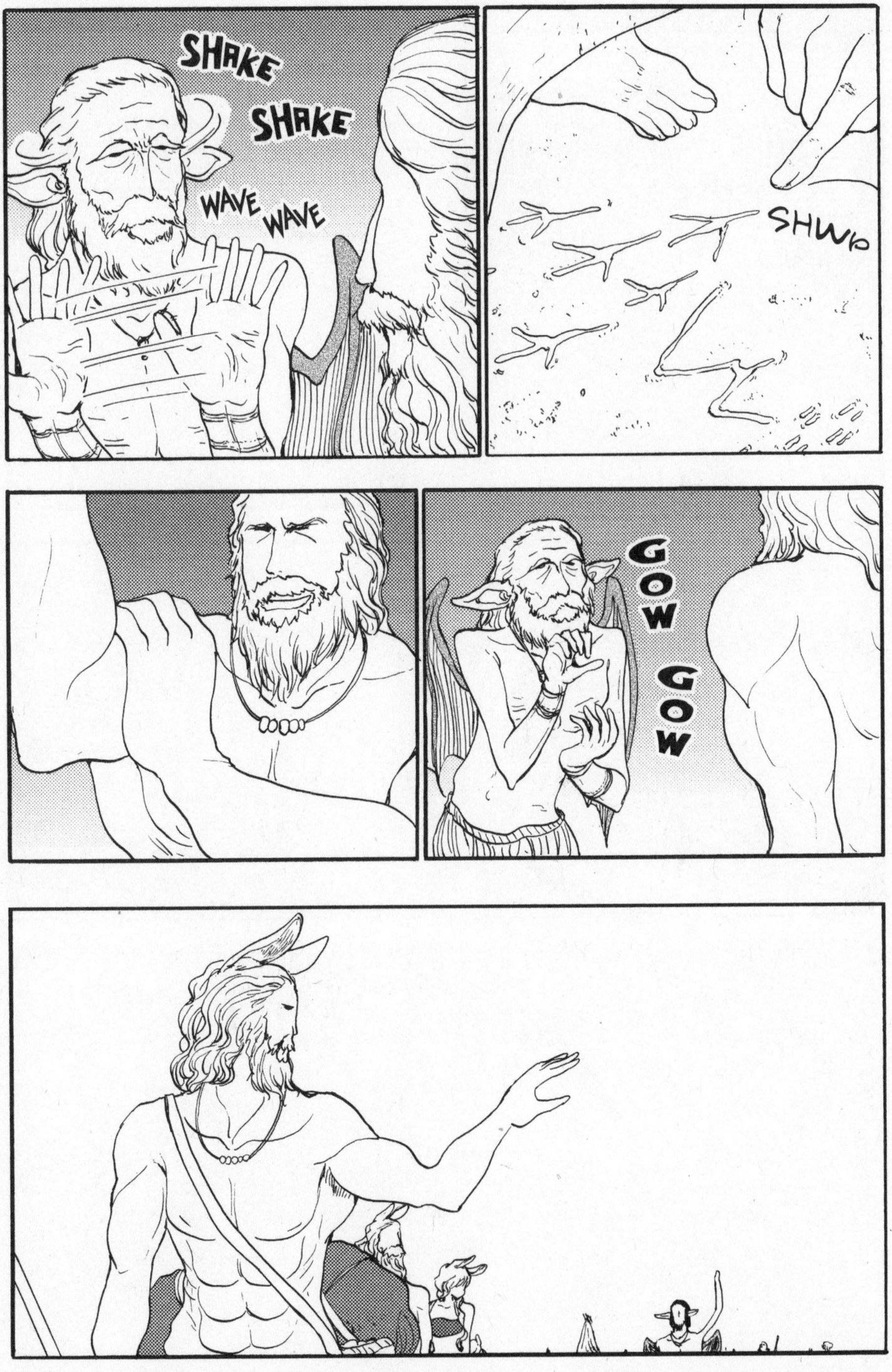
SHWP
SHAKE
SHAKE
WAVE
WAVE
GOW
GOW
GOW

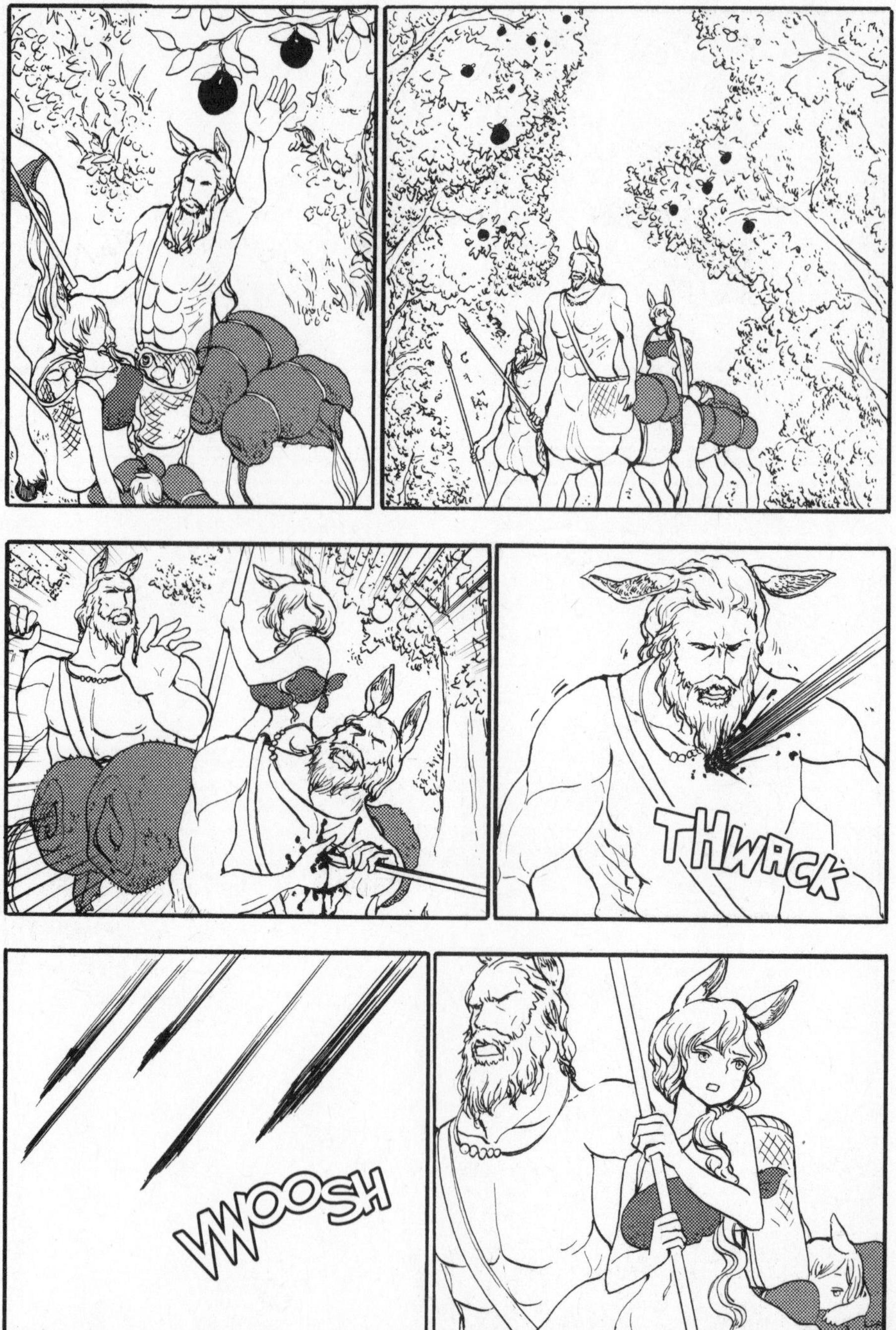
THWACK
WOOSH

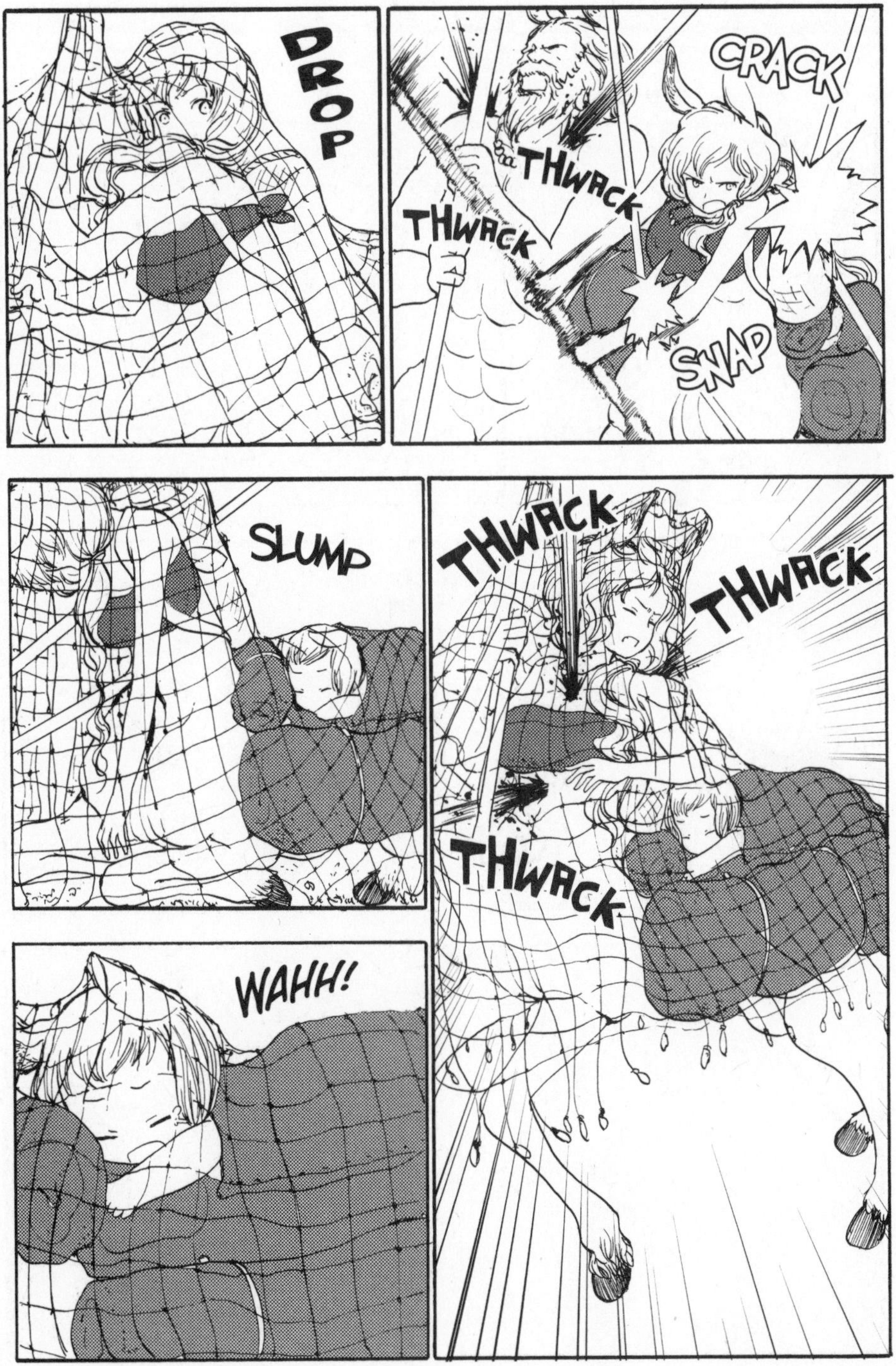
CRACK
THWACK
THWACK
SNAP
DROP
THWACK
THWACK
THWACK
SLUMP
WAHH!

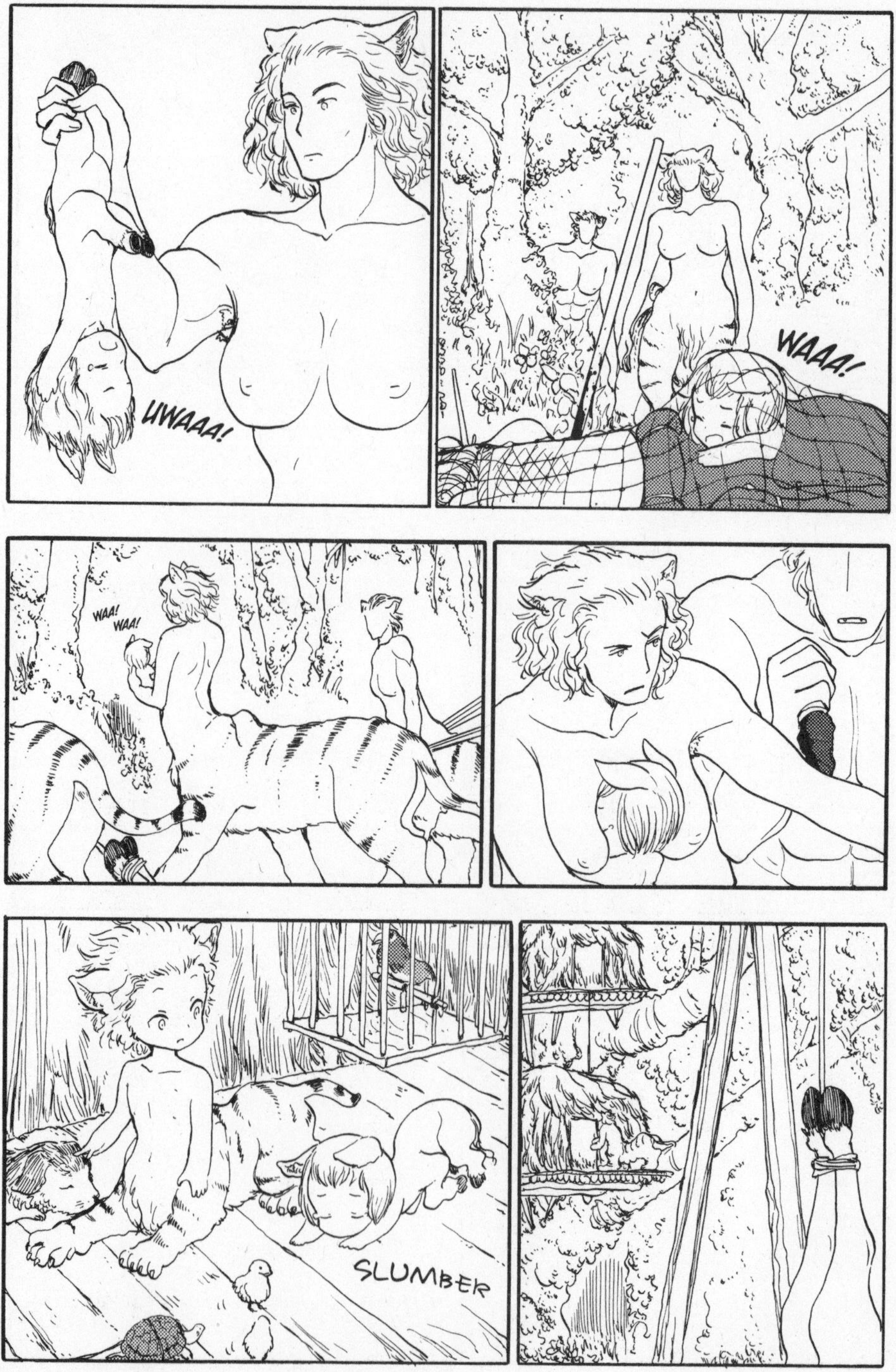
WAAA!
UWAAA!
WAA! WAA!
SLUMBER

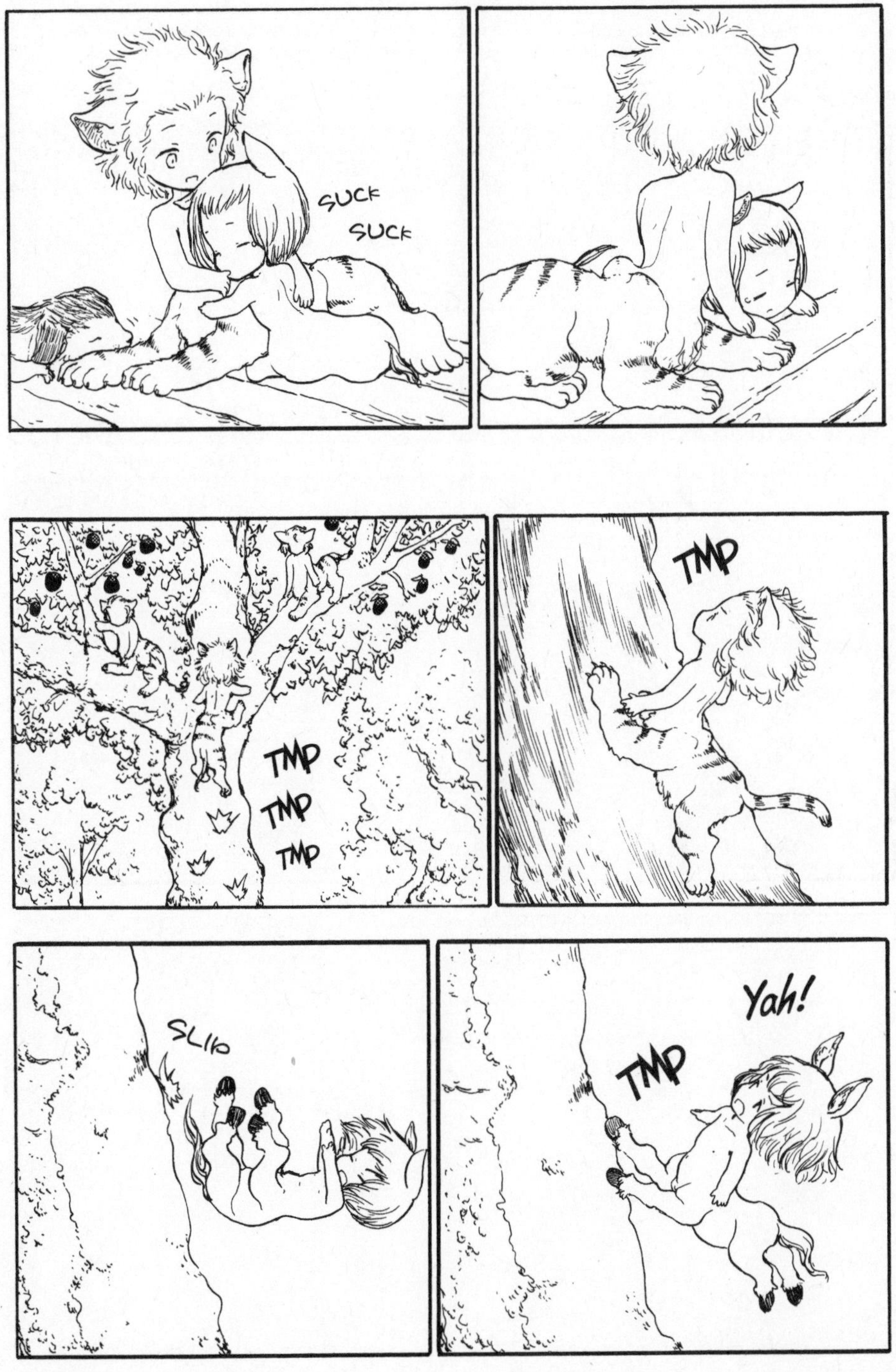
SUCK
SUCK
TMP
TMP
TMP
TMP
Yah!
TMP
SLIP

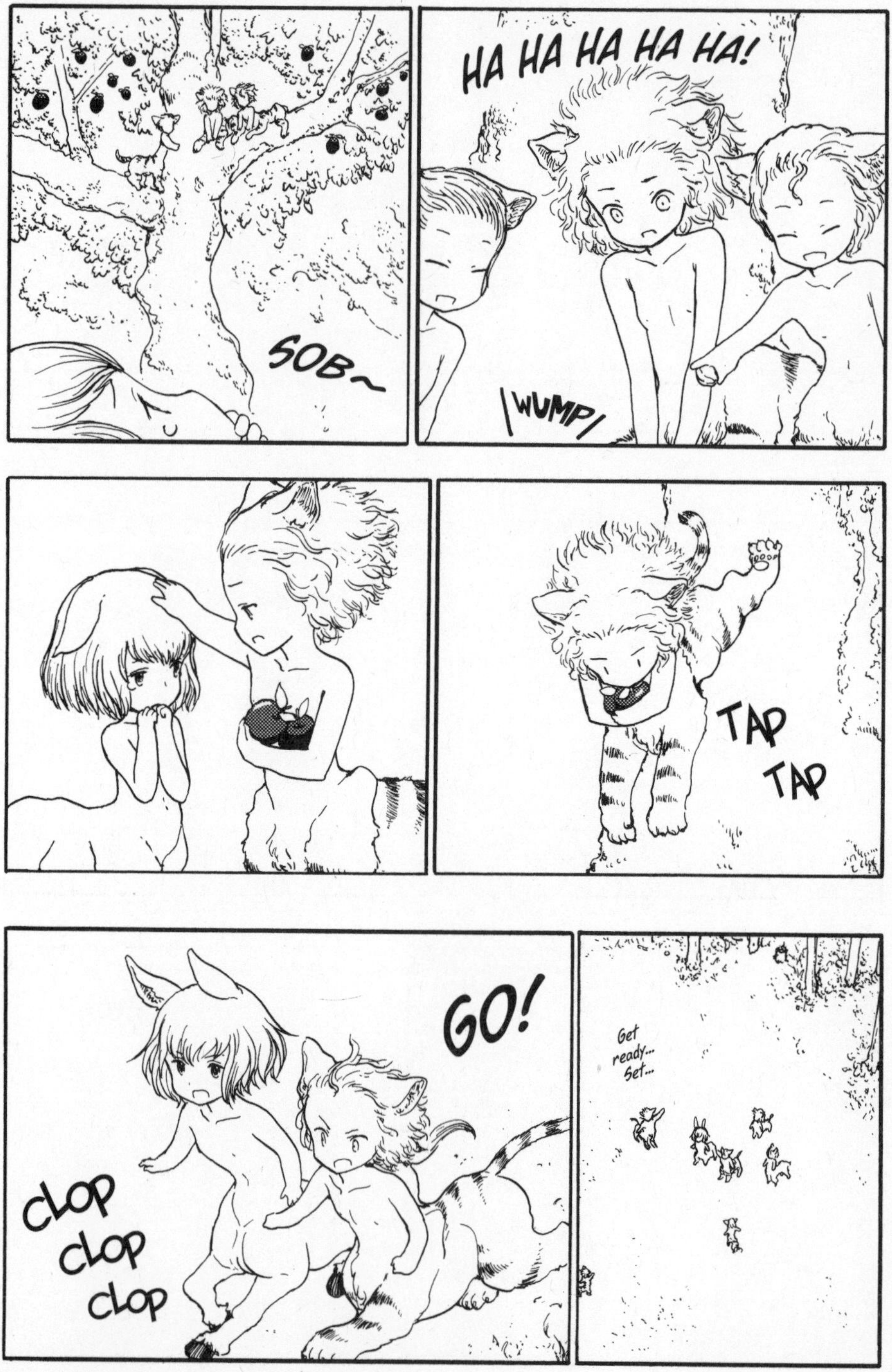
HA HA HA HA HA!
WUMP
SOB~
TAP
TAP
Get ready... Set...
GO!
CLOP
CLOP
CLOP

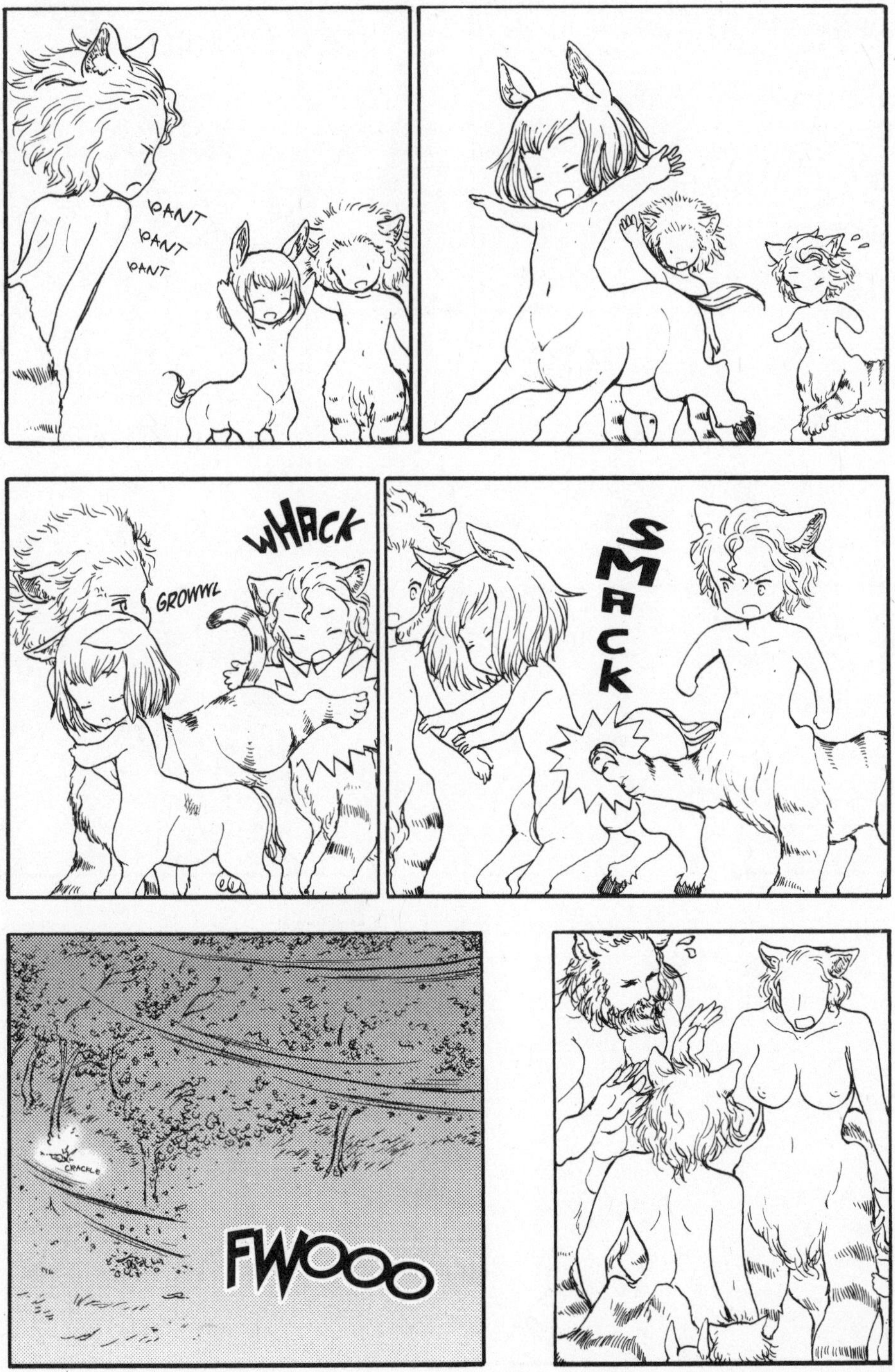
PANT
PANT
PANT
SMACK
WHACK
GROWWL
CRACKLE
FWOOO

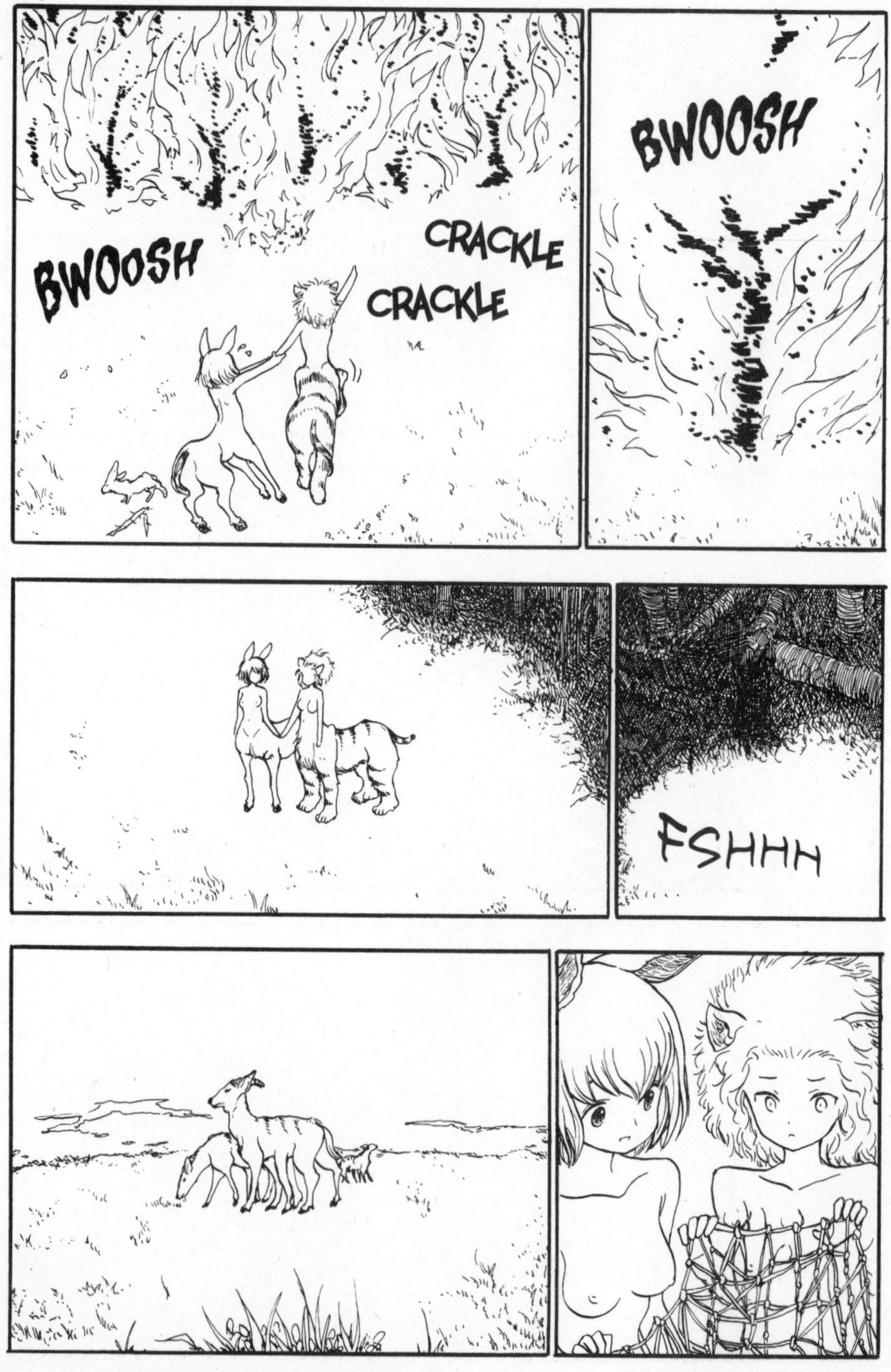
BWOOSH
CRACKLE
CRACKLE
BWOOSH
FSHHH

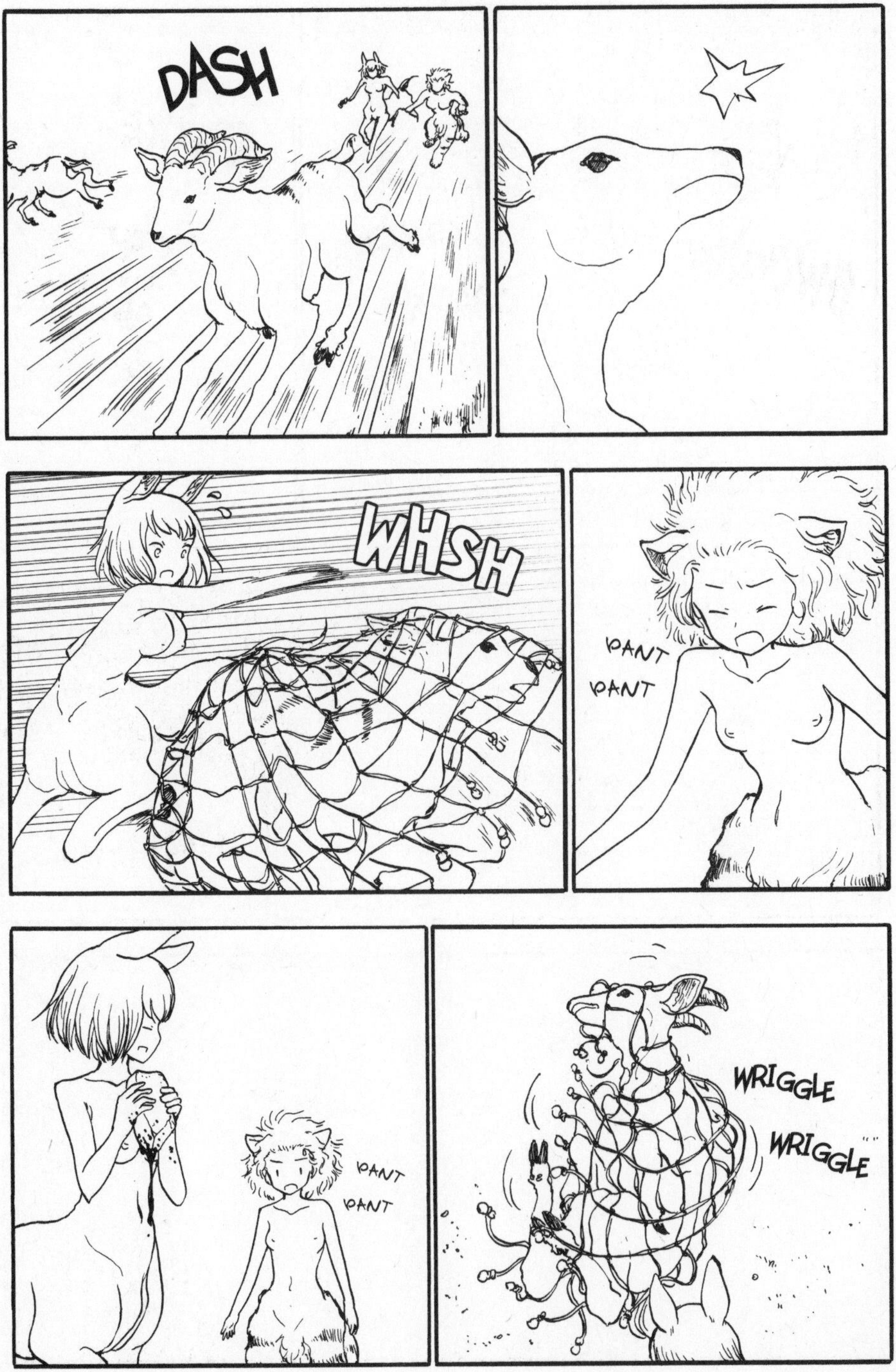
DASH
PANT
PANT
WHSH
WRIGGLE
WRIGGLE
PANT
PANT

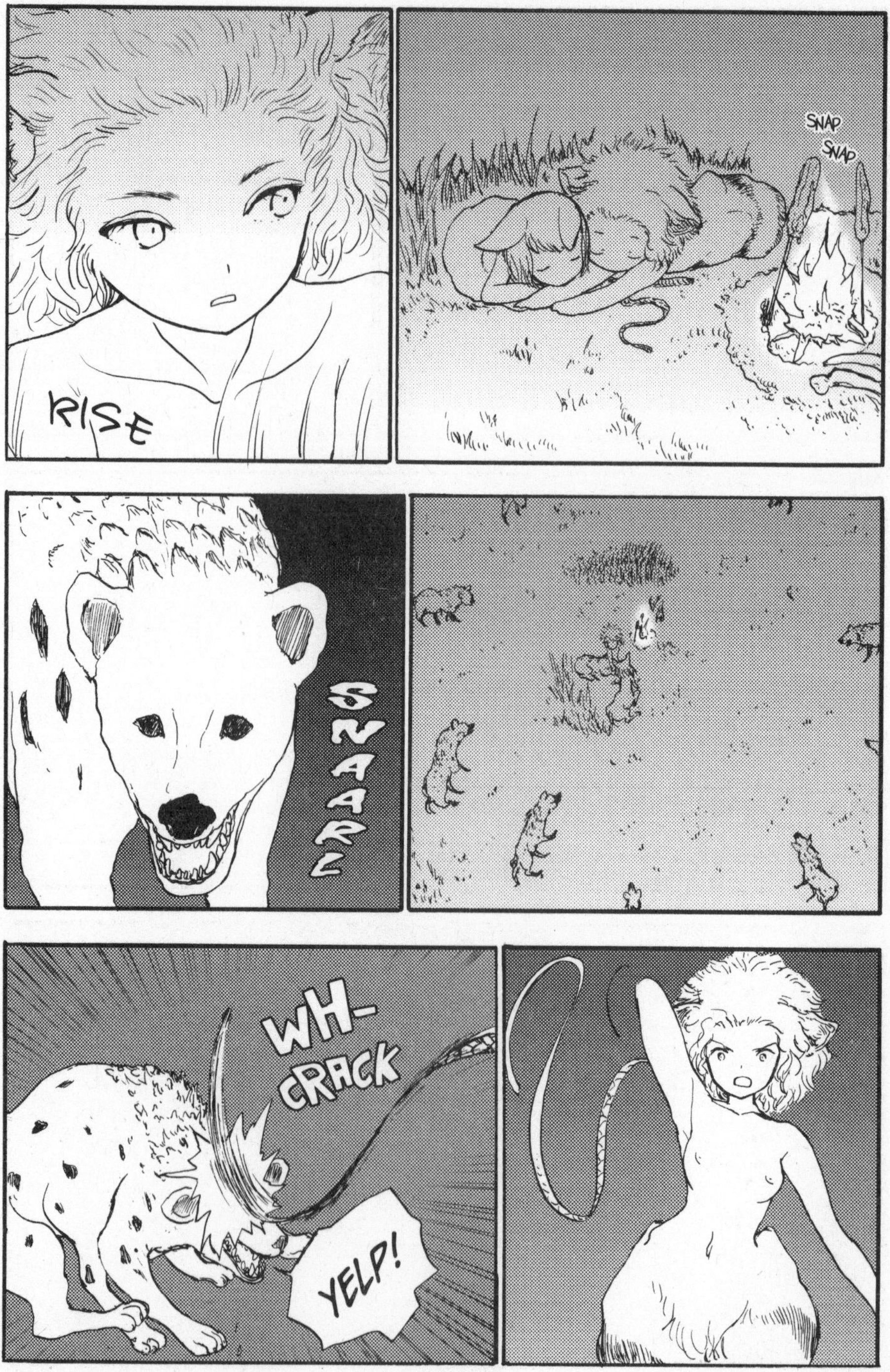
SNAP
SNAP
RISE
SNAARL
WH-
CRACK
YELP!

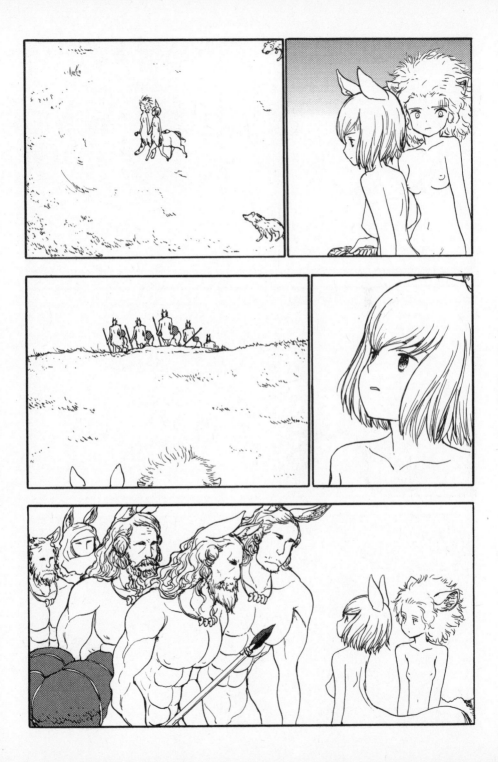

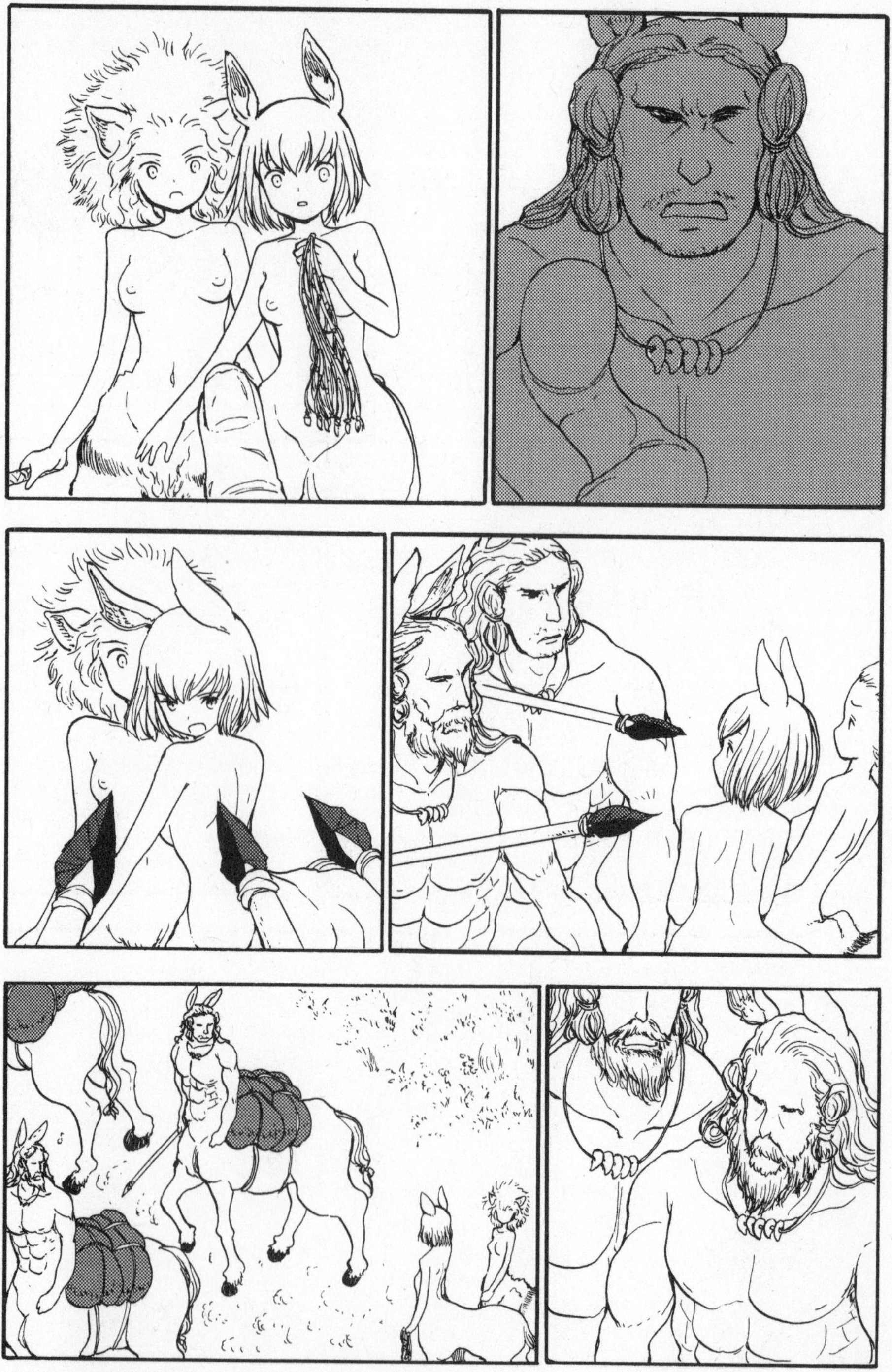

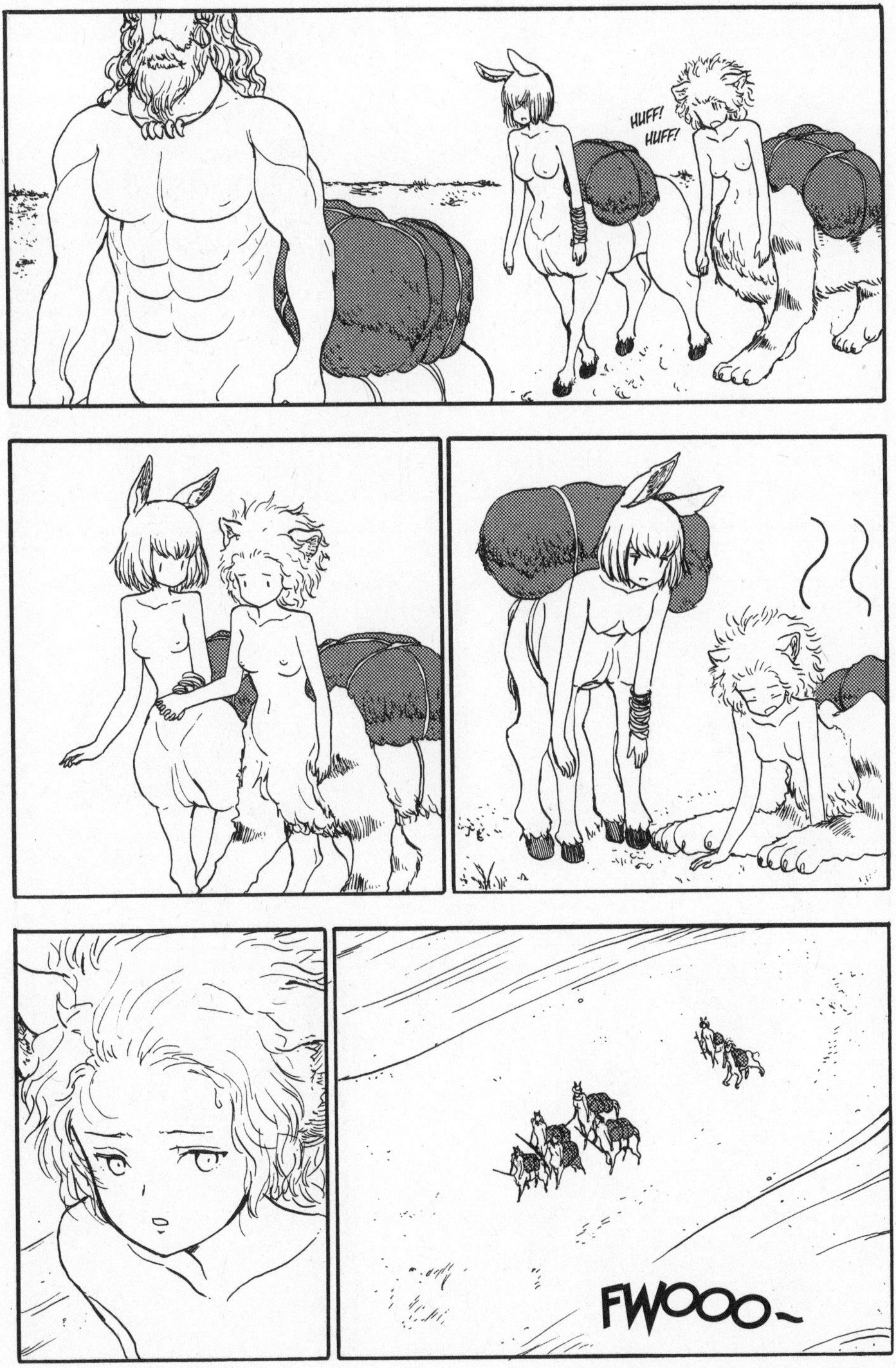
HUFF! HUFF!
FWOOO~

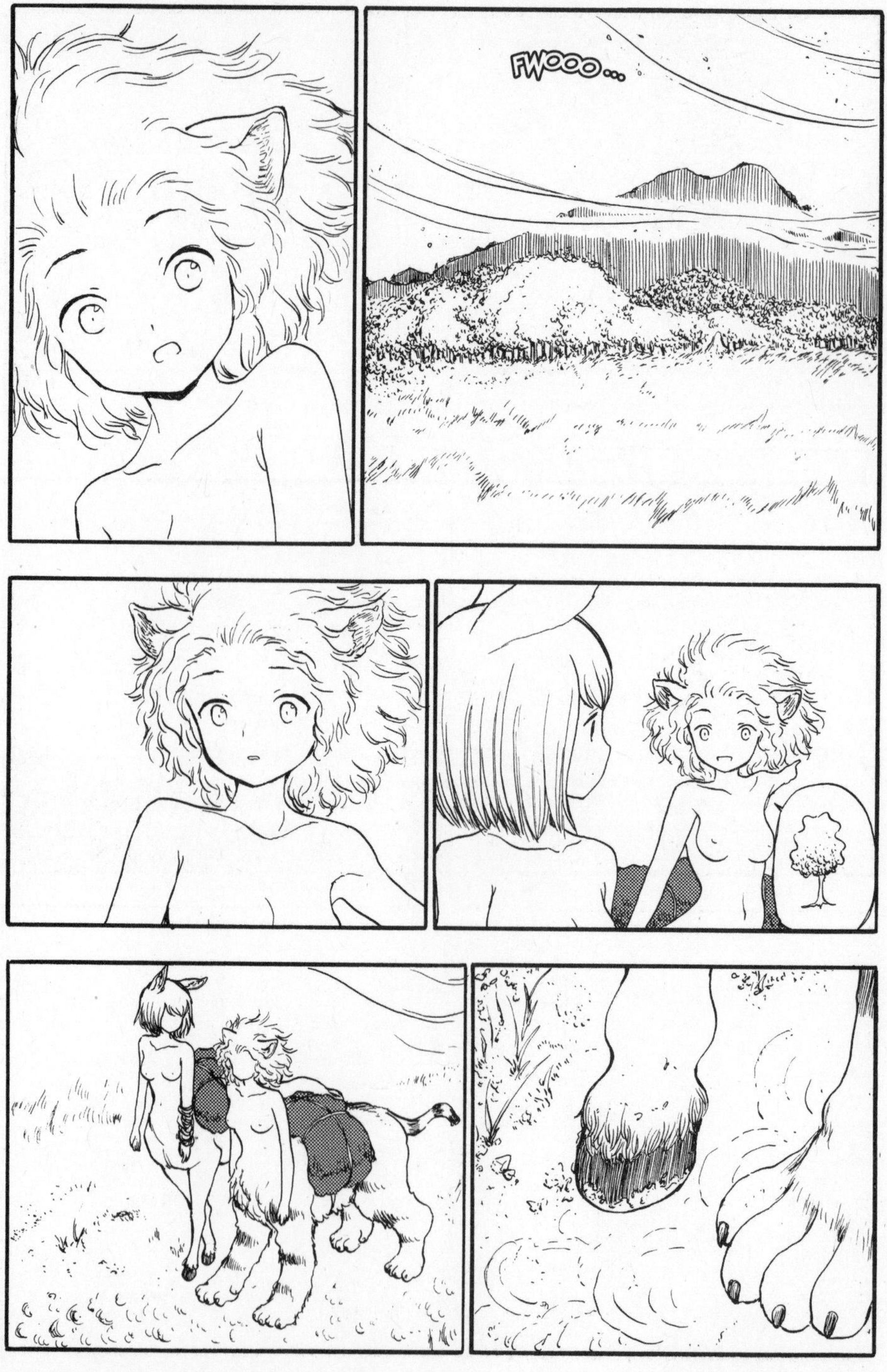
FWOOO...

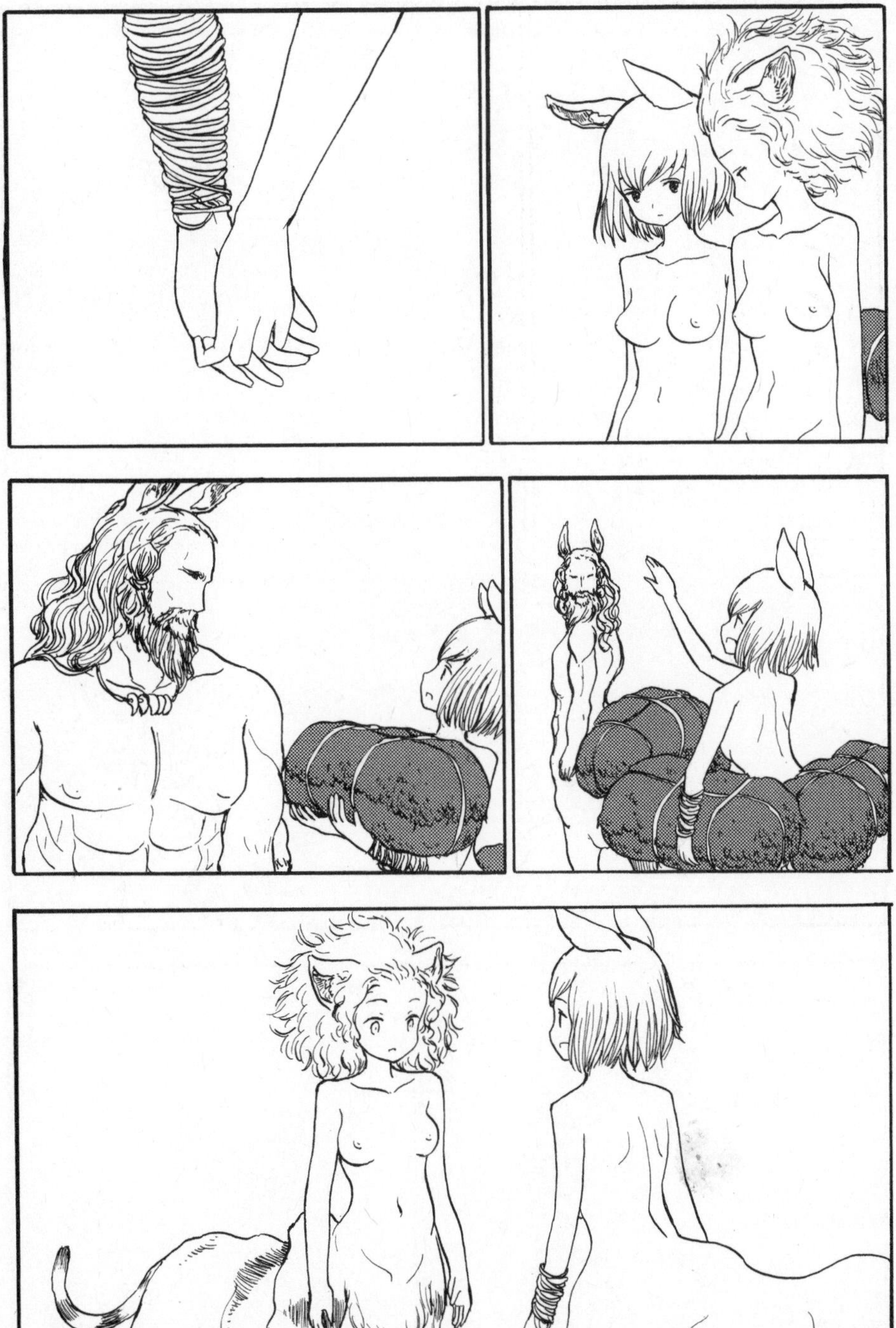

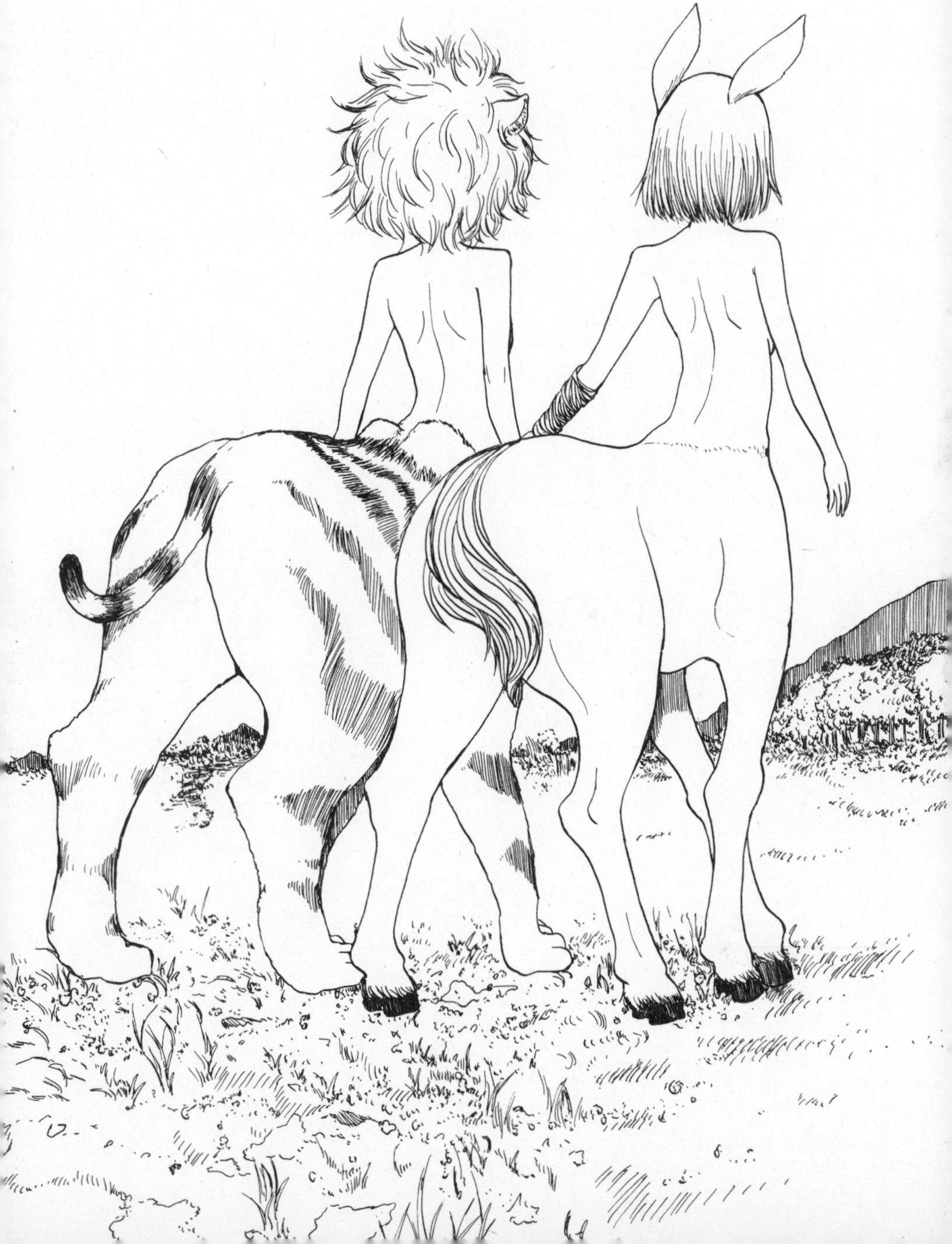

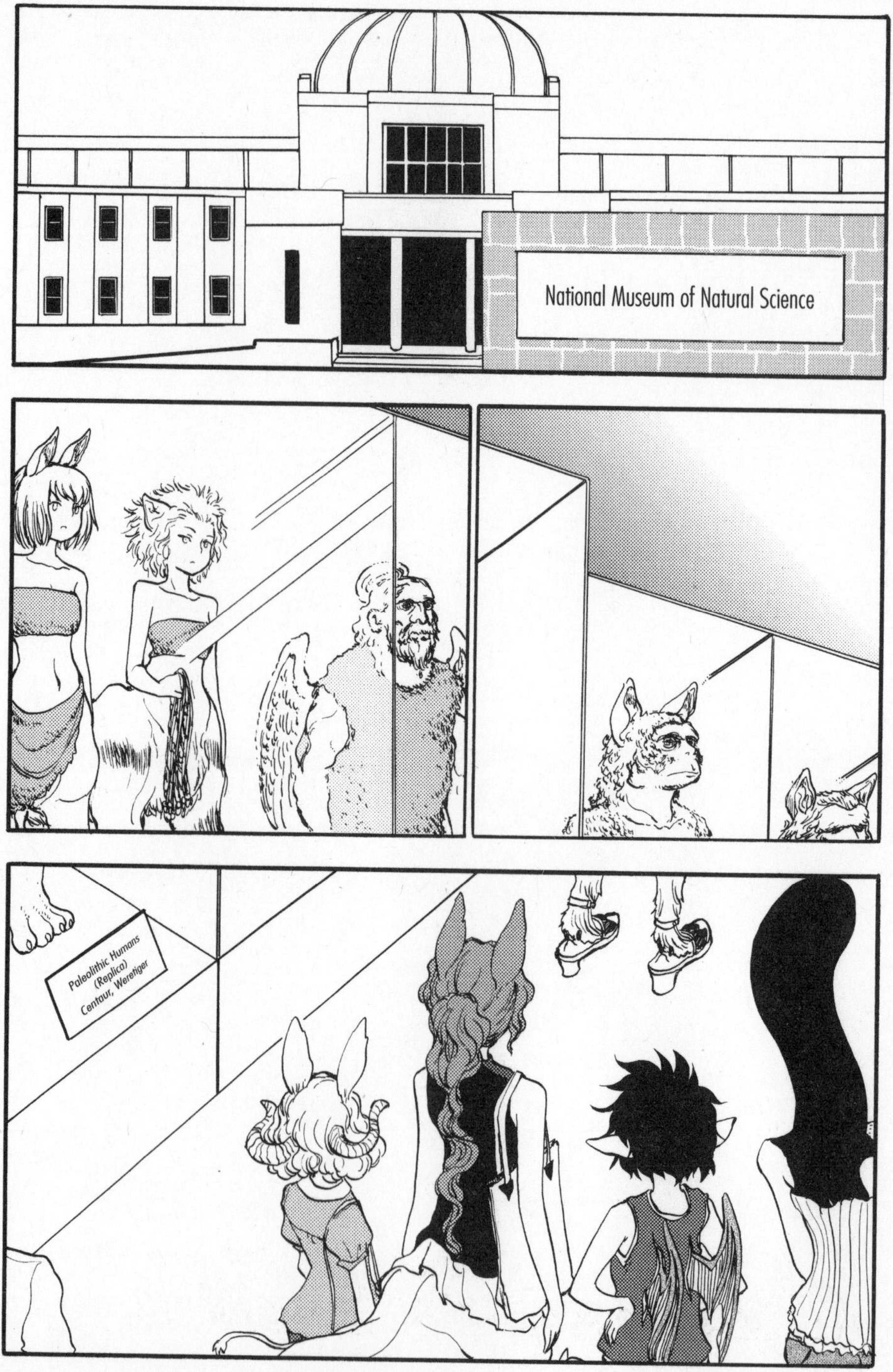
National Museum of Natural Science
Paleolithic Humans
(Replica)
Centaur, Weretiger

A Centaur's Life

UNDERSTANDING AMPHIBIANFOLK PART 1: AMPHIBIANFOLK AS A PEOPLE

AMPHIBIANFOLK ARE A NON-MAMMALIAN INTELLIGENT RACE THAT PRIMARILY LIVE NEAR RIVER A IN SOUTH AMERICA. THEY'VE BEEN COMMONLY CALLED FROGFOLK IN THE PAST, BUT ARE NOW THOUGHT TO BE CLOSER TO AN EXTINCT SUBCLASS OF PRIMITIVE AMPHIBIANS THAN TO MEMBERS OF ORDER ANURA (FROGS AND TOADS) OR ORDER URODELA (SALAMANDERS AND NEWTS). ALTHOUGH MOST AMPHIBIAN-FOLK ARE BELIEVED TO SUBSIST BY FISHING AND HUNTING, SOME HAVE BEEN SEEN ENTERTAINING TOURISTS BY PER-FORMING FOLK DANCES OR SELLING SOUVENIRS IN EASTERN TAWANTINSUYU. A SMALL NUMBER HAVE ESTABLISHED THEMSELVES IN MAMMALIAN COMMUNITIES. HOWEVER, THE AMPHIBIANFOLK GUERRILLA ORGANIZATION KNOWN AS CTHULCTHUL* IS GARNERING A GREAT DEAL OF MAMMALIAN ATTENTION WITH THEIR RECENT ACTIVITIES; NOW THAT THE CTHULCTHUL HAVE OCCUPIED THE UPSTREAM AREA OF RIVER A, THEY POSE A THREAT TO A MAMMALIAN NATION.

*NOTE: Cthulcthul means "Horizon of God" in the Gloloctl dialect of the amphibianfolk language.

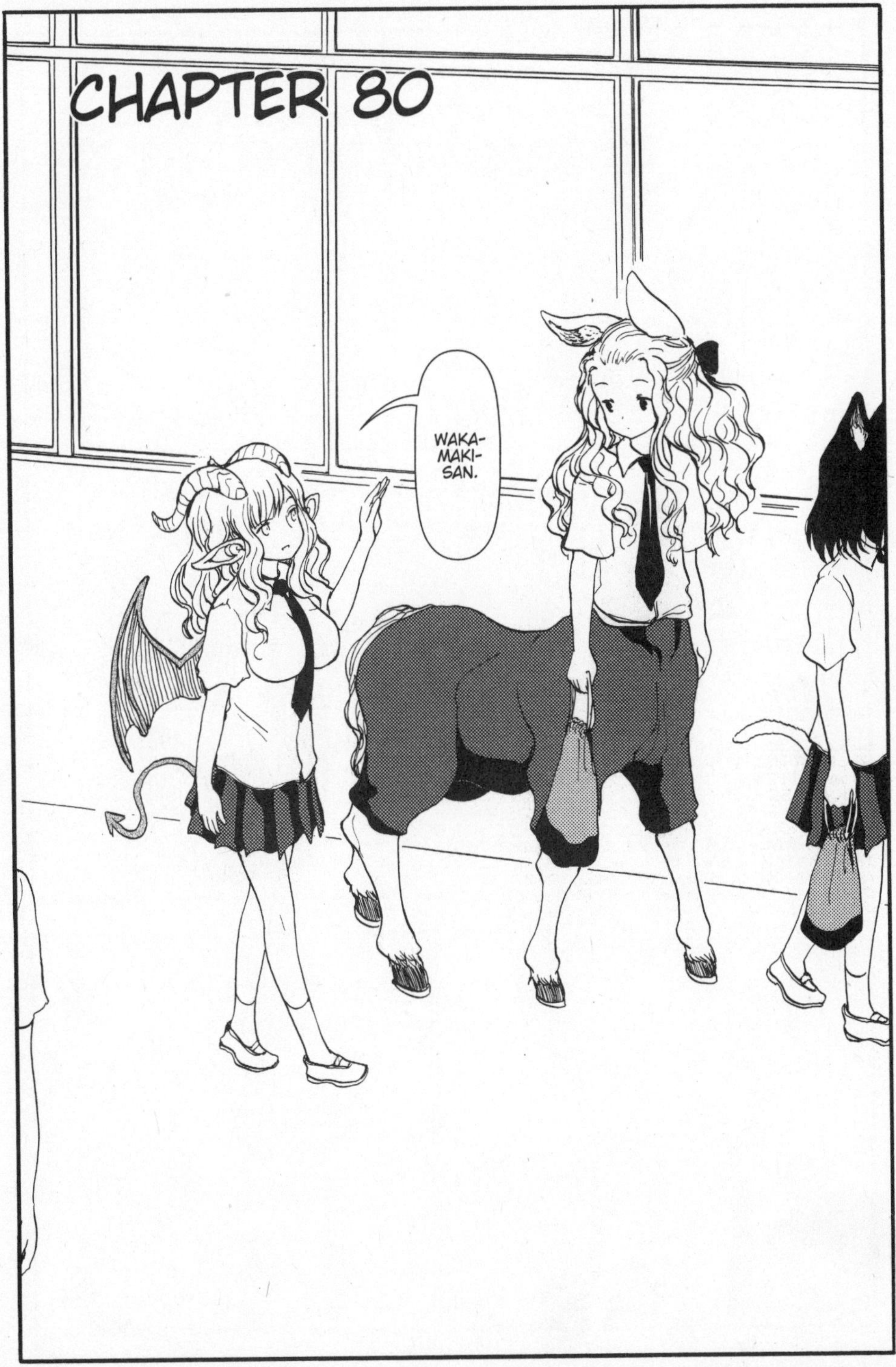
CHAPTER 80
WAKA-MAKI-SAN.

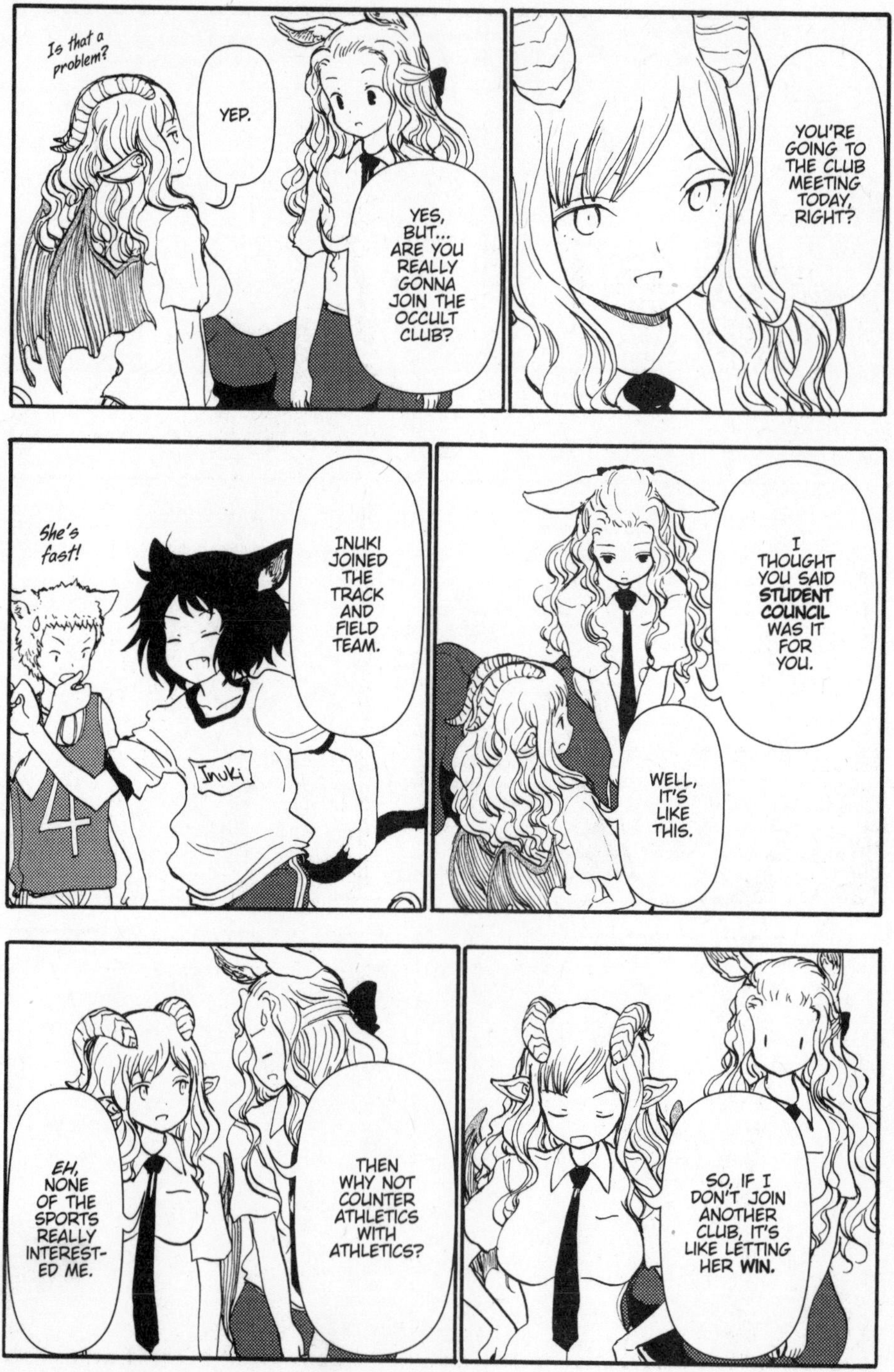
YOU'RE GOING TO THE CLUB MEETING TODAY, RIGHT?
YES, BUT... ARE YOU REALLY GONNA JOIN THE OCCULT CLUB?
YEP.
Is that a problem?
I THOUGHT YOU SAID **STUDENT COUNCIL** WAS IT FOR YOU.
WELL, IT'S LIKE THIS.
INUKI JOINED THE TRACK AND FIELD TEAM.
Inuki
She's fast!
SO, IF I DON'T JOIN ANOTHER CLUB, IT'S LIKE LETTING HER **WIN.**
THEN WHY NOT COUNTER ATHLETICS WITH ATHLETICS?
EH, NONE OF THE SPORTS REALLY INTEREST-ED ME.

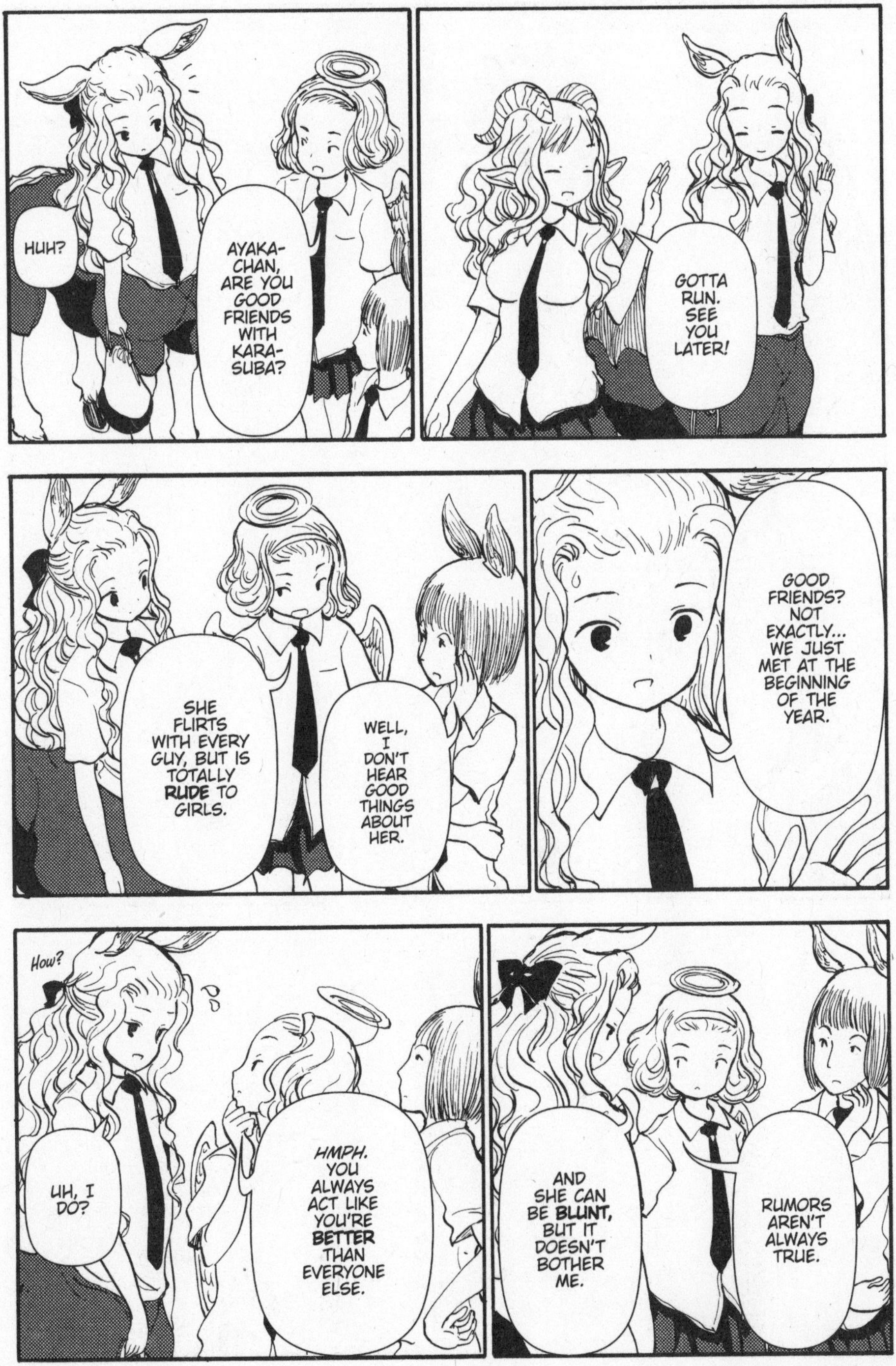
GOTTA RUN. SEE YOU LATER!
AYAKA-CHAN, ARE YOU GOOD FRIENDS WITH KARA-SUBA?
HUH?
GOOD FRIENDS? NOT EXACTLY... WE JUST MET AT THE BEGINNING OF THE YEAR.
WELL, I DON'T HEAR GOOD THINGS ABOUT HER.
SHE FLIRTS WITH EVERY GUY, BUT IS TOTALLY RUDE TO GIRLS.
RUMORS AREN'T ALWAYS TRUE.
AND SHE CAN BE BLUNT, BUT IT DOESN'T BOTHER ME.
HMPH. YOU ALWAYS ACT LIKE YOU'RE BETTER THAN EVERYONE ELSE.
How?
UH, I DO?

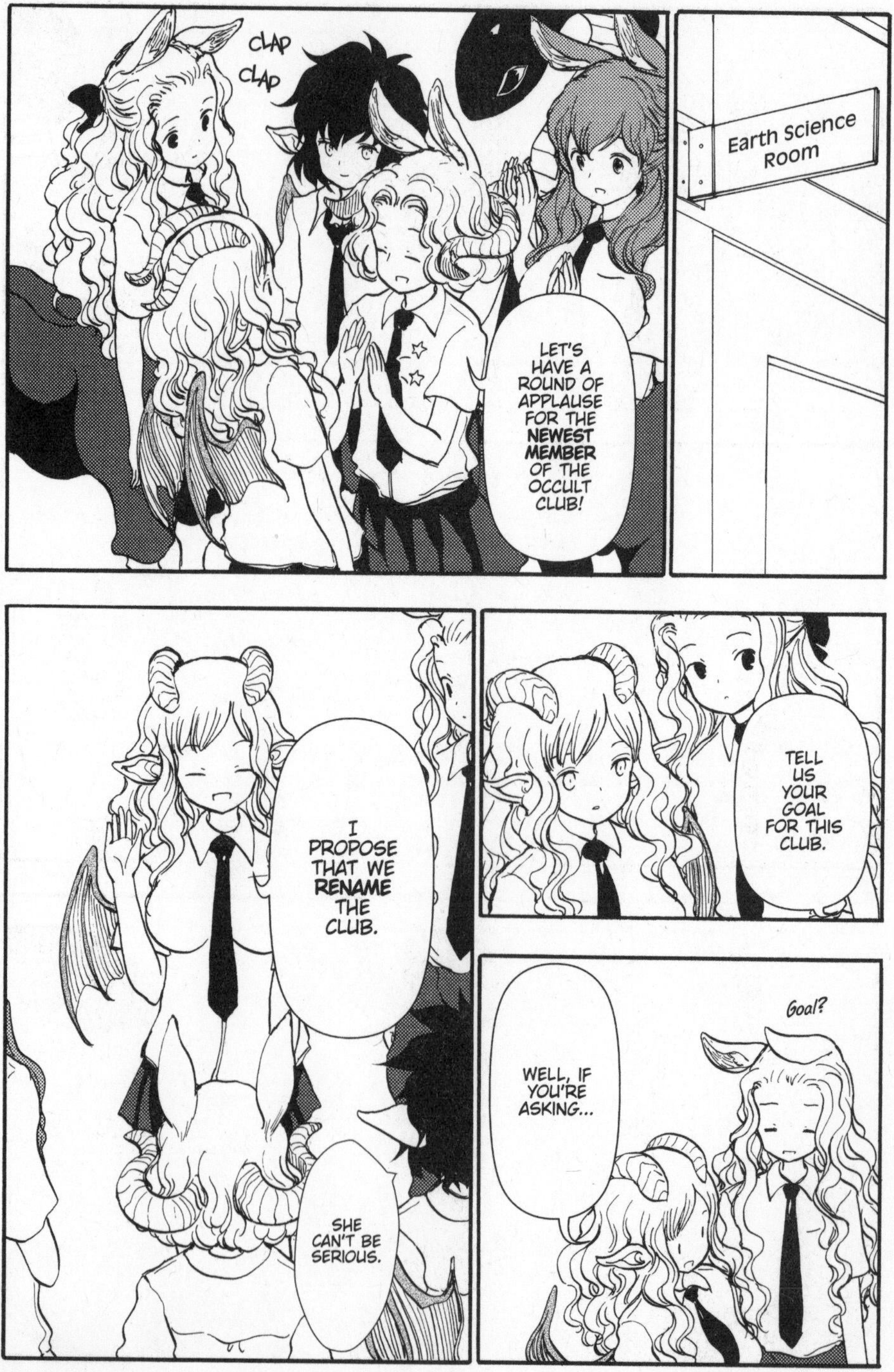
Earth Science Room
CLAP
CLAP
LET'S HAVE A ROUND OF APPLAUSE FOR THE NEWEST MEMBER OF THE OCCULT CLUB!
TELL US YOUR GOAL FOR THIS CLUB.
Goal?
WELL, IF YOU'RE ASKING...
I PROPOSE THAT WE RENAME THE CLUB.
SHE CAN'T BE SERIOUS.

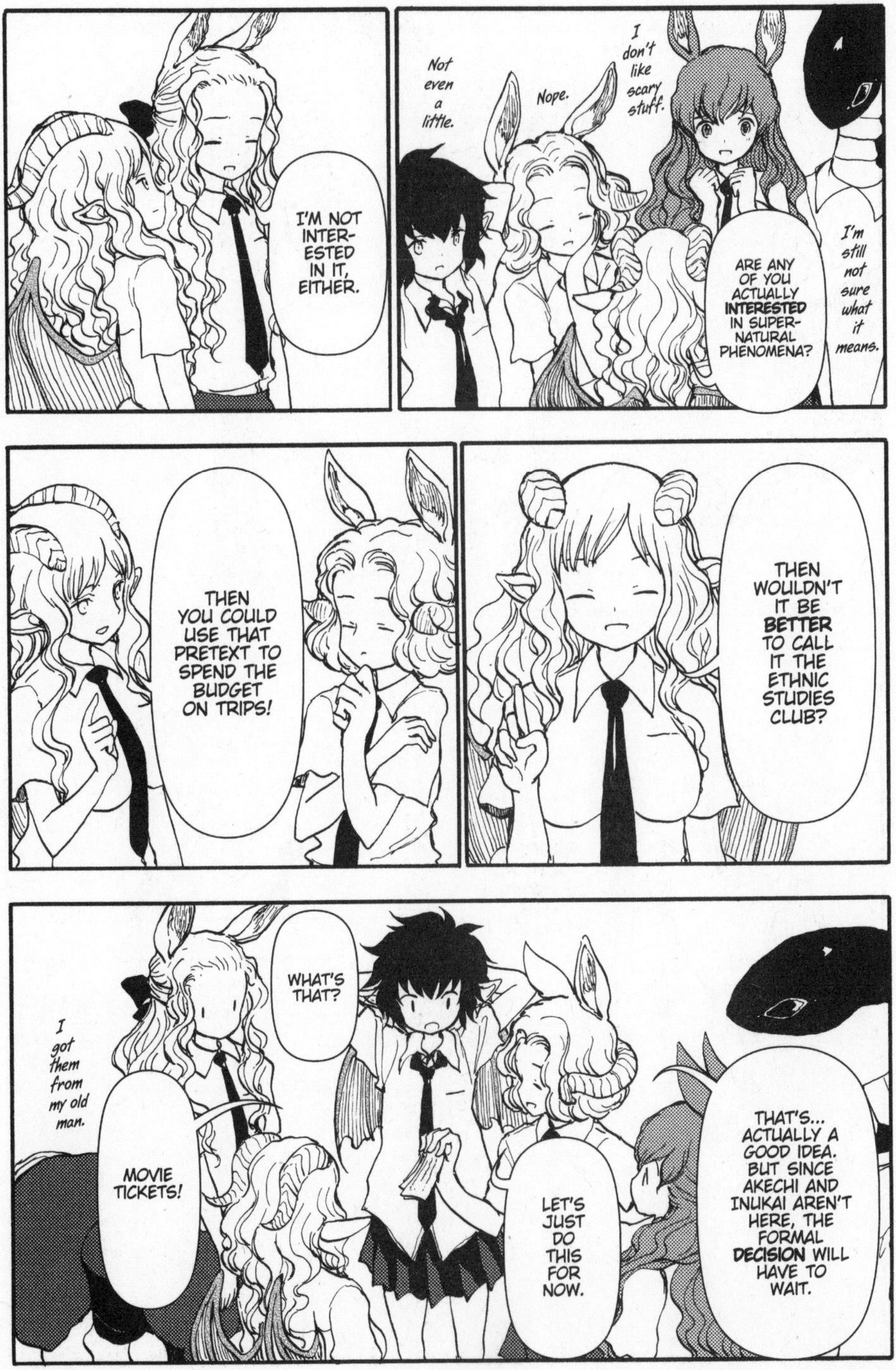
ARE ANY OF YOU ACTUALLY **INTERESTED** IN SUPER-NATURAL PHENOMENA?
I'm still not sure what it means.
I don't like scary stuff.
Nope.
Not even a little.
I'M NOT INTER-ESTED IN IT, EITHER.
THEN WOULDN'T IT BE **BETTER** TO CALL IT THE ETHNIC STUDIES CLUB?
THEN YOU COULD USE THAT PRETEXT TO SPEND THE BUDGET ON TRIPS!
THAT'S... ACTUALLY A GOOD IDEA. BUT SINCE AKECHI AND INUKAI AREN'T HERE, THE FORMAL **DECISION** WILL HAVE TO WAIT.
LET'S JUST DO THIS FOR NOW.
WHAT'S THAT?
MOVIE TICKETS!
I got them from my old man.

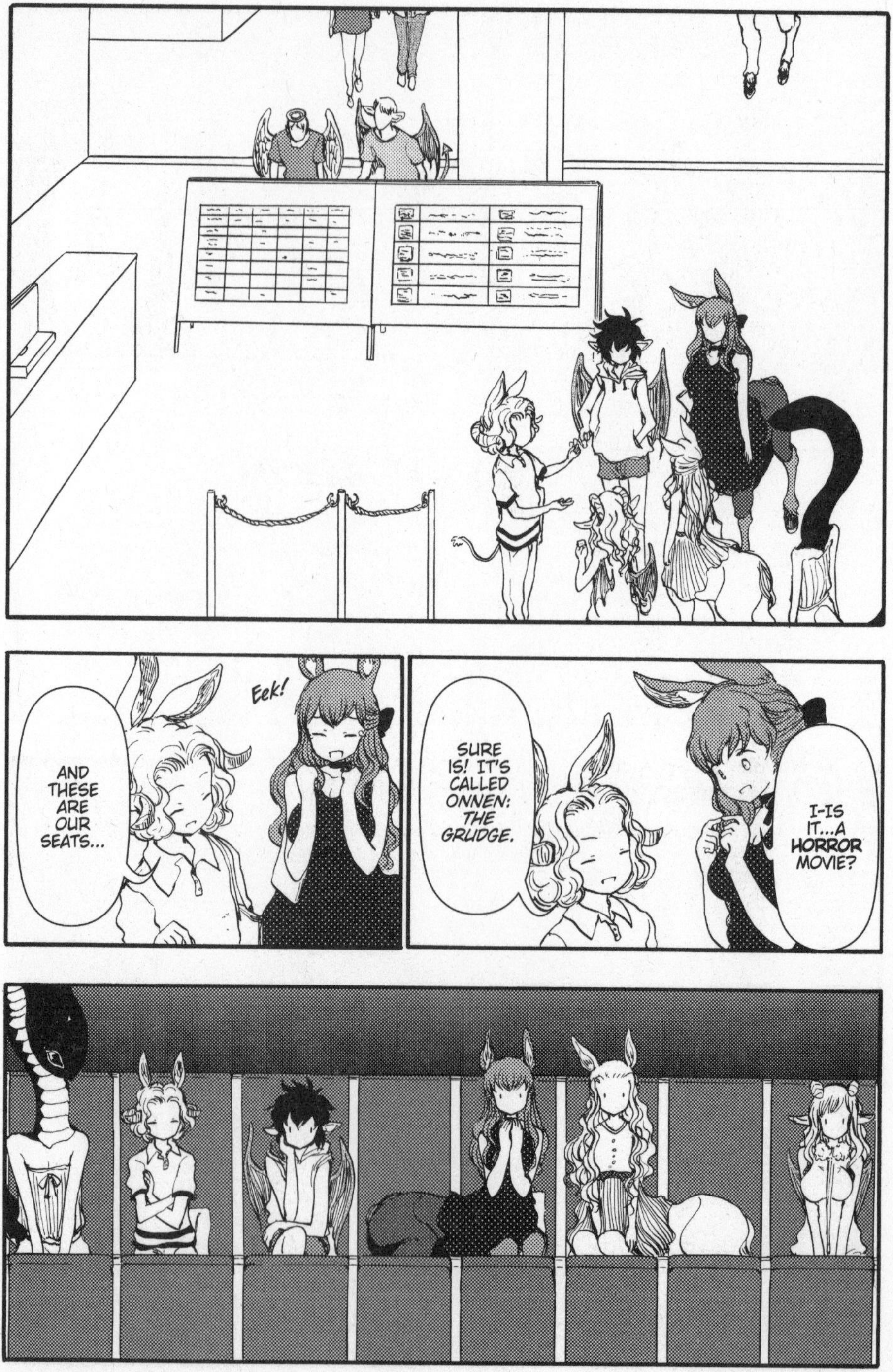
I-IS IT...A HORROR MOVIE?
SURE IS! IT'S CALLED ONNEN: THE GRUDGE.
Eek!
AND THESE ARE OUR SEATS...

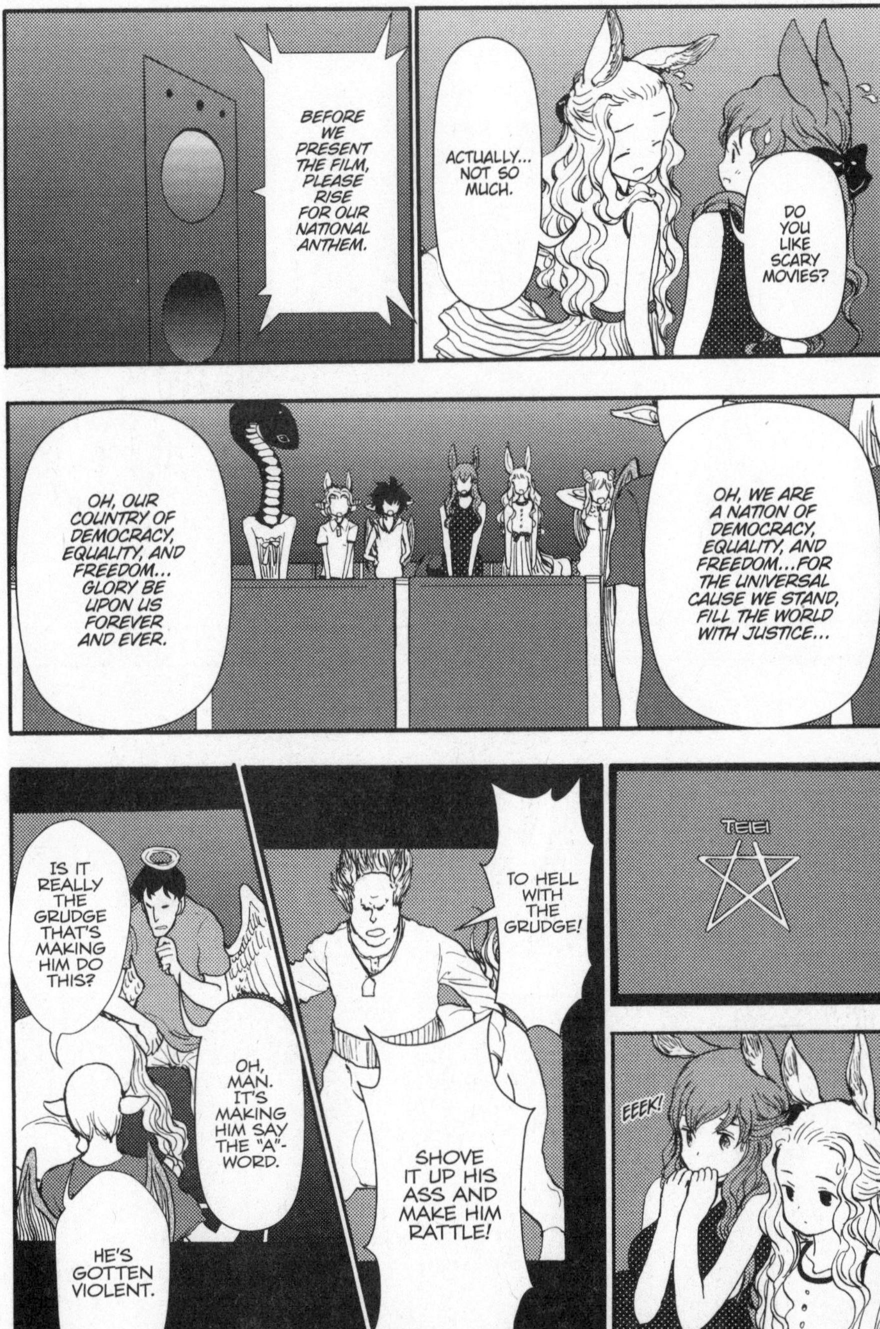
DO YOU LIKE SCARY MOVIES?
ACTUALLY... NOT SO MUCH.
BEFORE WE PRESENT THE FILM, PLEASE RISE FOR OUR NATIONAL ANTHEM.
OH, WE ARE A NATION OF DEMOCRACY, EQUALITY, AND FREEDOM...FOR THE UNIVERSAL CAUSE WE STAND, FILL THE WORLD WITH JUSTICE...
OH, OUR COUNTRY OF DEMOCRACY, EQUALITY, AND FREEDOM... GLORY BE UPON US FOREVER AND EVER.
TEIEI
EEEK!
TO HELL WITH THE GRUDGE!
SHOVE IT UP HIS ASS AND MAKE HIM RATTLE!
IS IT REALLY THE GRUDGE THAT'S MAKING HIM DO THIS?
OH, MAN. IT'S MAKING HIM SAY THE "A"-WORD.
HE'S GOTTEN VIOLENT.

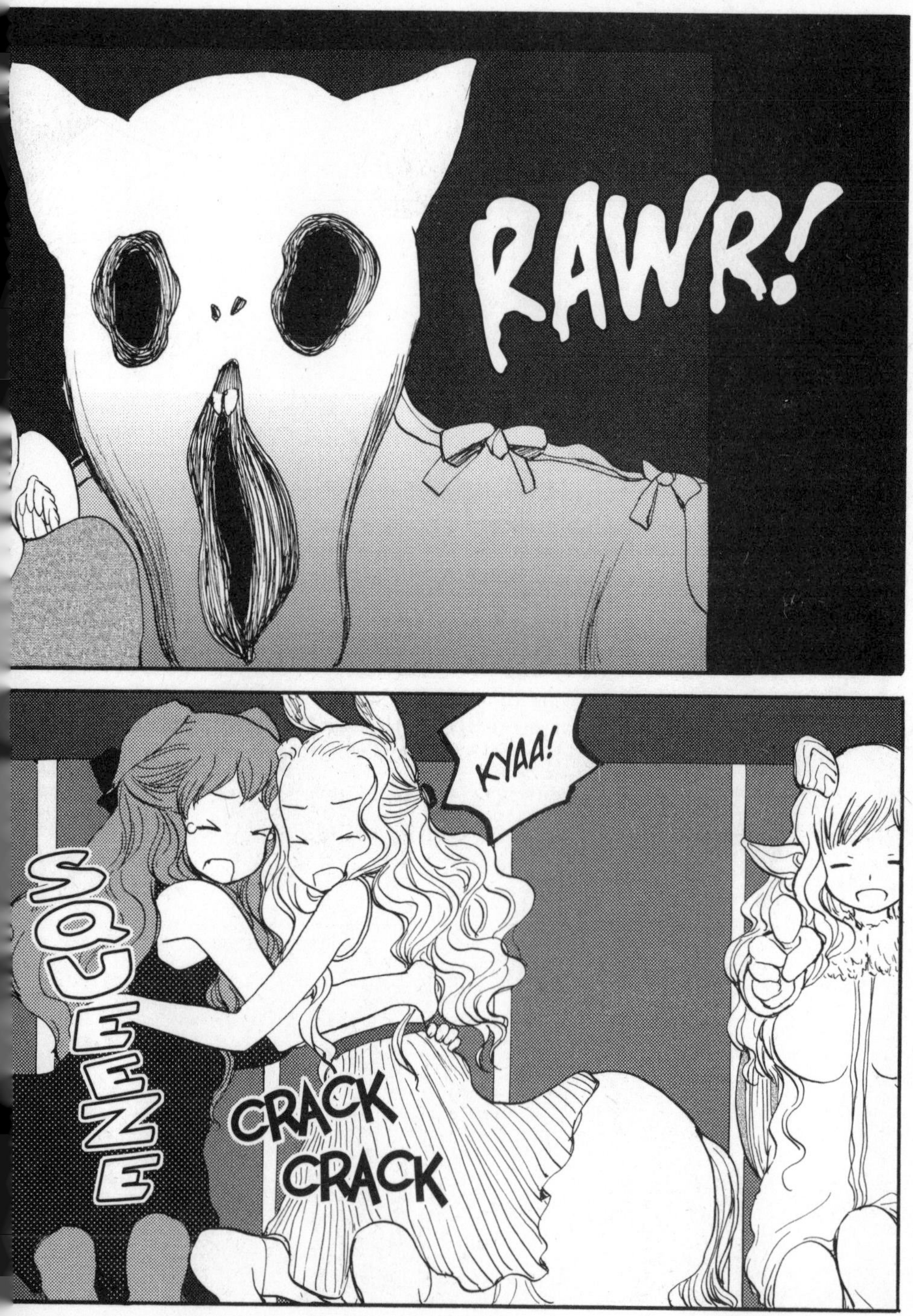
RAWR!
KYAA!
CRACK CRACK
SQUEEZE

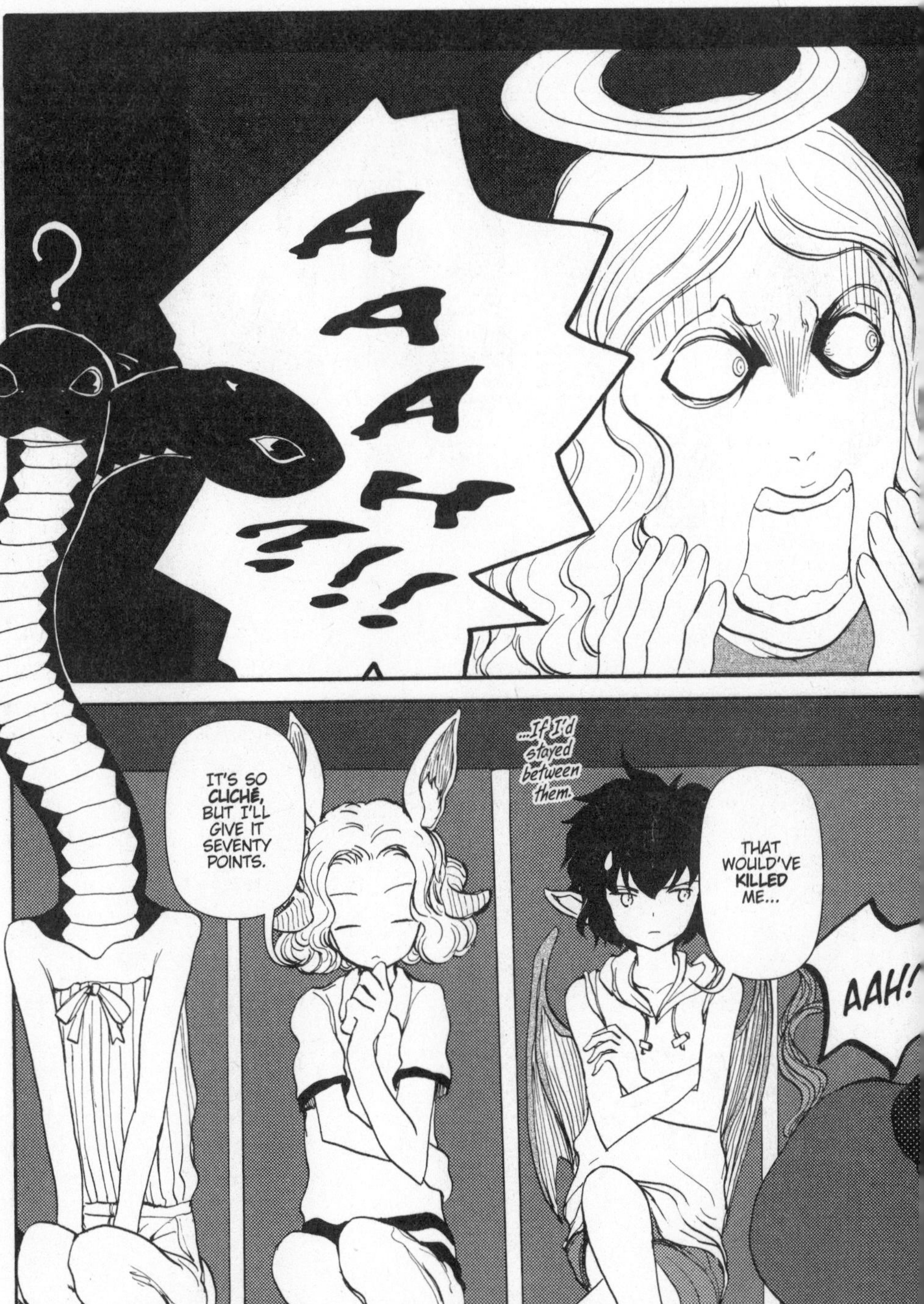
AAAH?!!
?
AAH!
THAT WOULD'VE KILLED ME...
...If I'd stayed between them.
IT'S SO CLICHÉ, BUT I'LL GIVE IT SEVENTY POINTS.

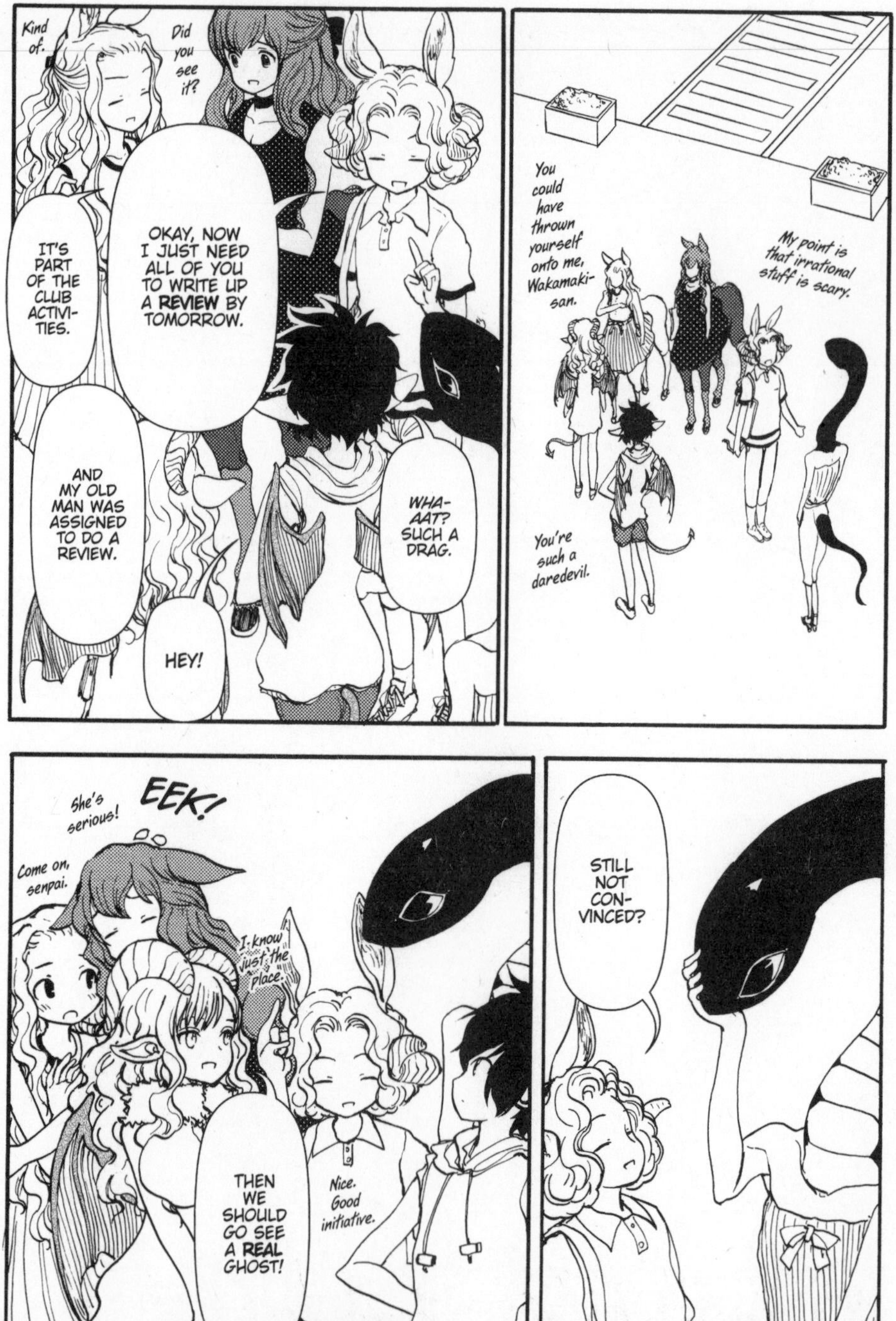
You could have thrown yourself onto me, Wakamaki-san.
My point is that irrational stuff is scary.
You're such a daredevil.
Did you see it?
Kind of.
OKAY, NOW I JUST NEED ALL OF YOU TO WRITE UP A **REVIEW** BY TOMORROW.
IT'S PART OF THE CLUB ACTIVITIES.
WHA-AAT? SUCH A DRAG.
AND MY OLD MAN WAS ASSIGNED TO DO A REVIEW.
HEY!
STILL NOT CON-VINCED?
THEN WE SHOULD GO SEE A **REAL** GHOST!
Nice. Good initiative.
I know just the place.
EEK!
She's serious!
Come on, senpai.

A Centaur's Life

UNDERSTANDING AMPHIBIANFOLK PART 2: THE MISUNDERSTANDING OF AMPHIBIANFOLK

BECAUSE OF THEIR APPEARANCE, SOME PEOPLE MISTAKENLY BELIEVE THAT AMPHIBIANFOLK ARE NOTHING MORE THAN WALKING FROGS, BUT THEY ARE IN FACT ADVANCED LIFE FORMS. DESPITE THE NAME OF THEIR RACE, THEY DO NOT FIT THE TYPICAL CLASSIFICATION OF AMPHIBIANS. INSPECTING THEIR GENETIC MAKEUP SHOWS US THAT THE GENETIC DISTANCE BETWEEN A BULLFROG AND AN AMPHIBIANFOLK IS SIMILAR TO THE DISTANCE BETWEEN A FROG AND A MAMMALIAN HUMAN. THIS AND MANY OTHER FACTORS HAVE LED SCIENTISTS TO CONCLUDE THAT AMPHIBIANFOLK CAN BE CONSIDERED BIOLOGICALLY EQUIVALENT, AND IN SOME WAYS POSSIBLY SUPERIOR, TO MAMMALIAN HUMANS.

UNLIKE TYPICAL AMPHIBIANS, THEIR SKIN ISN'T A MUCUS MEMBRANE--THIS MEANS THAT THEY ARE ABLE TO TOLERATE DRY CONDITIONS, ALBEIT IN A LIMITED FASHION. THEIR EYES ARE POSITIONED CLOSER TO THE FRONT OF THEIR HEADS THAN IS SEEN IN FROGS, GIVING THEM EXCELLENT BINOCULAR VISION. RESEARCH SHOWS THAT THEY ARE HOMEOTHERMIC AND JUST AS INTELLIGENT AS MAMMALIAN HUMANS. THEIR RELATIVELY PRIMITIVE WAY OF LIFE SEEMS TO BE DUE TO THEIR GEOGRAPHICAL AND HISTORICAL BACK-GROUND, WHICH WILL BE EXPLAINED LATER, RATHER THAN BECAUSE THEY ARE SOMEHOW INFERIOR. THOSE WHO CONSIDER THEM INFERIOR SHOULD BE REMINDED THAT THERE ARE MAMMALIAN HUMANS LIVING RELATIVELY PRIMITIVELY OUTSIDE OF THE CULTURAL CENTERS OF CIVILIZATION, AND SOME WHO ARE INTELLECTUALLY IGNORANT WITHIN.

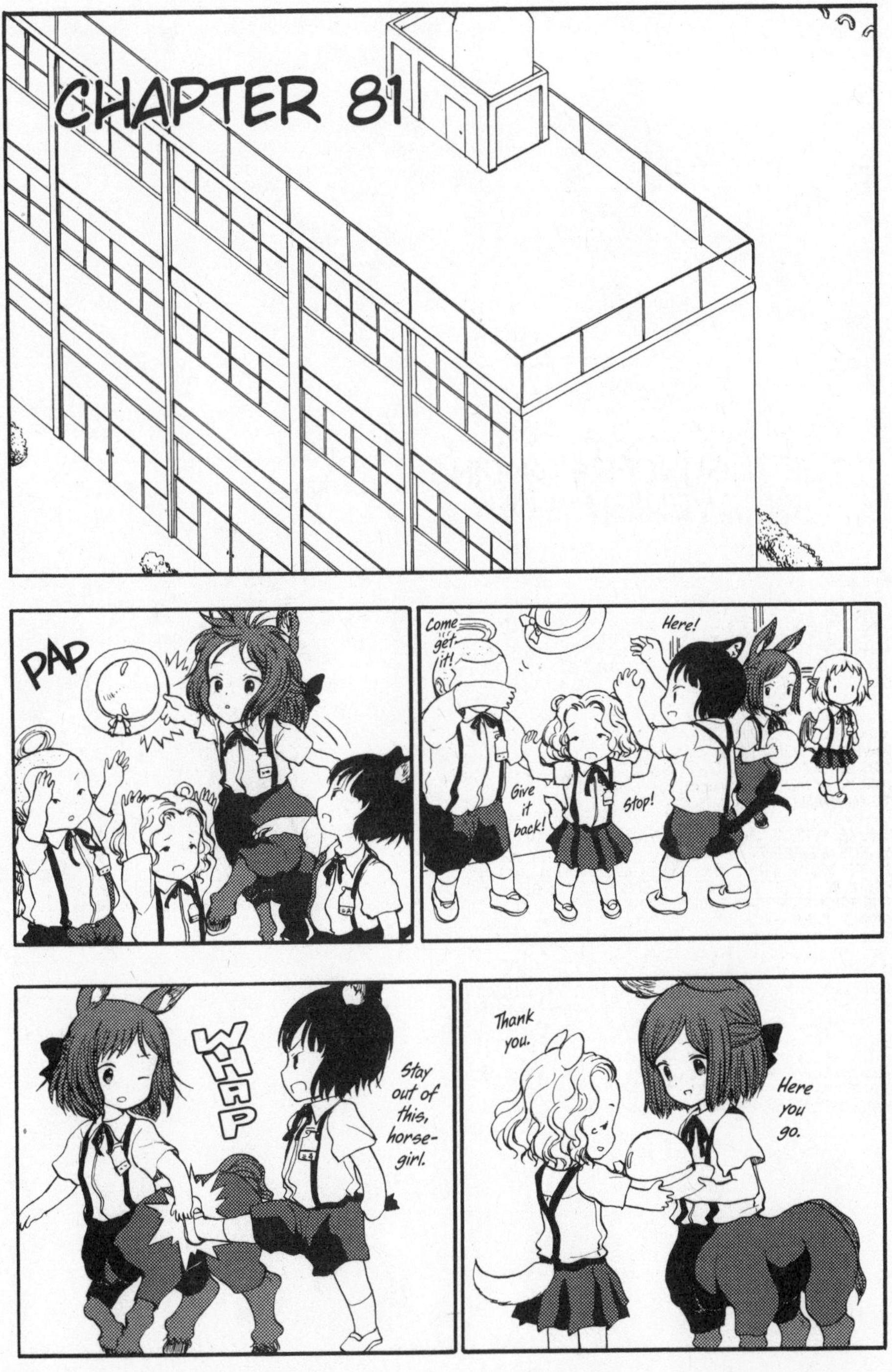
CHAPTER 81
Here!
Come get it!
Stop!
Give it back!
PAP
Here you go.
Thank you.
Stay out of this, horse-girl.
WHAP

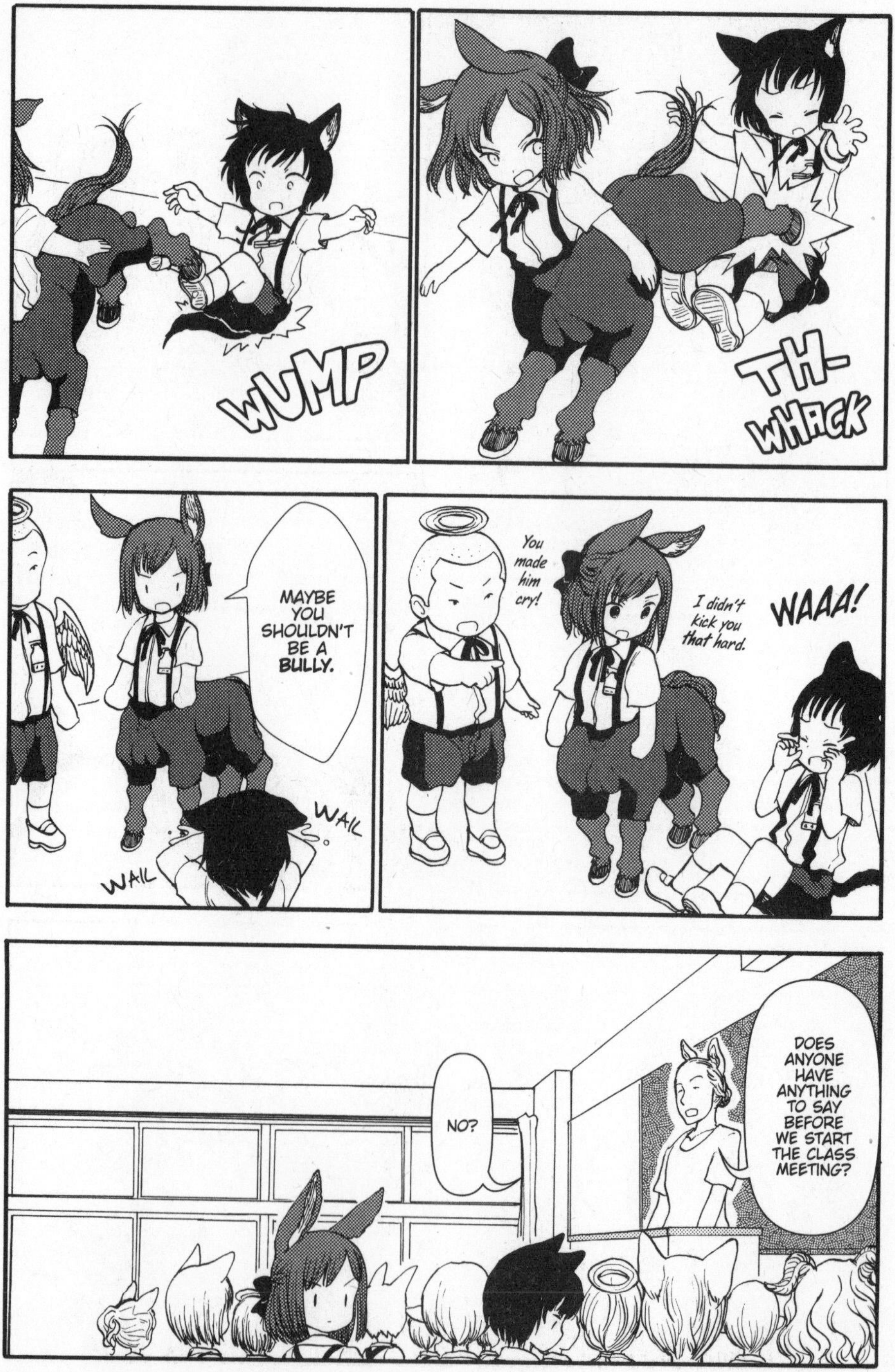
TH-WHACK
WUMP
WAAA!
I didn't kick you that hard.
You made him cry!
MAYBE YOU SHOULDN'T BE A BULLY.
WAIL
WAIL
DOES ANYONE HAVE ANYTHING TO SAY BEFORE WE START THE CLASS MEETING?
NO?

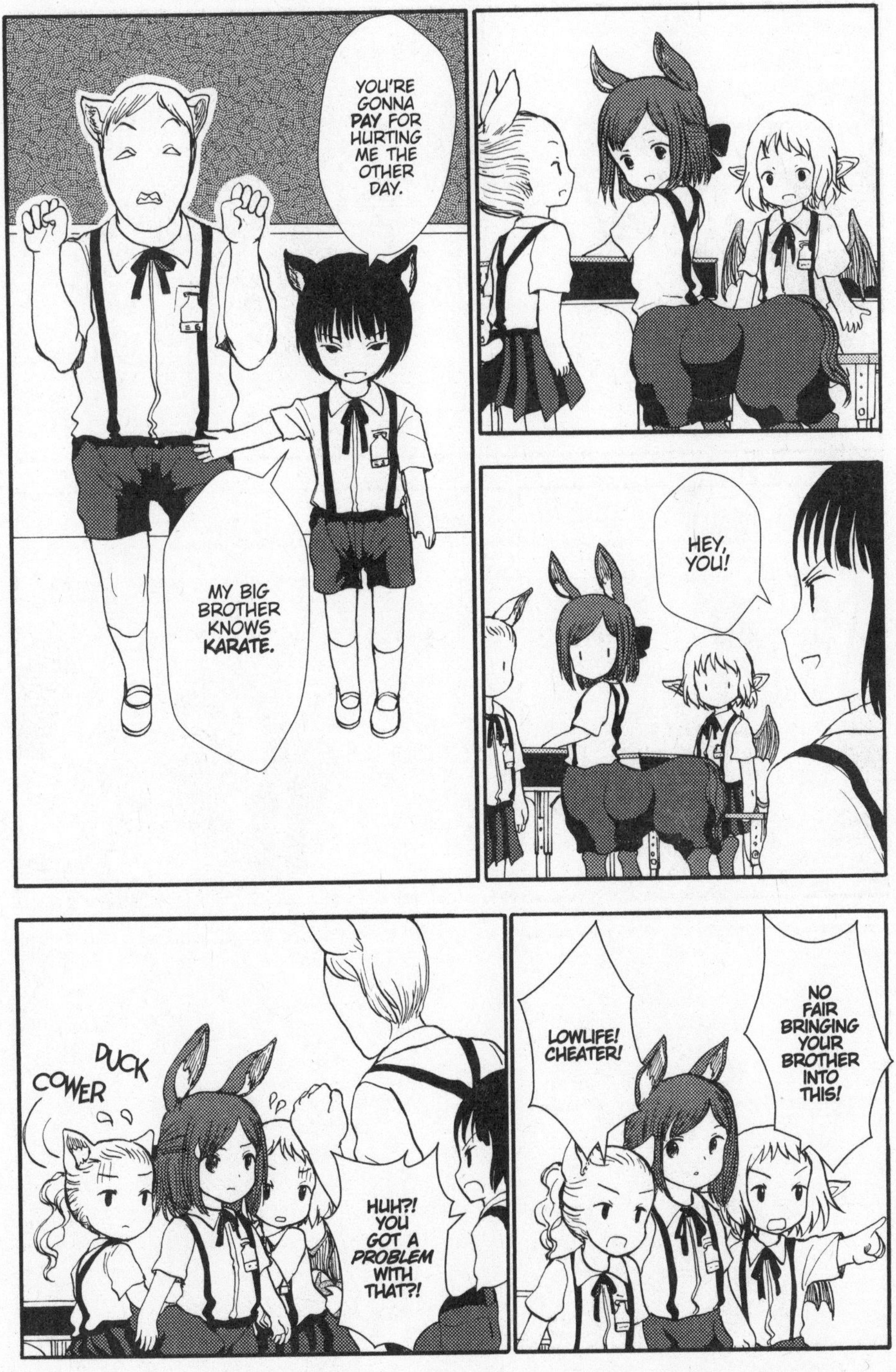
HEY, YOU!
YOU'RE GONNA PAY FOR HURTING ME THE OTHER DAY.
MY BIG BROTHER KNOWS KARATE.
NO FAIR BRINGING YOUR BROTHER INTO THIS!
LOWLIFE! CHEATER!
HUH?! YOU GOT A PROBLEM WITH THAT?!
DUCK
COWER

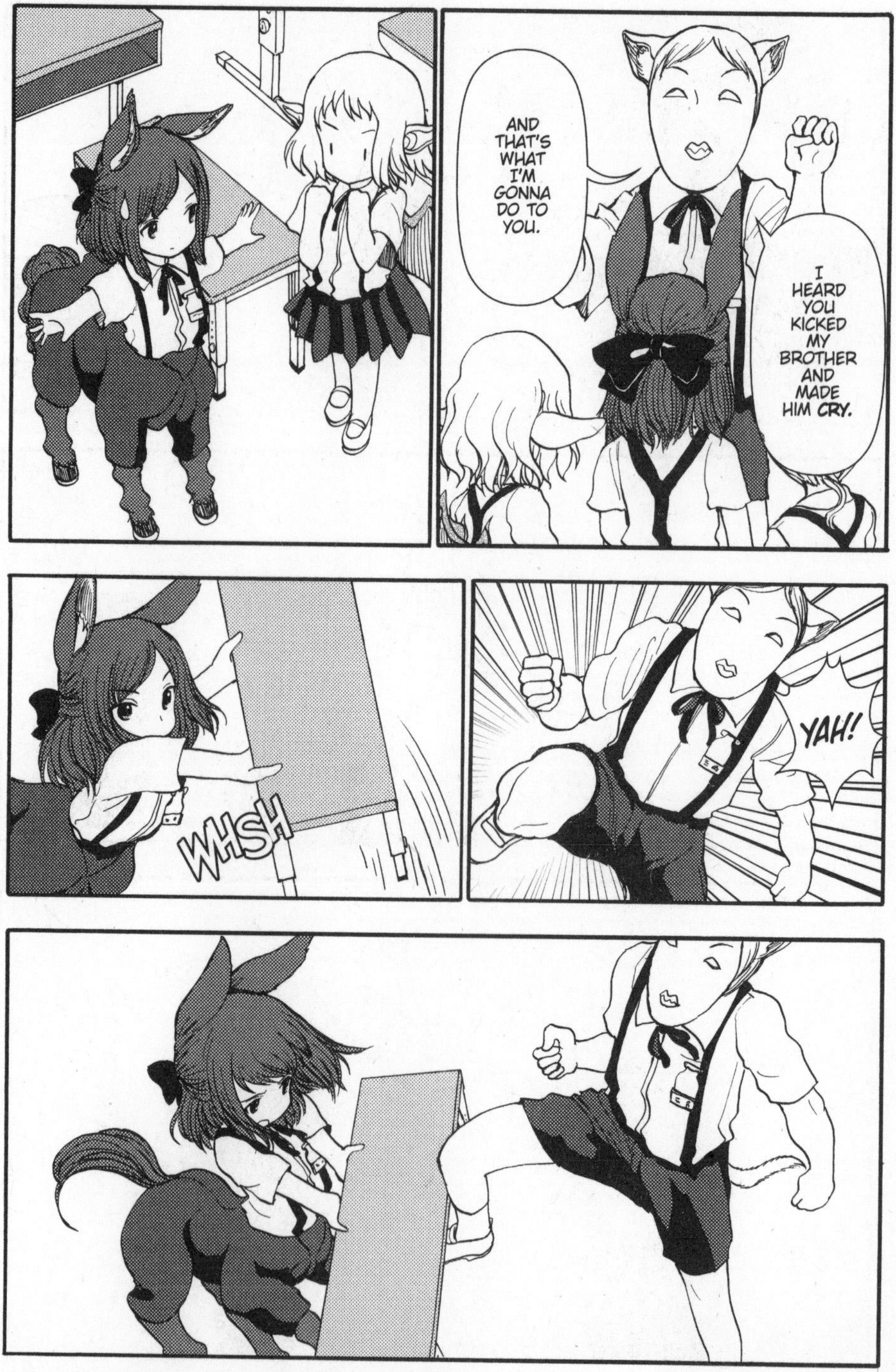
I HEARD YOU KICKED MY BROTHER AND MADE HIM CRY.
AND THAT'S WHAT I'M GONNA DO TO YOU.
YAH!
WHSH

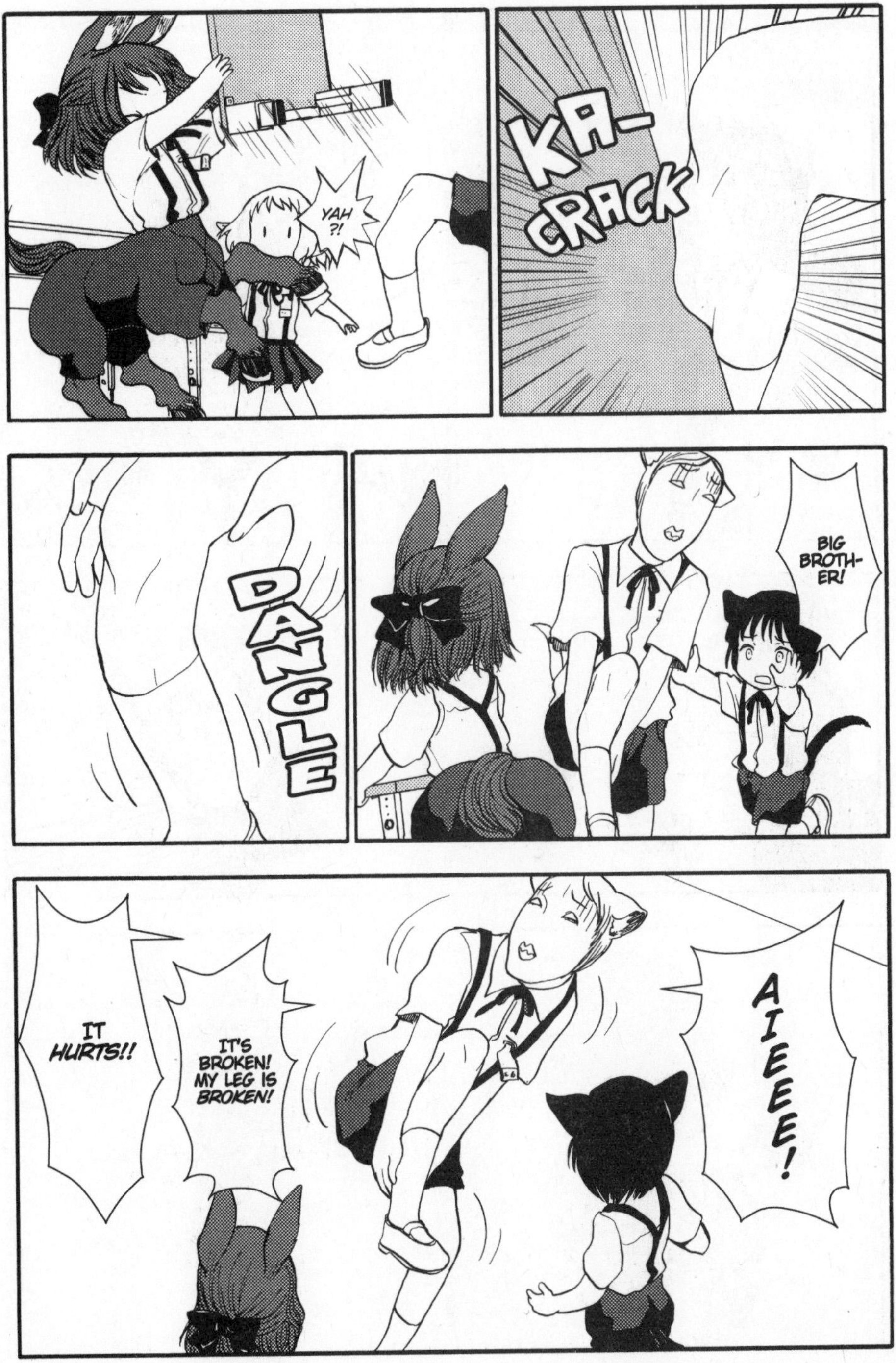
KA-CRACK
YAH?!
BIG BROTHER!
DANGLE
AIEEE!
IT'S BROKEN! MY LEG IS BROKEN!
IT HURTS!!

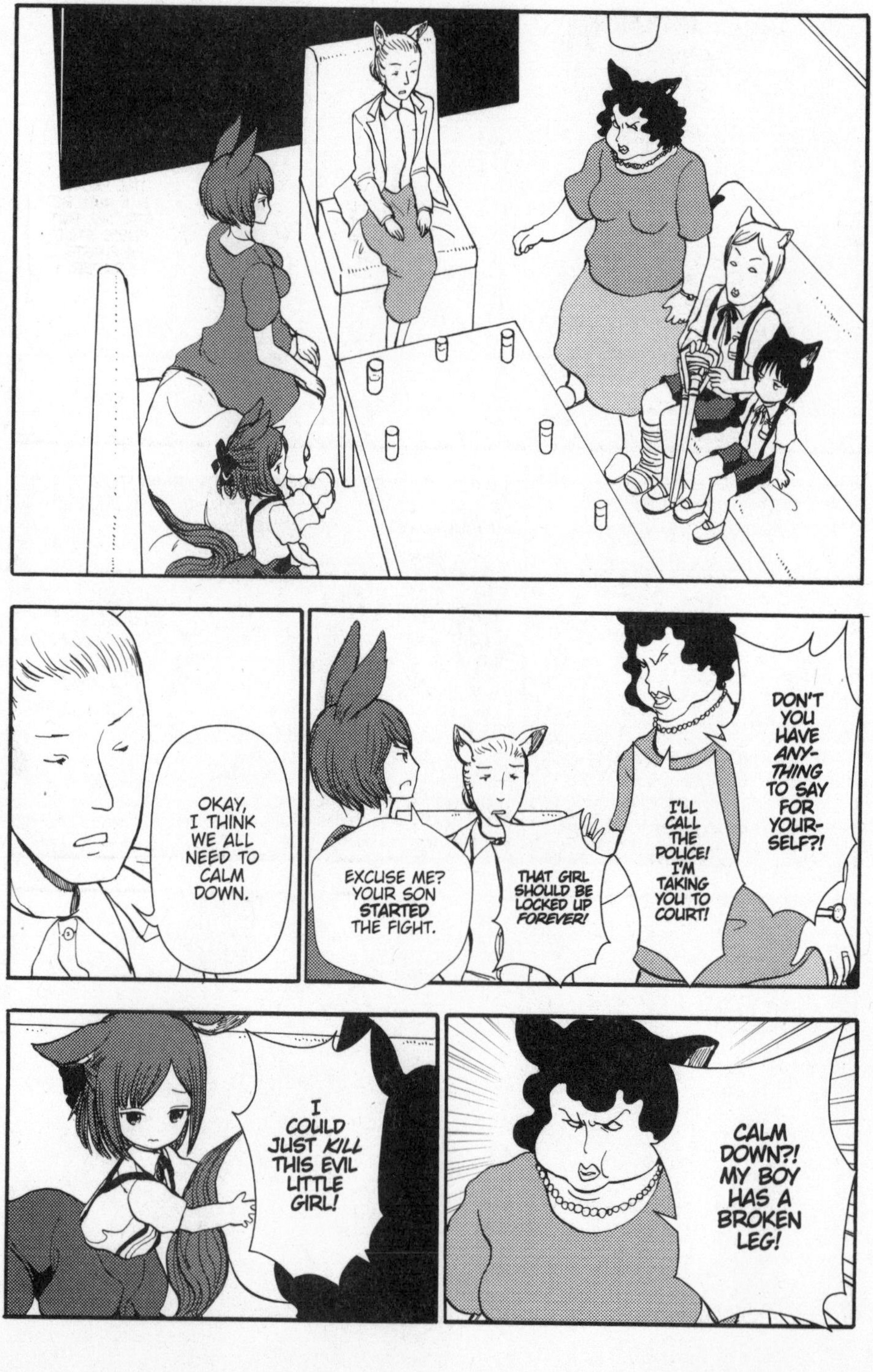
DON'T YOU HAVE *ANYTHING* TO SAY FOR YOURSELF?!
I'LL CALL THE POLICE! I'M TAKING YOU TO COURT!
THAT GIRL SHOULD BE LOCKED UP *FOREVER!*
EXCUSE ME? YOUR SON STARTED THE FIGHT.
OKAY, I THINK WE ALL NEED TO CALM DOWN.
CALM DOWN?! MY BOY HAS A BROKEN LEG!
I COULD JUST *KILL* THIS EVIL LITTLE GIRL!

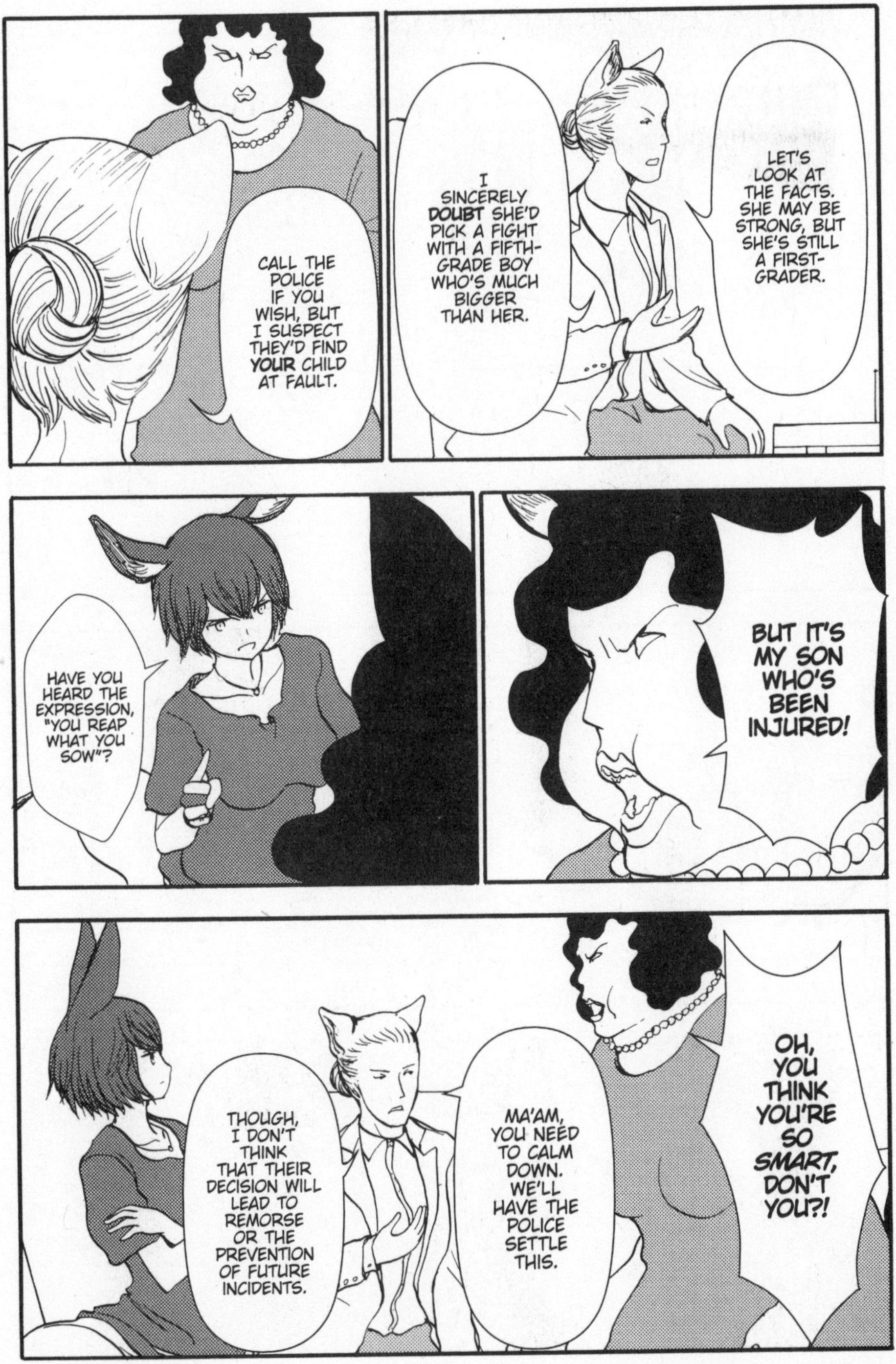
LET'S LOOK AT THE FACTS. SHE MAY BE STRONG, BUT SHE'S STILL A FIRST-GRADER.
I SINCERELY **DOUBT** SHE'D PICK A FIGHT WITH A FIFTH-GRADE BOY WHO'S MUCH BIGGER THAN HER.
CALL THE POLICE IF YOU WISH, BUT I SUSPECT THEY'D FIND **YOUR** CHILD AT FAULT.
BUT IT'S MY SON WHO'S BEEN INJURED!
HAVE YOU HEARD THE EXPRESSION, "YOU REAP WHAT YOU SOW"?
OH, YOU THINK YOU'RE SO *SMART*, DON'T YOU?!
MA'AM, YOU NEED TO CALM DOWN. WE'LL HAVE THE POLICE SETTLE THIS.
THOUGH, I DON'T THINK THAT THEIR DECISION WILL LEAD TO REMORSE OR THE PREVENTION OF FUTURE INCIDENTS.

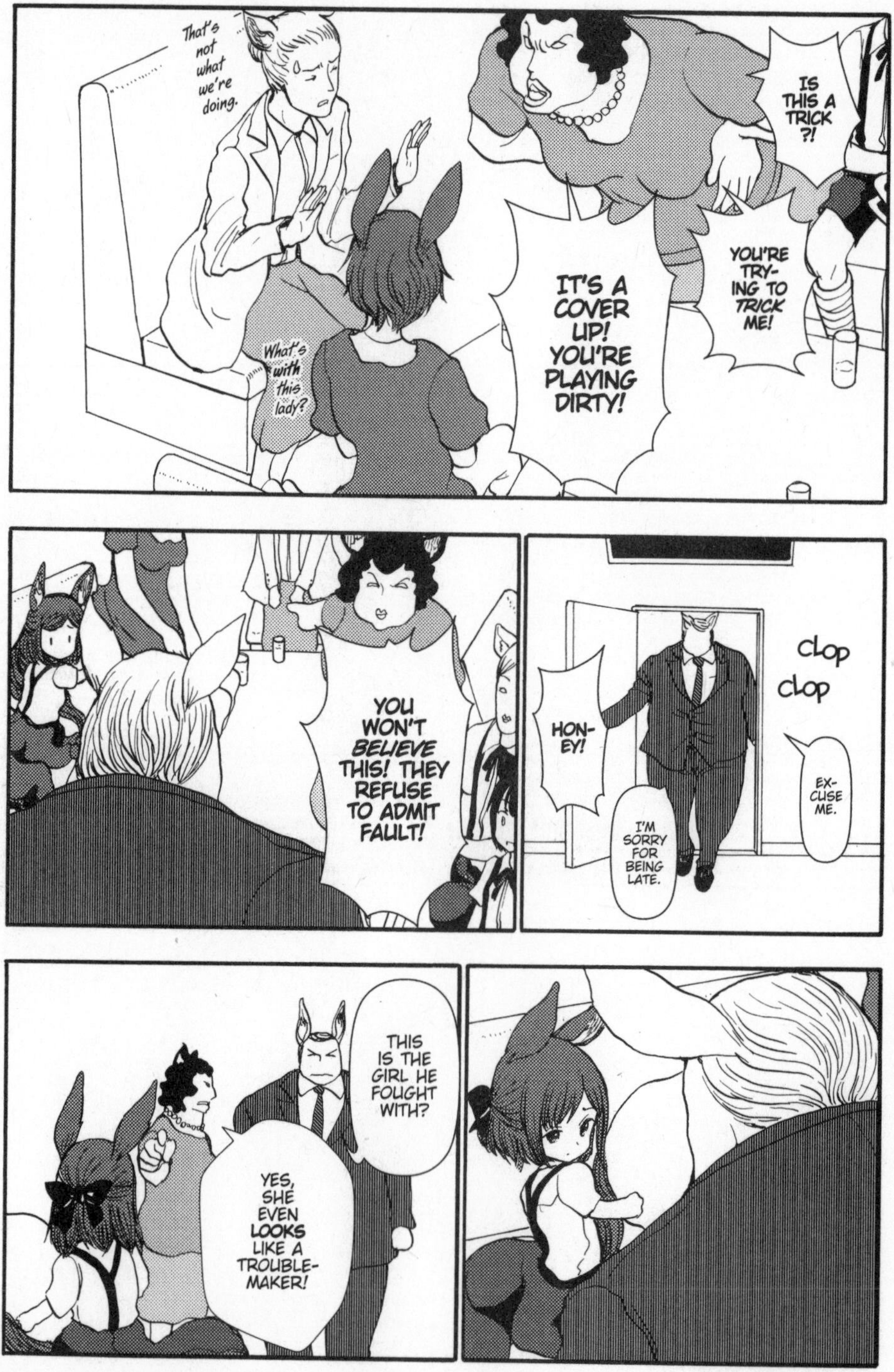
IS THIS A TRICK?!
YOU'RE TRYING TO *TRICK* ME!
IT'S A COVER UP! YOU'RE PLAYING DIRTY!
That's not what we're doing.
What's with this lady?
CLOP CLOP
EXCUSE ME.
HONEY!
I'M SORRY FOR BEING LATE.
YOU WON'T *BELIEVE* THIS! THEY REFUSE TO ADMIT FAULT!
THIS IS THE GIRL HE FOUGHT WITH?
YES, SHE EVEN **LOOKS** LIKE A TROUBLE-MAKER!

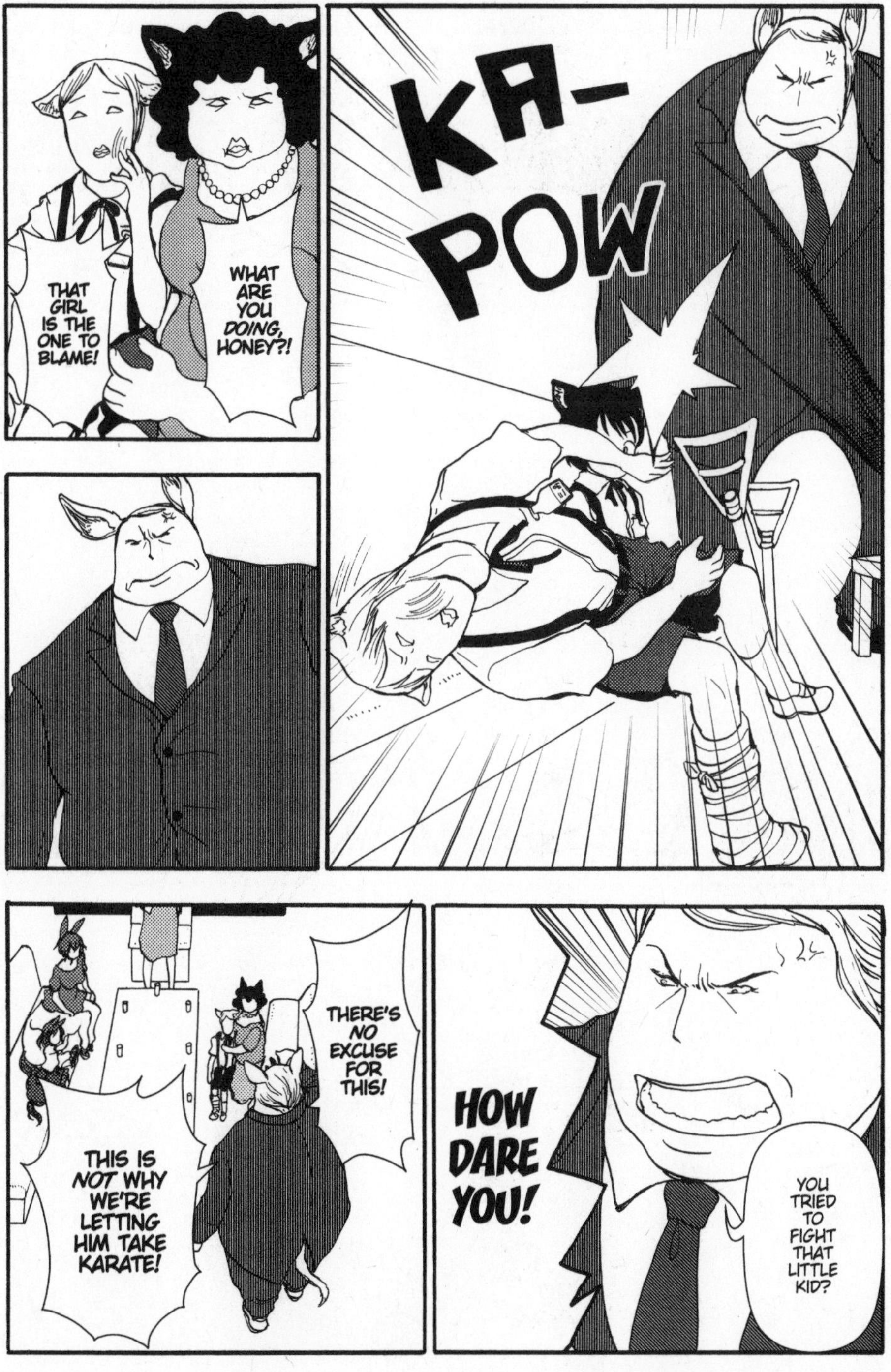
KA-POW
WHAT ARE YOU *DOING*, HONEY?!
THAT GIRL IS THE ONE TO BLAME!
HOW DARE YOU!
YOU TRIED TO FIGHT THAT LITTLE KID?
THERE'S *NO* EXCUSE FOR THIS!
THIS IS *NOT* WHY WE'RE LETTING HIM TAKE KARATE!

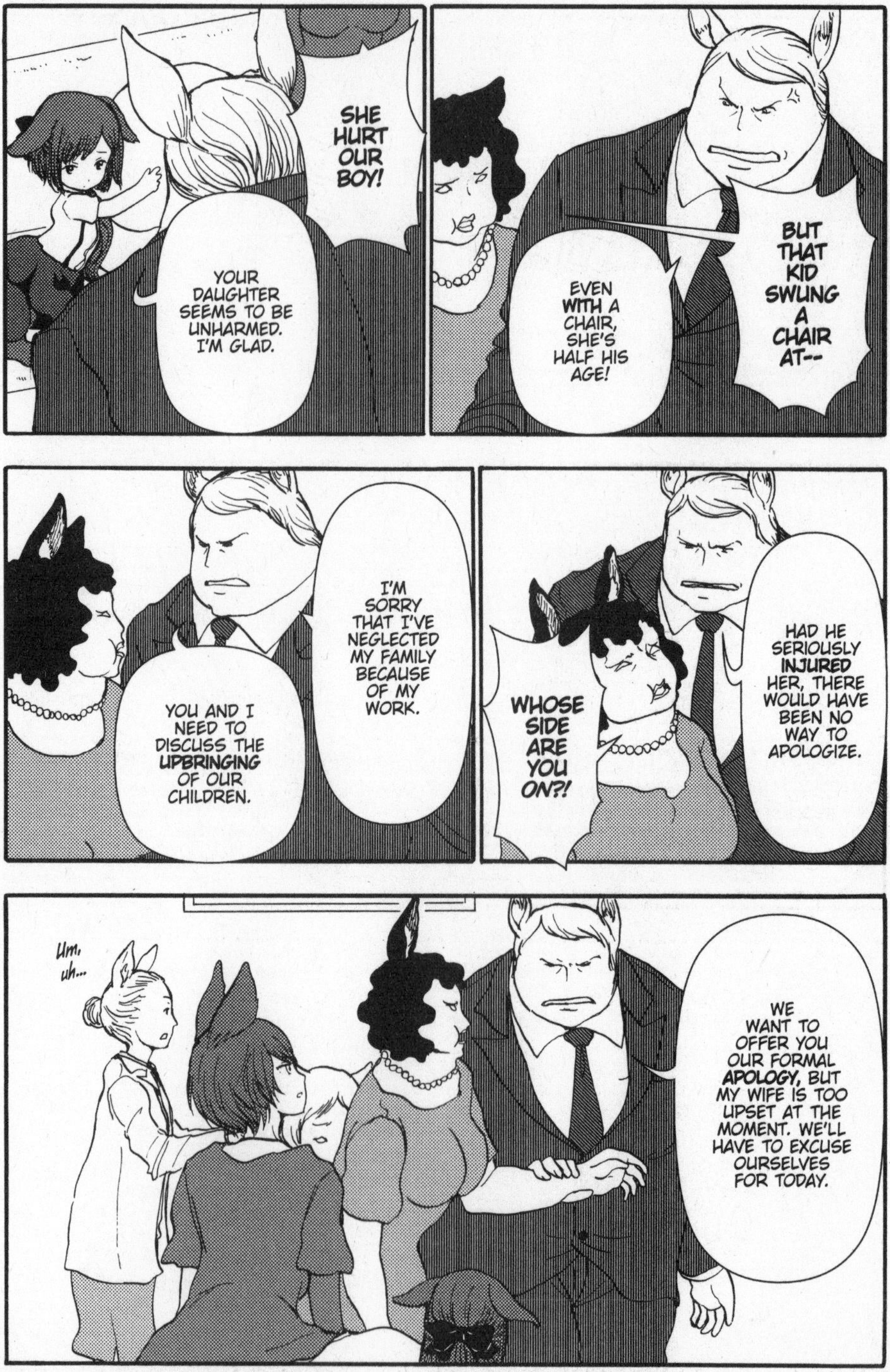
BUT THAT KID SWUNG A CHAIR AT--
EVEN WITH A CHAIR, SHE'S HALF HIS AGE!
SHE HURT OUR BOY!
YOUR DAUGHTER SEEMS TO BE UNHARMED. I'M GLAD.
HAD HE SERIOUSLY INJURED HER, THERE WOULD HAVE BEEN NO WAY TO APOLOGIZE.
WHOSE SIDE ARE YOU ON?!
I'M SORRY THAT I'VE NEGLECTED MY FAMILY BECAUSE OF MY WORK.
YOU AND I NEED TO DISCUSS THE UPBRINGING OF OUR CHILDREN.
WE WANT TO OFFER YOU OUR FORMAL APOLOGY, BUT MY WIFE IS TOO UPSET AT THE MOMENT. WE'LL HAVE TO EXCUSE OURSELVES FOR TODAY.
Um, uh...

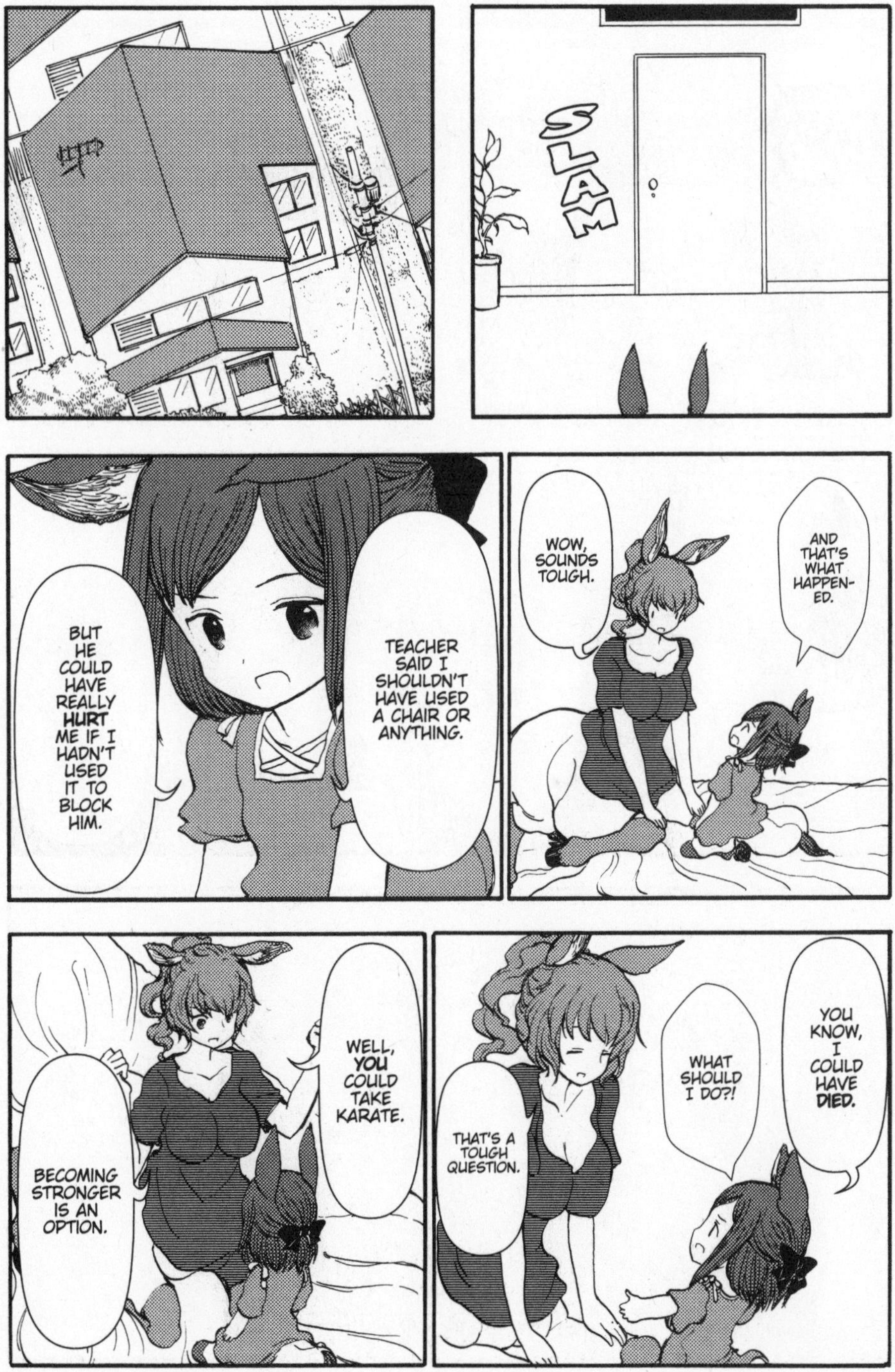
SLAM
AND THAT'S WHAT HAPPEN-ED.
WOW, SOUNDS TOUGH.
TEACHER SAID I SHOULDN'T HAVE USED A CHAIR OR ANYTHING.
BUT HE COULD HAVE REALLY HURT ME IF I HADN'T USED IT TO BLOCK HIM.
YOU KNOW, I COULD HAVE DIED.
WHAT SHOULD I DO?!
THAT'S A TOUGH QUESTION.
WELL, YOU COULD TAKE KARATE.
BECOMING STRONGER IS AN OPTION.

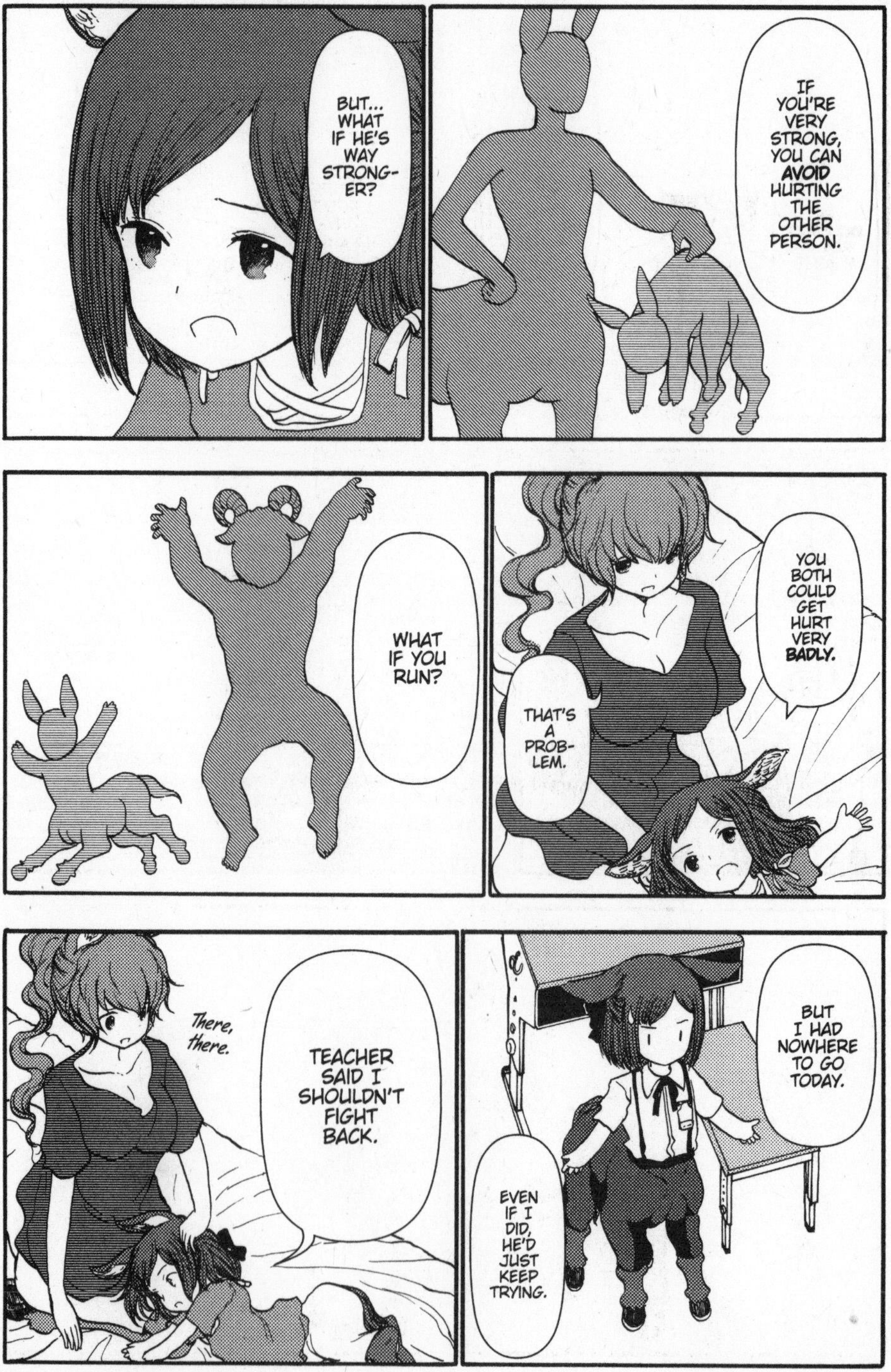
IF YOU'RE VERY STRONG, YOU CAN **AVOID** HURTING THE OTHER PERSON.
BUT... WHAT IF HE'S WAY STRONGER?
YOU BOTH COULD GET HURT VERY **BADLY.**
THAT'S A PROBLEM.
WHAT IF YOU RUN?
BUT I HAD NOWHERE TO GO TODAY.
EVEN IF I DID, HE'D JUST KEEP TRYING.
TEACHER SAID I SHOULDN'T FIGHT BACK.
There, there.

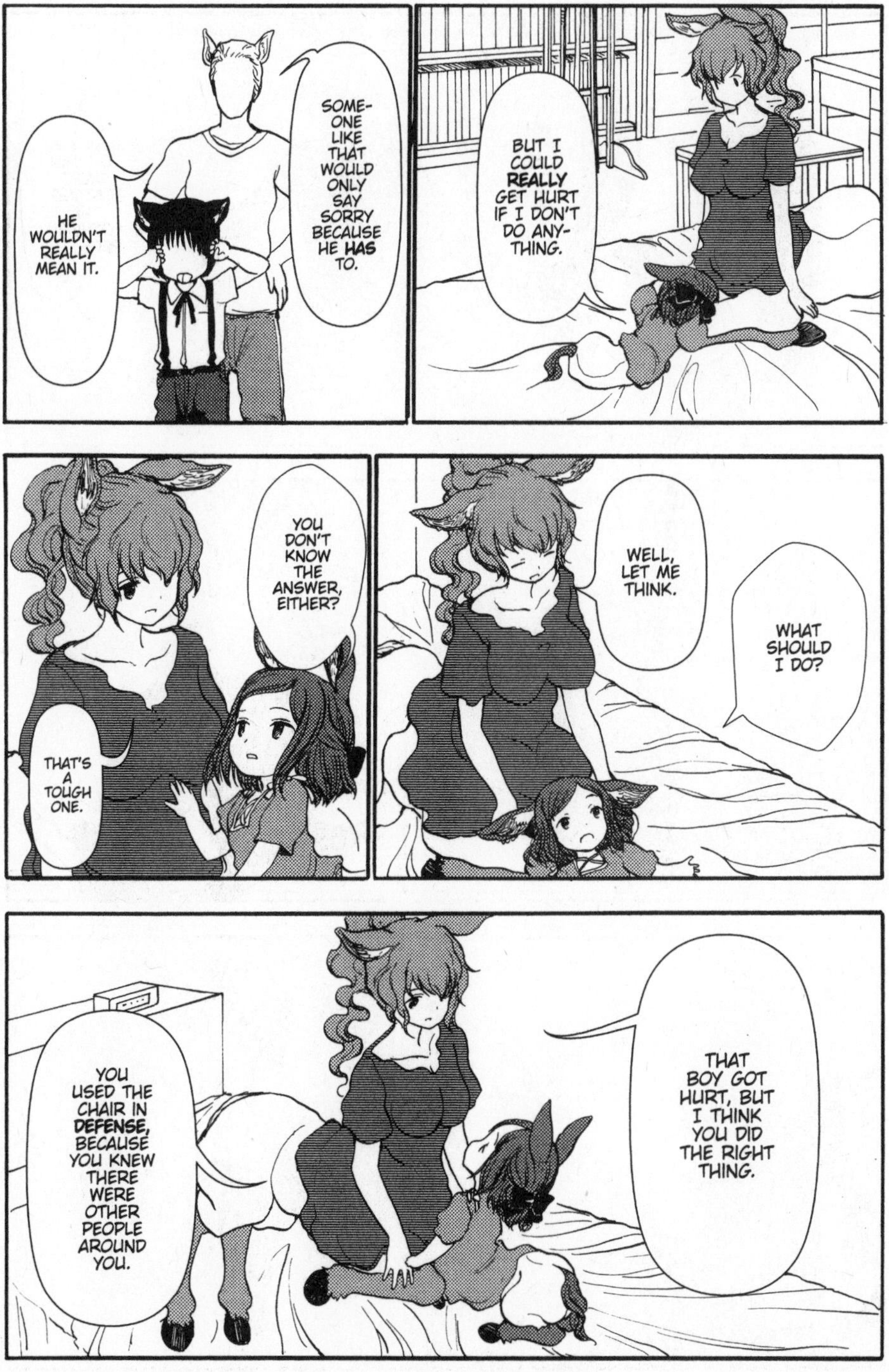
BUT I COULD REALLY GET HURT IF I DON'T DO ANYTHING.
SOMEONE LIKE THAT WOULD ONLY SAY SORRY BECAUSE HE HAS TO.
HE WOULDN'T REALLY MEAN IT.
WHAT SHOULD I DO?
WELL, LET ME THINK.
YOU DON'T KNOW THE ANSWER, EITHER?
THAT'S A TOUGH ONE.
THAT BOY GOT HURT, BUT I THINK YOU DID THE RIGHT THING.
YOU USED THE CHAIR IN DEFENSE, BECAUSE YOU KNEW THERE WERE OTHER PEOPLE AROUND YOU.

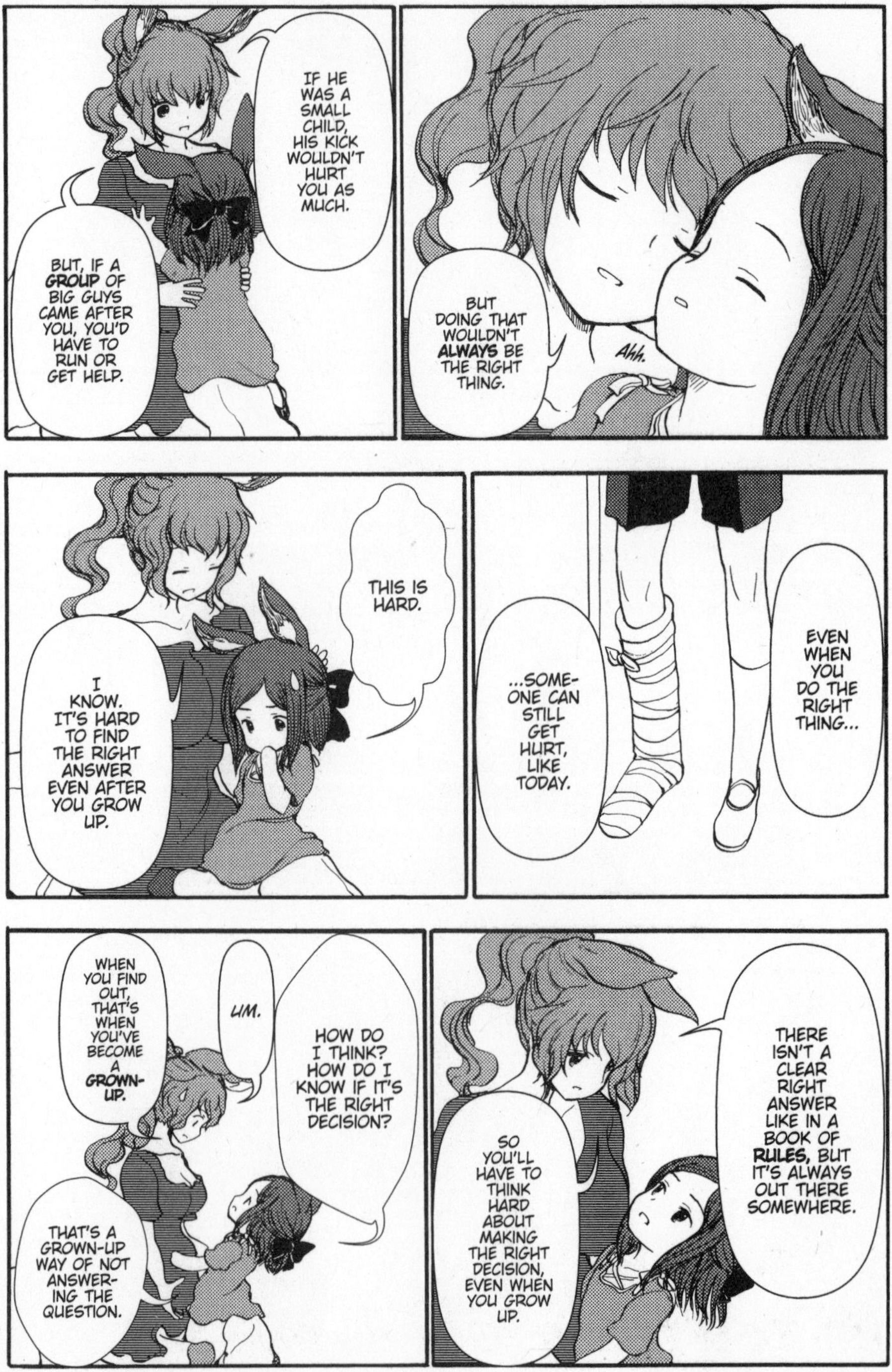
BUT DOING THAT WOULDN'T **ALWAYS** BE THE RIGHT THING.
Ahh.
IF HE WAS A SMALL CHILD, HIS KICK WOULDN'T HURT YOU AS MUCH.
BUT, IF A **GROUP** OF BIG GUYS CAME AFTER YOU, YOU'D HAVE TO RUN OR GET HELP.
EVEN WHEN YOU DO THE RIGHT THING...
...SOME-ONE CAN STILL GET HURT, LIKE TODAY.
THIS IS HARD.
I KNOW. IT'S HARD TO FIND THE RIGHT ANSWER EVEN AFTER YOU GROW UP.
THERE ISN'T A CLEAR RIGHT ANSWER LIKE IN A BOOK OF **RULES**, BUT IT'S ALWAYS OUT THERE SOMEWHERE.
SO YOU'LL HAVE TO THINK HARD ABOUT MAKING THE RIGHT DECISION, EVEN WHEN YOU GROW UP.
HOW DO I THINK? HOW DO I KNOW IF IT'S THE RIGHT DECISION?
UM.
WHEN YOU FIND OUT, THAT'S WHEN YOU'VE BECOME A **GROWN-UP.**
THAT'S A GROWN-UP WAY OF NOT ANSWERING THE QUESTION.

A Centaur's Life

UNDERSTANDING AMPHIBIANFOLK, PART 3: ARE AMPHIBIANFOLK KAPPA?

WHILE A KAPPA MIGHT BE CLASSIFIED AS A KIND OF AMPHIBIANFOLK IF IT WERE REAL, THE TRUTH IS THAT KAPPA ONLY EXIST IN FOLKLORE AND MYTH. THIS CREATURE IS VERY POPULAR AND HAS BEEN OPENLY REPORTED BY THE MEDIA IN JAPAN, BUT JUST LIKE MOST URBAN LEGENDS AND HORROR STORIES, KAPPA ARE PURELY FICTIONAL. THERE'S NO HISTORICAL EVIDENCE OF ANY REAL AMPHIBIANFOLK IN JAPAN, SO IT'S UNLIKELY THAT THE LEGEND OF THE KAPPA AROSE FROM A CASE OF MISTAKEN IDENTITY SURROUNDING TRUE AMPHIBIANFOLK. IN FACT, SINCE KAPPA SUPPOSEDLY CAME IN VARIOUS FORMS RANGING FROM MONKEYS TO HUMAN-TURTLE CHIMERAS, THE MOST LIKELY HYPOTHESIS IS THAT THEIR MODERN IMAGE WAS CREATED BY AN ARTIST.

IT IS ONLY IN THIS WAY THAT THERE IS A SMALL POSSIBILITY THAT THE AMPHIBIANFOLK APPEARANCE HAD AN IMPACT ON THE IMAGE OF KAPPA--SPECIFICALLY, THAT THE ARTIST MAY HAVE SEEN AND BEEN INFLUENCED BY A DEPICTION OF AMPHIBIANFOLK. THEY WERE NOT DISCOVERED BY THE WESTERN WORLD UNTIL THE TURN OF THE NINETEENTH CENTURY, BUT HAD BEEN KNOWN AS LEGEND OR UNIDENTIFIED MYSTERIOUS CREATURES THROUGHOUT SOUTH AMERICA, INCLUDING TAWANTINSUYU, FOR SOME TIME BEFORE THAT. IN PAINTINGS DONE BY ARTISTS FROM MAMMALIAN CIVILIZATION, THEY WERE OCCASIONALLY DEPICTED AS HIDDEN SYMBOLIC ICONS OF PRIMITIVE CHARACTERS.

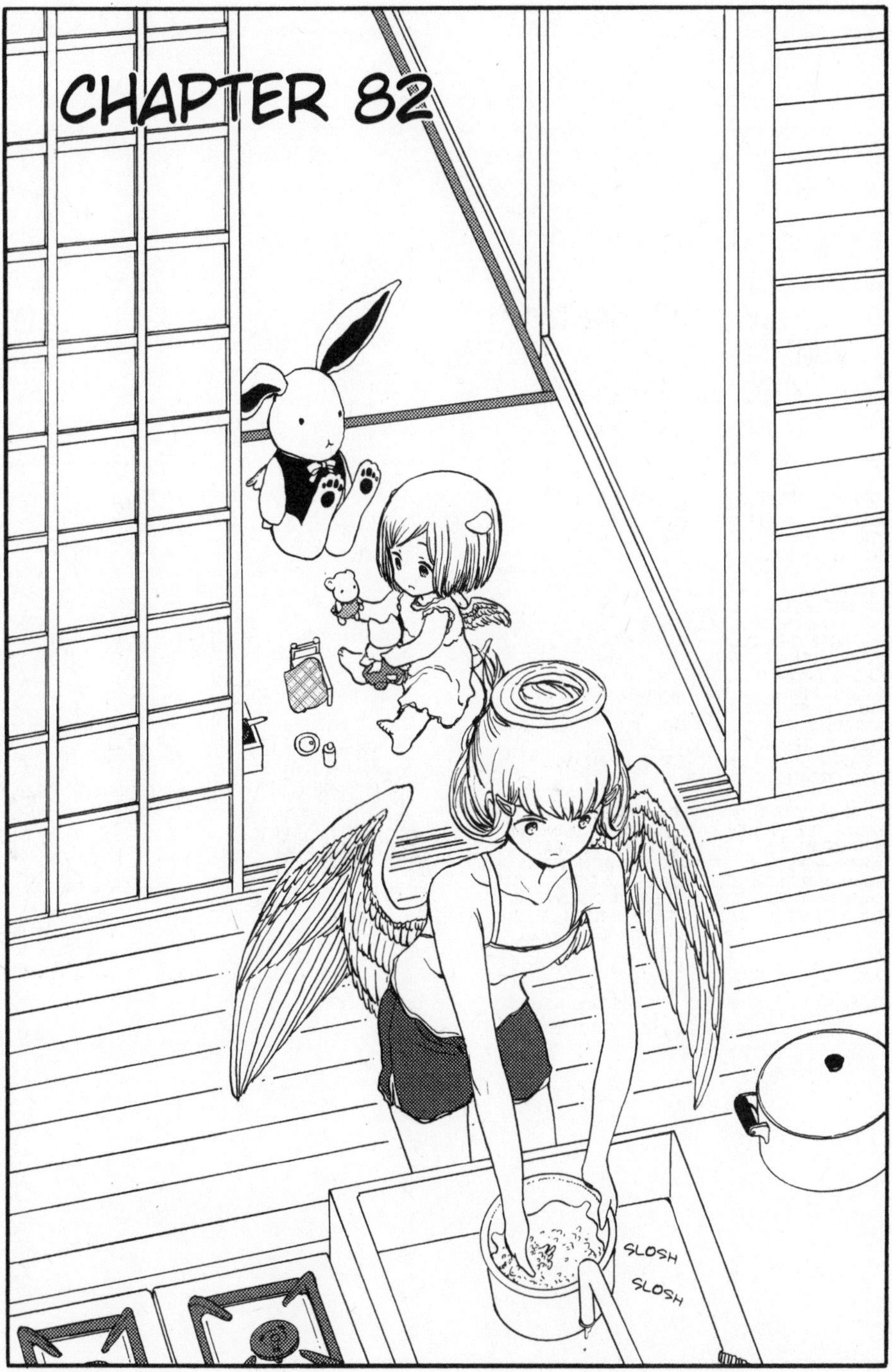
CHAPTER 82
SLOSH
SLOSH

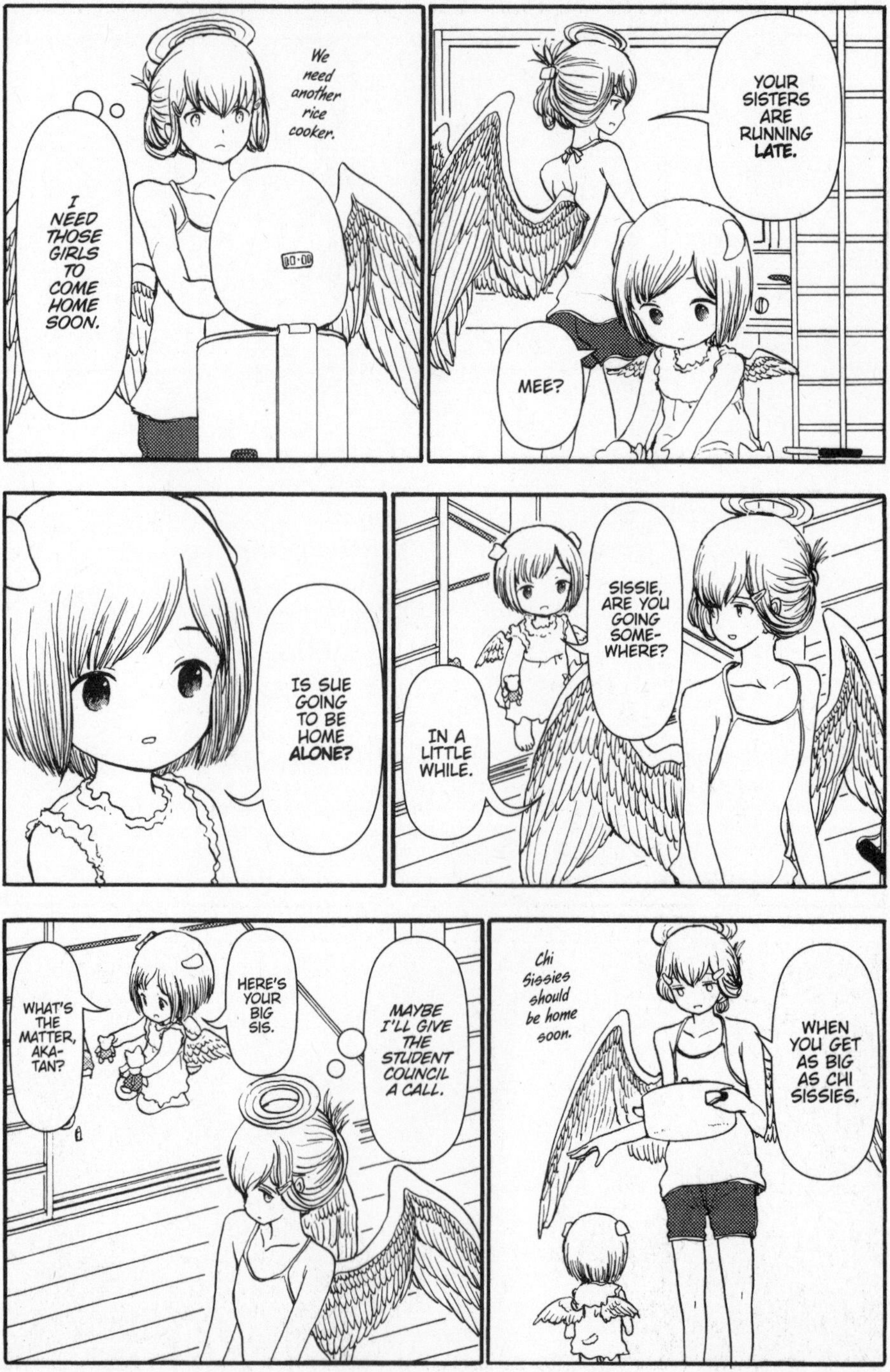
YOUR SISTERS ARE RUNNING LATE.
MEE?
We need another rice cooker.
I NEED THOSE GIRLS TO COME HOME SOON.
SISSIE, ARE YOU GOING SOME-WHERE?
IN A LITTLE WHILE.
IS SUE GOING TO BE HOME ALONE?
WHEN YOU GET AS BIG AS CHI SISSIES.
Chi Sissies should be home soon.
MAYBE I'LL GIVE THE STUDENT COUNCIL A CALL.
HERE'S YOUR BIG SIS.
WHAT'S THE MATTER, AKA-TAN?

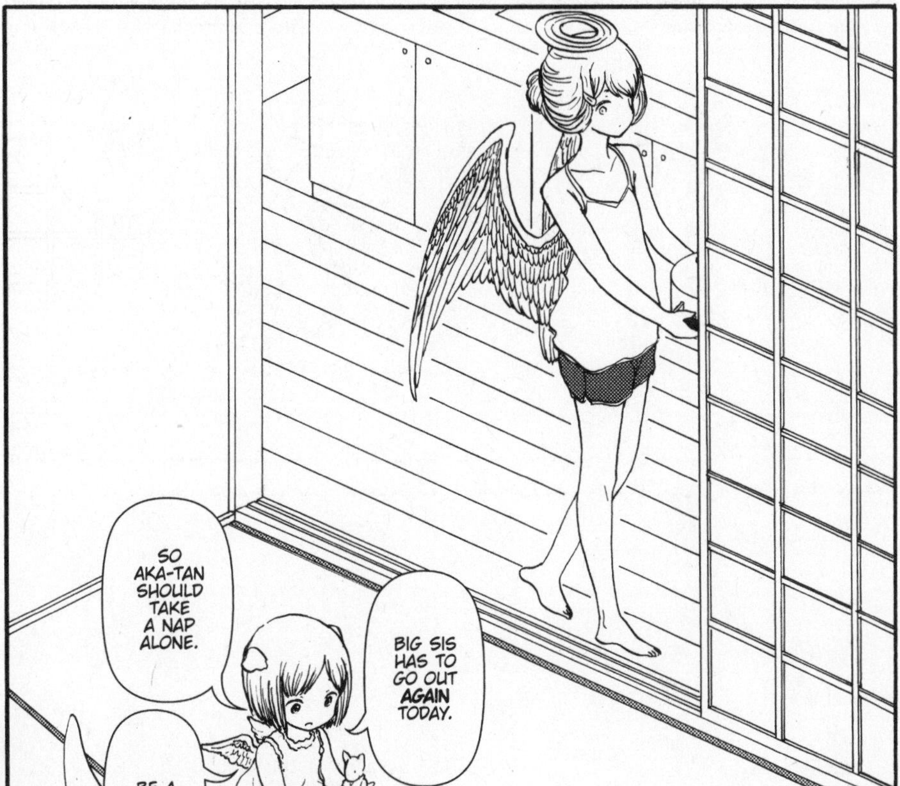
BIG SIS HAS TO GO OUT **AGAIN** TODAY.
SO AKA-TAN SHOULD TAKE A NAP ALONE.
BE A GOOD GIRL.

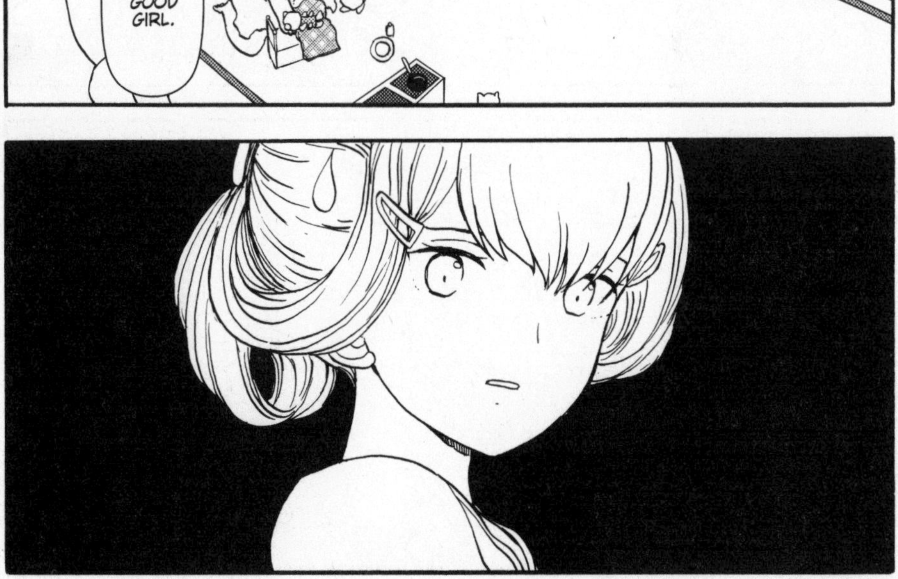

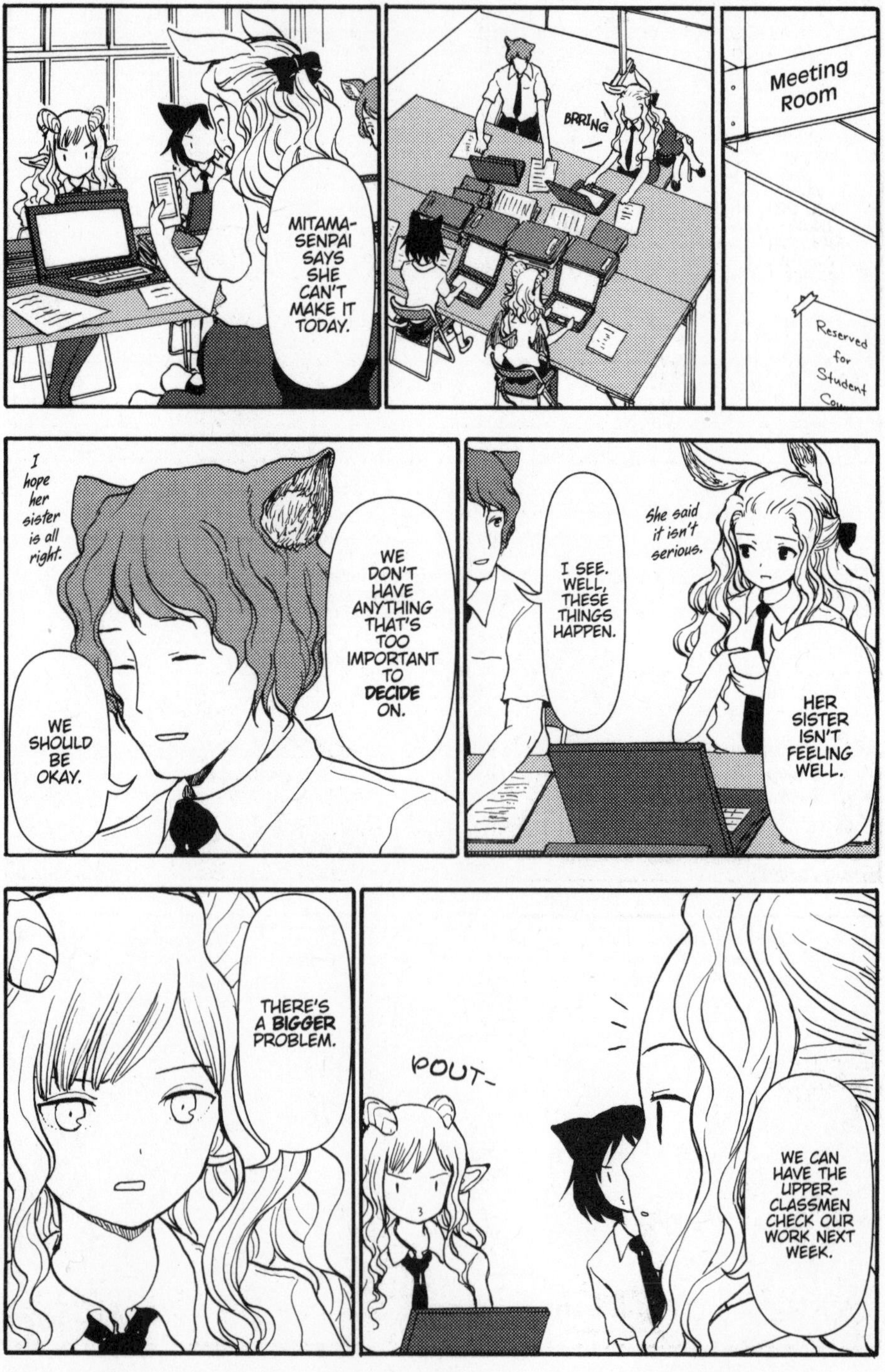
Meeting Room
Reserved for Student
BRRING
MITAMA-SENPAI SAYS SHE CAN'T MAKE IT TODAY.
HER SISTER ISN'T FEELING WELL.
She said it isn't serious.
I SEE. WELL, THESE THINGS HAPPEN.
WE DON'T HAVE ANYTHING THAT'S TOO IMPORTANT TO **DECIDE** ON.
WE SHOULD BE OKAY.
I hope her sister is all right.
WE CAN HAVE THE UPPERCLASSMEN CHECK OUR WORK NEXT WEEK.
POUT-
THERE'S A **BIGGER** PROBLEM.

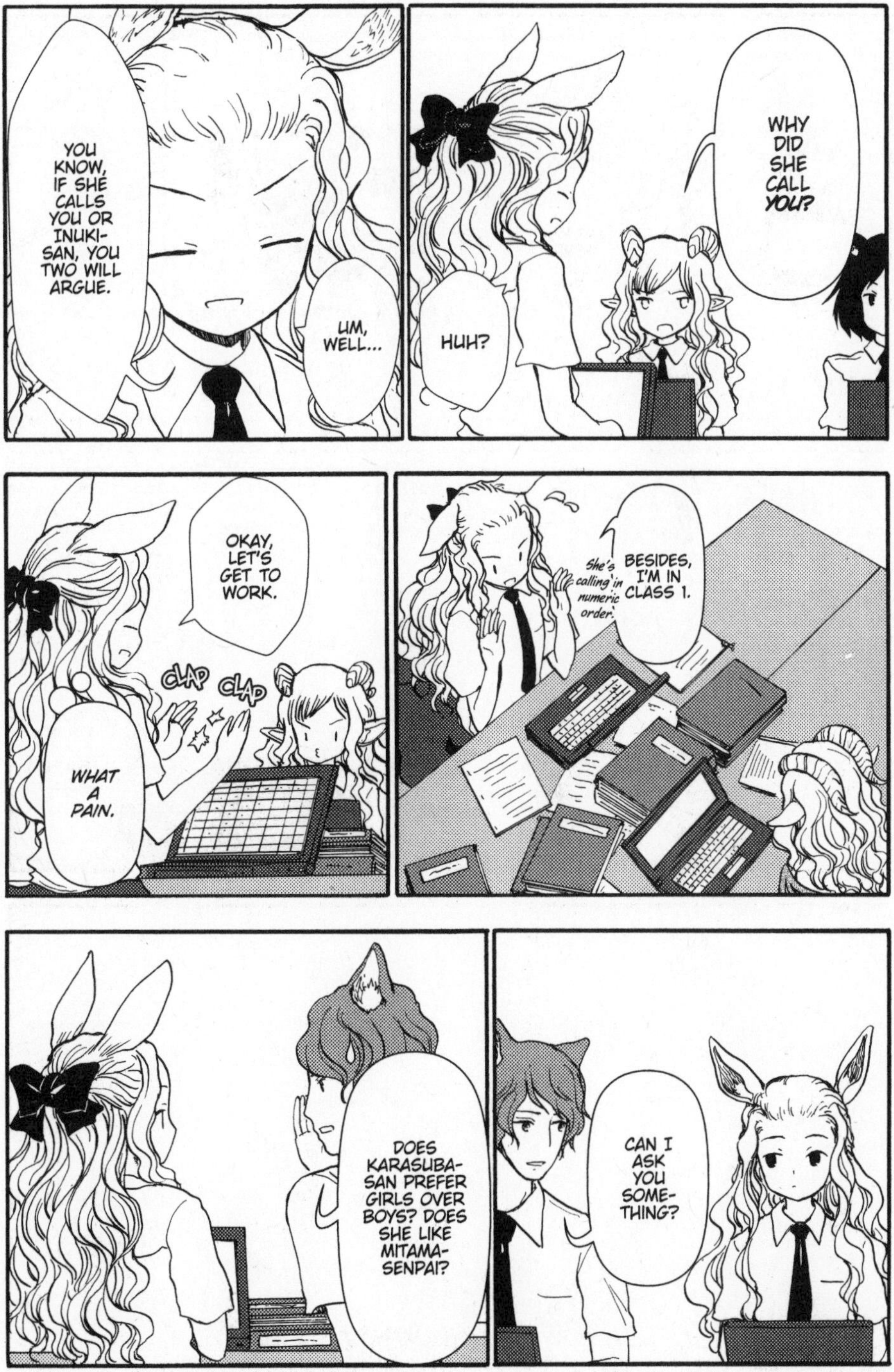
WHY DID SHE CALL *YOU?*
HUH?
UM, WELL...
YOU KNOW, IF SHE CALLS YOU OR INUKI-SAN, YOU TWO WILL ARGUE.
BESIDES, I'M IN CLASS 1.
She's calling in numeric order.
OKAY, LET'S GET TO WORK.
CLAP CLAP
WHAT A PAIN.
CAN I ASK YOU SOMETHING?
DOES KARASUBA-SAN PREFER GIRLS OVER BOYS? DOES SHE LIKE MITAMA-SENPAI?

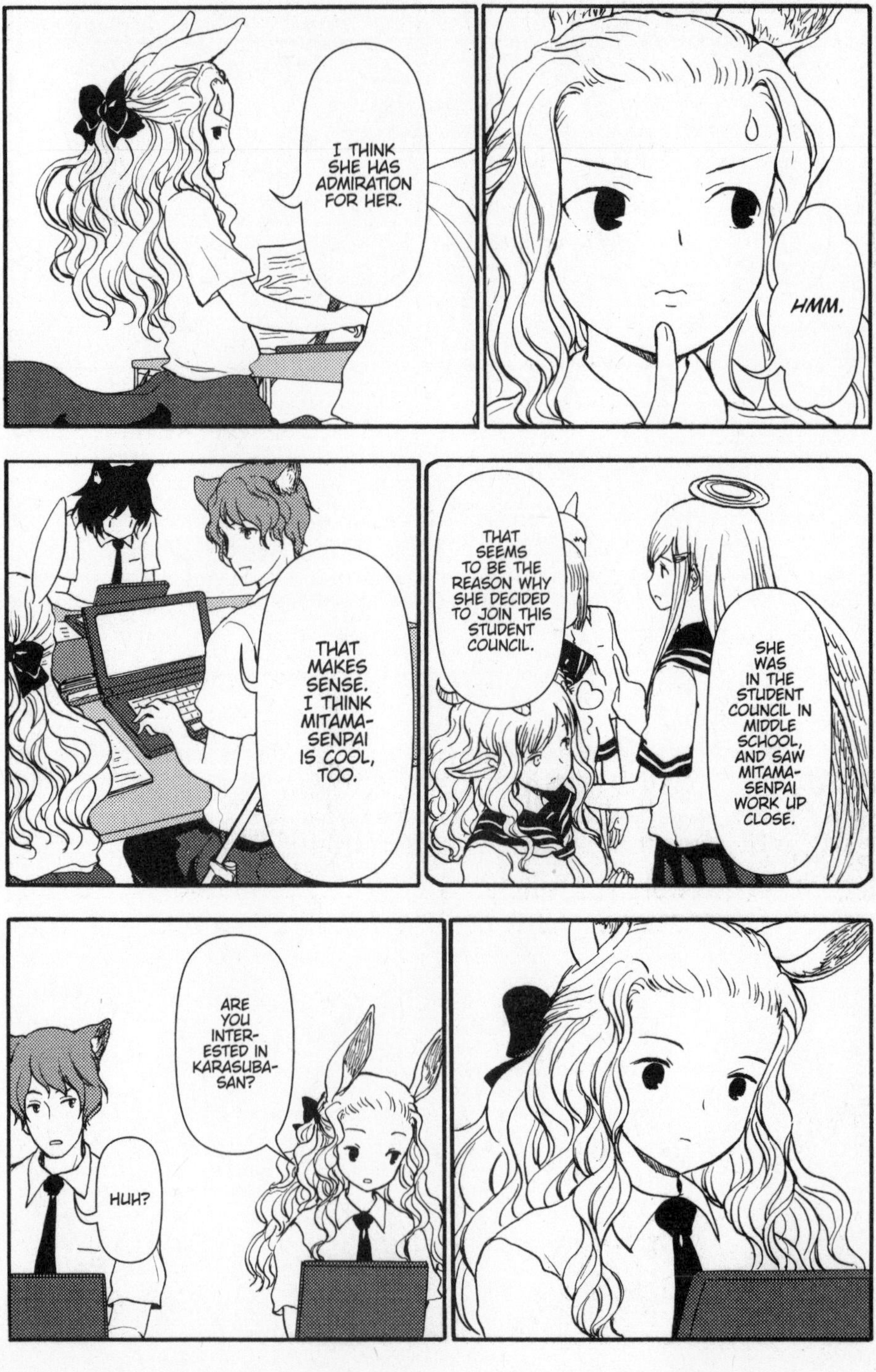
HMM.
I THINK SHE HAS ADMIRATION FOR HER.
SHE WAS IN THE STUDENT COUNCIL IN MIDDLE SCHOOL, AND SAW MITAMA-SENPAI WORK UP CLOSE.
THAT SEEMS TO BE THE REASON WHY SHE DECIDED TO JOIN THIS STUDENT COUNCIL.
THAT MAKES SENSE. I THINK MITAMA-SENPAI IS COOL, TOO.
ARE YOU INTER-ESTED IN KARASUBA-SAN?
HUH?

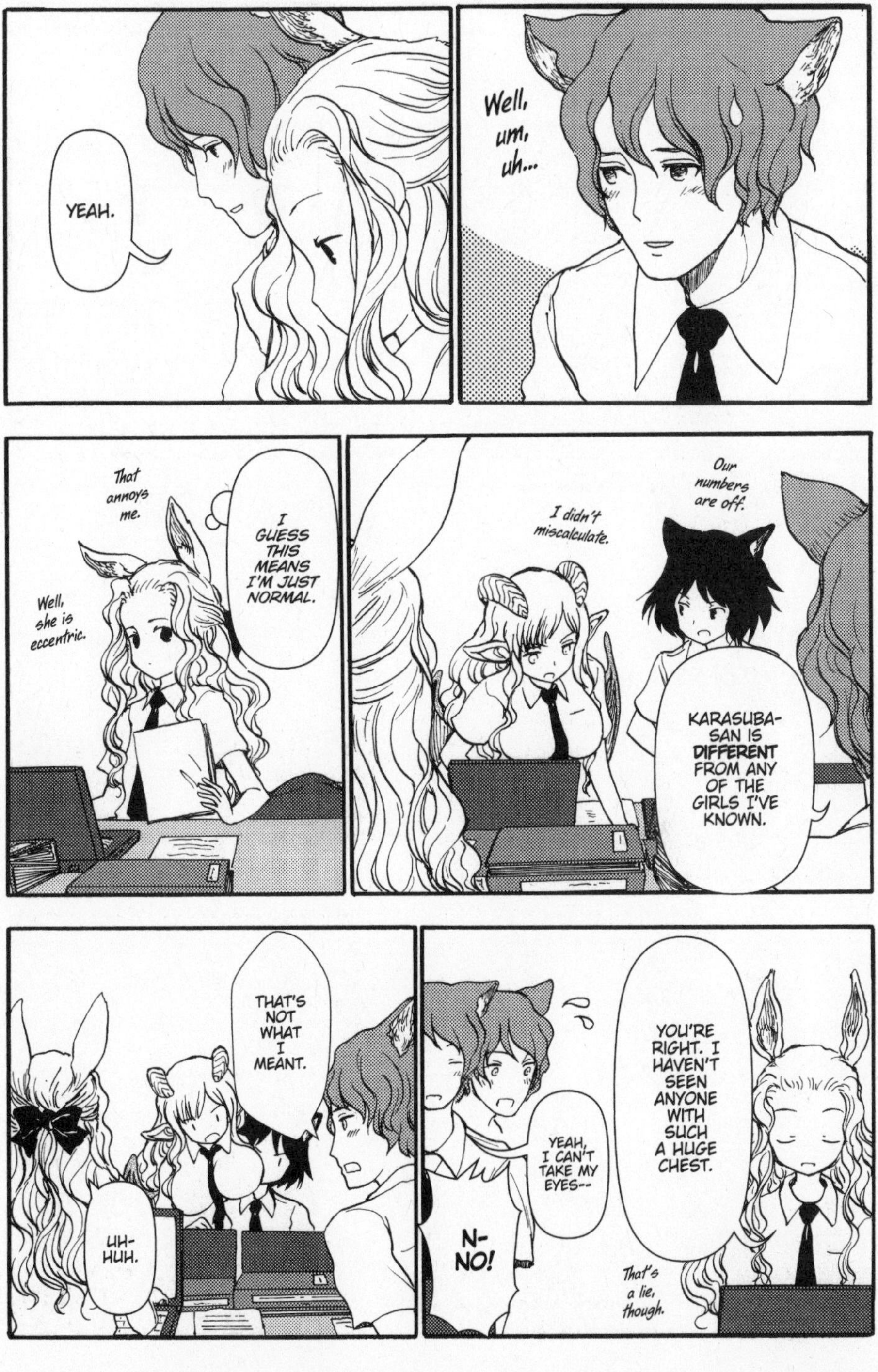
Well, um, uh...
YEAH.
Our numbers are off.
I didn't miscalculate.
KARASUBA-SAN IS **DIFFERENT** FROM ANY OF THE GIRLS I'VE KNOWN.
I GUESS THIS MEANS I'M JUST NORMAL.
That annoys me.
Well, she is eccentric.
YOU'RE RIGHT. I HAVEN'T SEEN ANYONE WITH SUCH A HUGE CHEST.
YEAH, I CAN'T TAKE MY EYES--
N-NO!
That's a lie, though.
THAT'S NOT WHAT I MEANT.
UH-HUH.

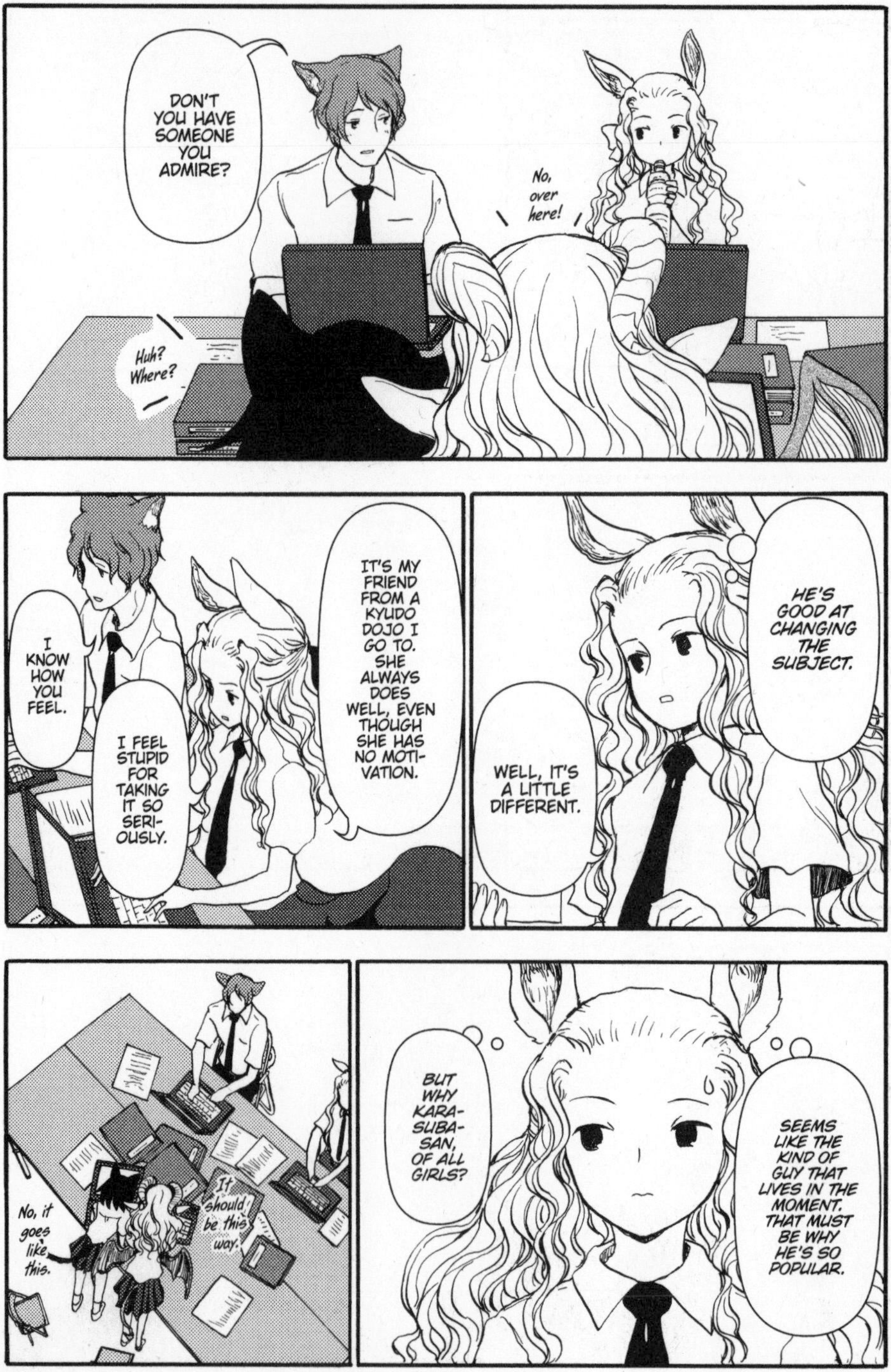
DON'T YOU HAVE SOMEONE YOU ADMIRE?
No, over here!
Huh? Where?
HE'S GOOD AT CHANGING THE SUBJECT.
WELL, IT'S A LITTLE DIFFERENT.
IT'S MY FRIEND FROM A KYUDO DOJO I GO TO. SHE ALWAYS DOES WELL, EVEN THOUGH SHE HAS NO MOTI-VATION.
I FEEL STUPID FOR TAKING IT SO SERI-OUSLY.
I KNOW HOW YOU FEEL.
SEEMS LIKE THE KIND OF GUY THAT LIVES IN THE MOMENT. THAT MUST BE WHY HE'S SO POPULAR.
BUT WHY KARA-SUBA-SAN, OF ALL GIRLS?
It should be this way.
No, it goes like this.

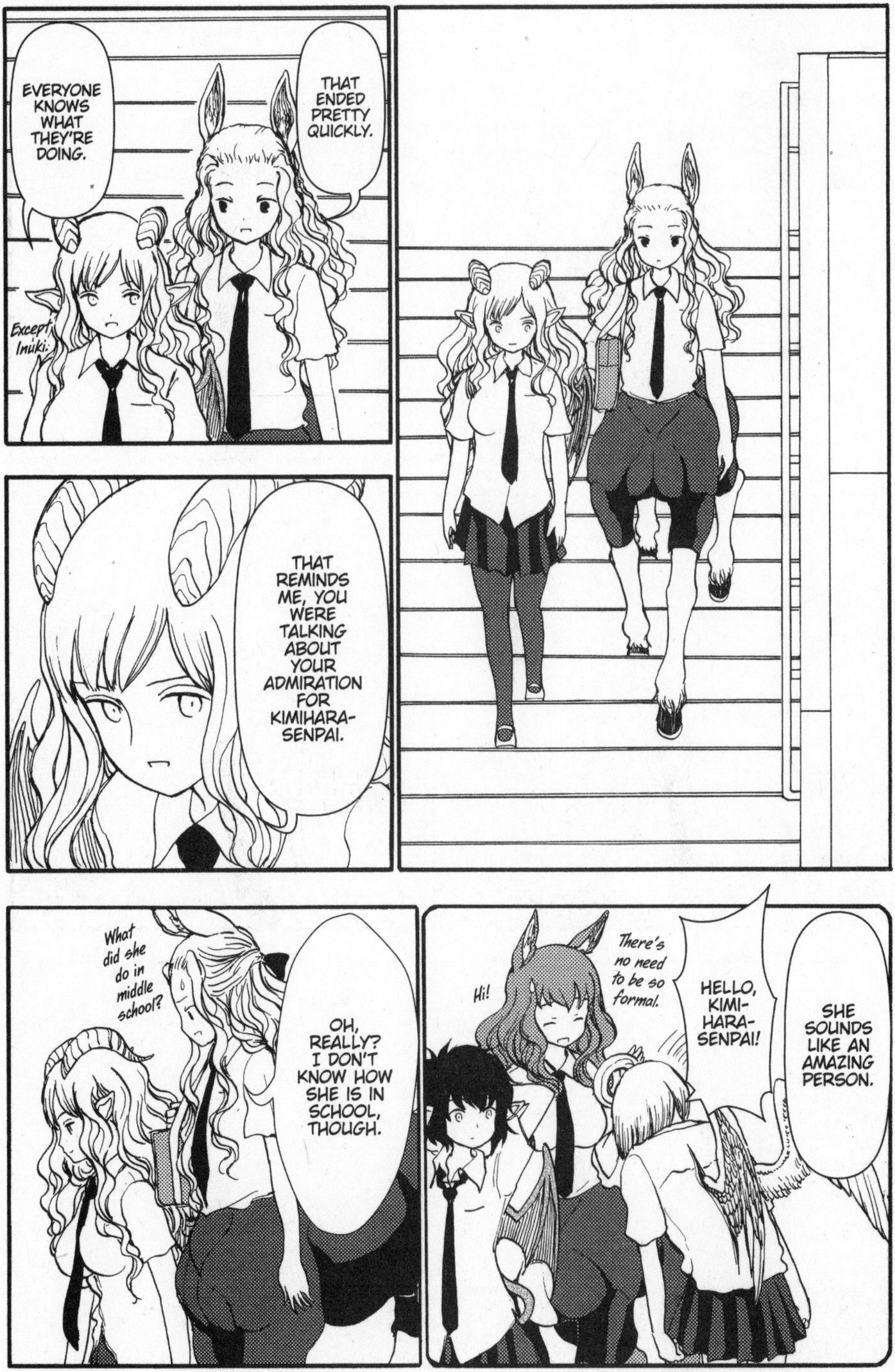
THAT ENDED PRETTY QUICKLY.
EVERYONE KNOWS WHAT THEY'RE DOING.
Except Inuki.
THAT REMINDS ME, YOU WERE TALKING ABOUT YOUR ADMIRATION FOR KIMIHARA-SENPAI.
SHE SOUNDS LIKE AN AMAZING PERSON.
HELLO, KIMI-HARA-SENPAI!
There's no need to be so formal.
Hi!
OH, REALLY? I DON'T KNOW HOW SHE IS IN SCHOOL, THOUGH.
What did she do in middle school?

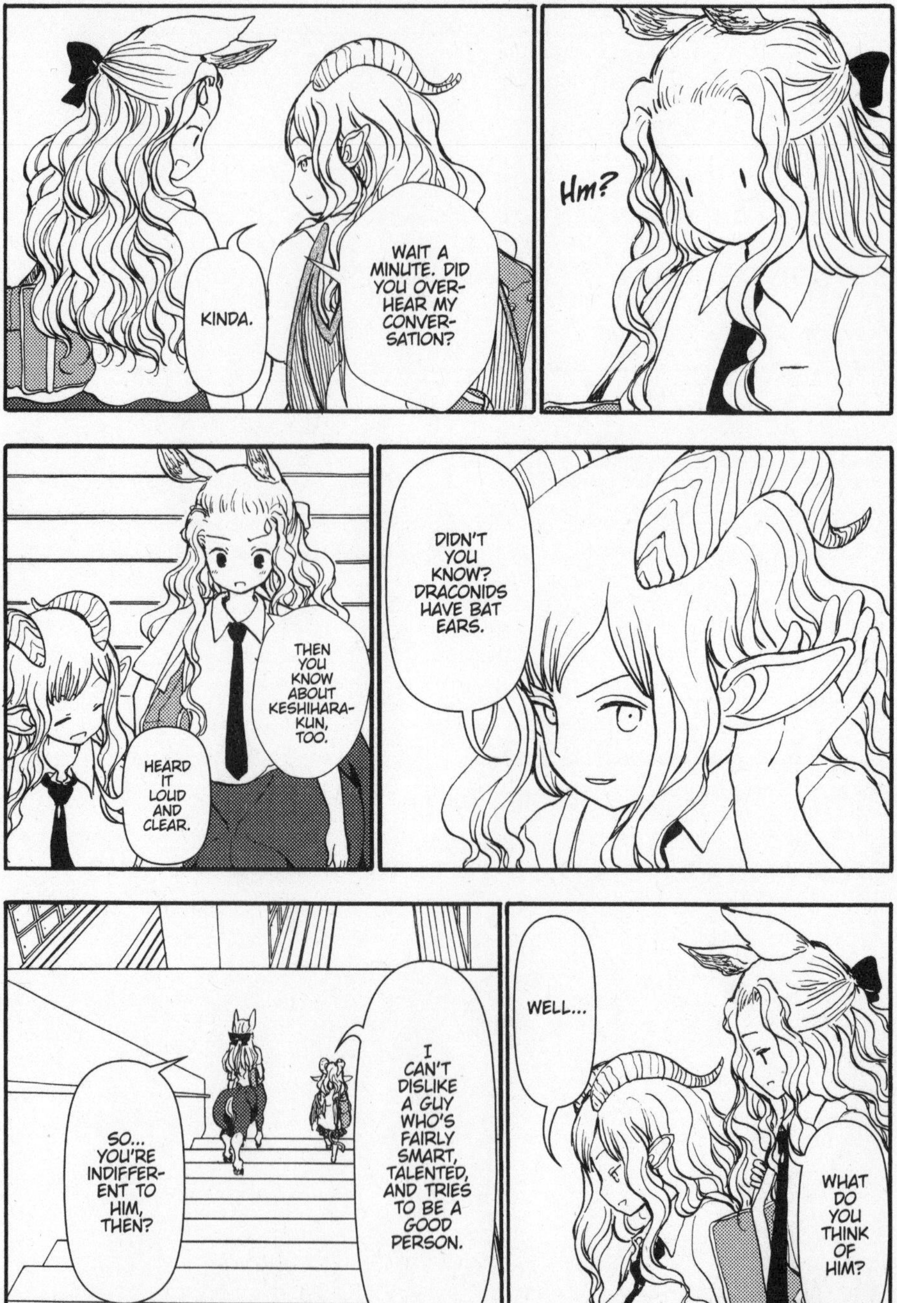
Hm?
WAIT A MINUTE. DID YOU OVERHEAR MY CONVERSATION?
KINDA.
DIDN'T YOU KNOW? DRACONIDS HAVE BAT EARS.
THEN YOU KNOW ABOUT KESHIHARA-KUN, TOO.
HEARD IT LOUD AND CLEAR.
WHAT DO YOU THINK OF HIM?
WELL...
I CAN'T DISLIKE A GUY WHO'S FAIRLY SMART, TALENTED, AND TRIES TO BE A GOOD PERSON.
SO... YOU'RE INDIFFERENT TO HIM, THEN?

A CentaUr's Life

UNDERSTANDING AMPHIBIANFOLK PART 4: AMPHIBIANFOLK SOCIETY

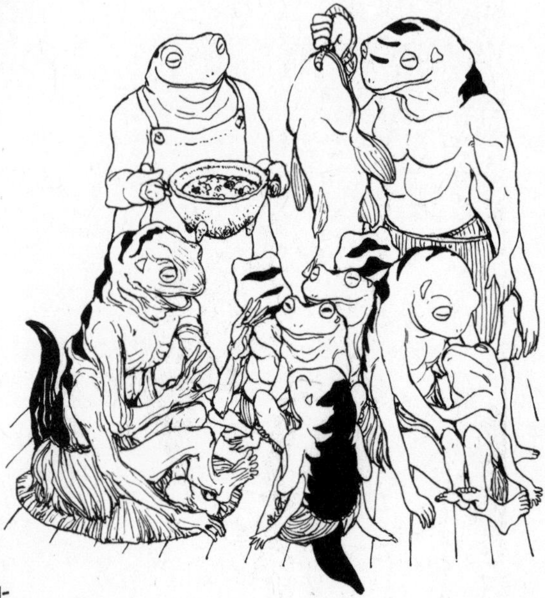

AMPHIBIANFOLK DIDN'T HAVE A RECOGNIZED COUNTRY UNTIL VERY RECENTLY. IT'S BELIEVED THAT THEY WERE A TRIBAL SOCIETY, WITH EACH TRIBE MADE UP OF MULTIPLE FAMILIES THRIVING ON FISHING, HUNTING, AND GATHERING. THE FAMILY UNIT INCLUDES THE ENTIRE EXTENDED FAMILY RATHER THAN SIMPLY THE NUCLEAR FAMILY, AND THEIR REPRODUCTION IS PROLIFIC--IT IS NOT UNCOMMON FOR AN AMPHIBIAN-FOLK WOMAN TO HAVE MORE THAN TEN CHILDREN. THEIR TROPICAL RAINFOREST HOME IS NOT IDEAL FOR FARMING, AS IT IS DIFFICULT FOR CROPS TO RISE FROM MASSES OF DECOMPOSED FALLEN LEAVES. NEITHER POVERTY NOR SOCIAL STATUS WERE KNOWN TO THEM; IT WAS THE QUINT-ESSENTIAL PRIMITIVE FORAGING SOCIETY.

IN RECENT YEARS, HOWEVER, THERE WERE SIGNS OF THE TRIBES MERGING. THE REASON FOR THIS SEEMS TO BE RELATED TO FLOURISHING TRADE WITH MAMMALIANS, WHICH FOR THE AMPHIBIAN-FOLK BROUGHT ABOUT AN INTRODUCTION TO THE CONCEPT OF SAVING THEIR WEALTH AND THE NEED FOR LEADERS WHO COULD HANDLE NEW SITUATIONS WITH WISDOM. THERE'S SPECULATION THAT THE AMPHIBIAN-FOLK-LED, ANTI-GOVERNMENT MILITIA GROUP CTHULCTHUL IS CURRENTLY PLAYING THE ROLE OF A CENTRAL GOVERNMENT, CREATING A UNIFIED STATE FOR THEIR PEOPLE. THEIR UNPRECEDENTED ATTACKS AGAINST MAMMALIAN SOCIETY AND MODERN MILITARY FORCE DEMONSTRATE THAT THEY HAVE STRONG ORGANIZATION AND LEADERSHIP. SOME EXPERTS SAY THAT MAMMALIANS ARE RESPONSIBLE FOR THE CREATION OF MODERN AMPHIBIANFOLK SOCIETY, INCLUDING CTHULCTHUL.

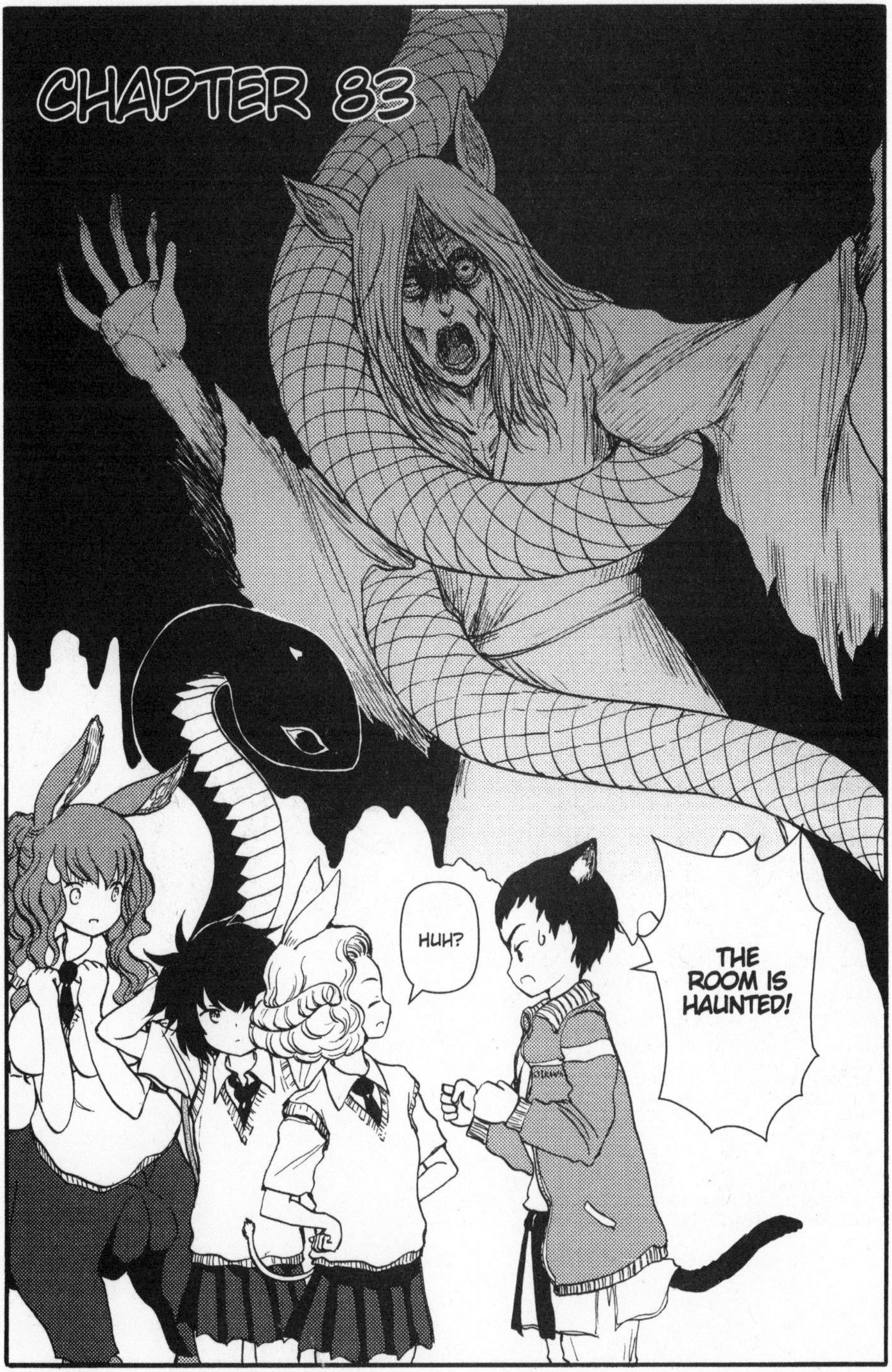
CHAPTER 83
THE ROOM IS HAUNTED!
HUH?

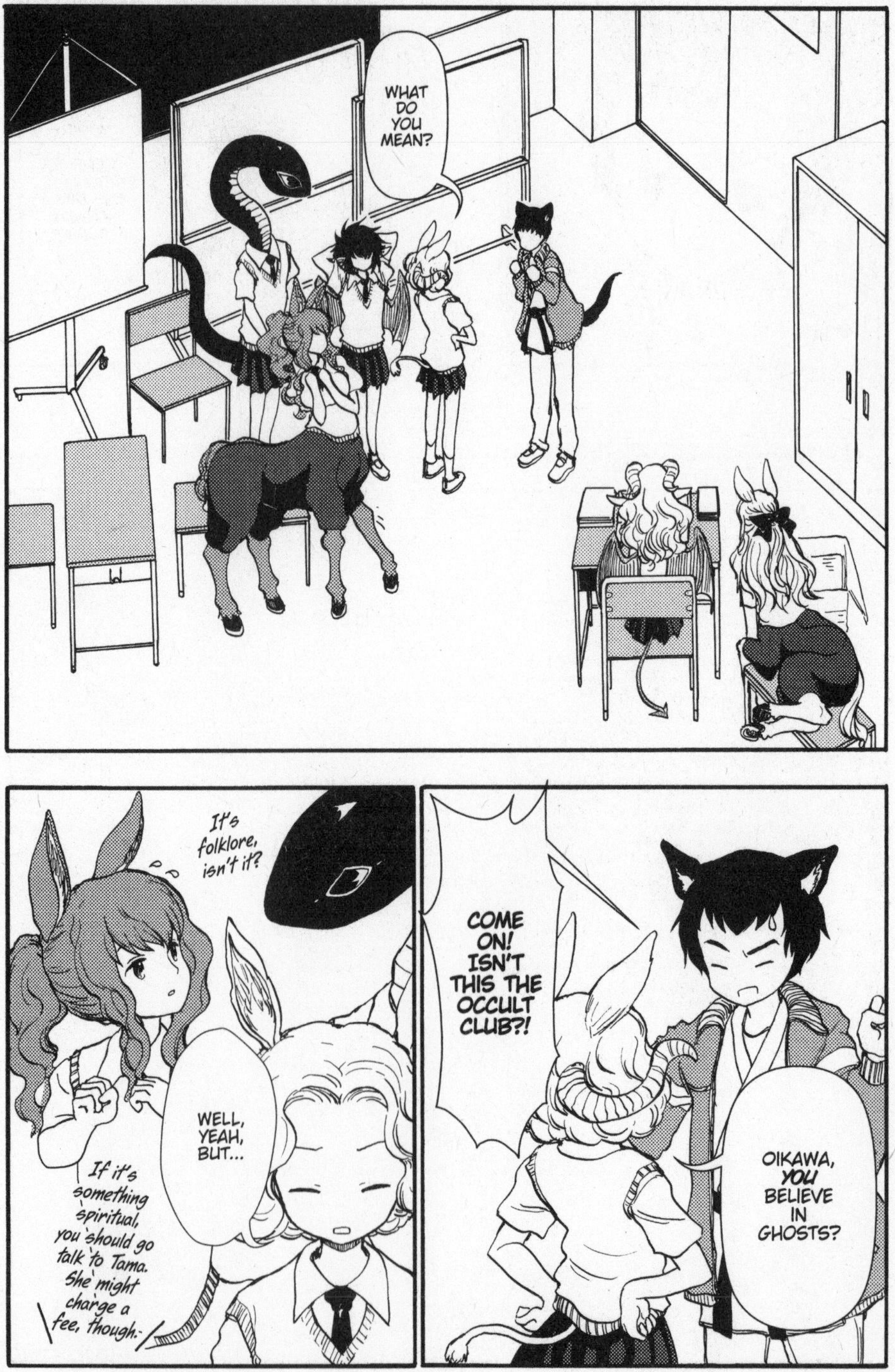
WHAT DO YOU MEAN?
COME ON! ISN'T THIS THE OCCULT CLUB?!
OIKAWA, YOU BELIEVE IN GHOSTS?
It's folklore, isn't it?
WELL, YEAH, BUT...
If it's something spiritual, you should go talk to Tama. She might charge a fee, though.

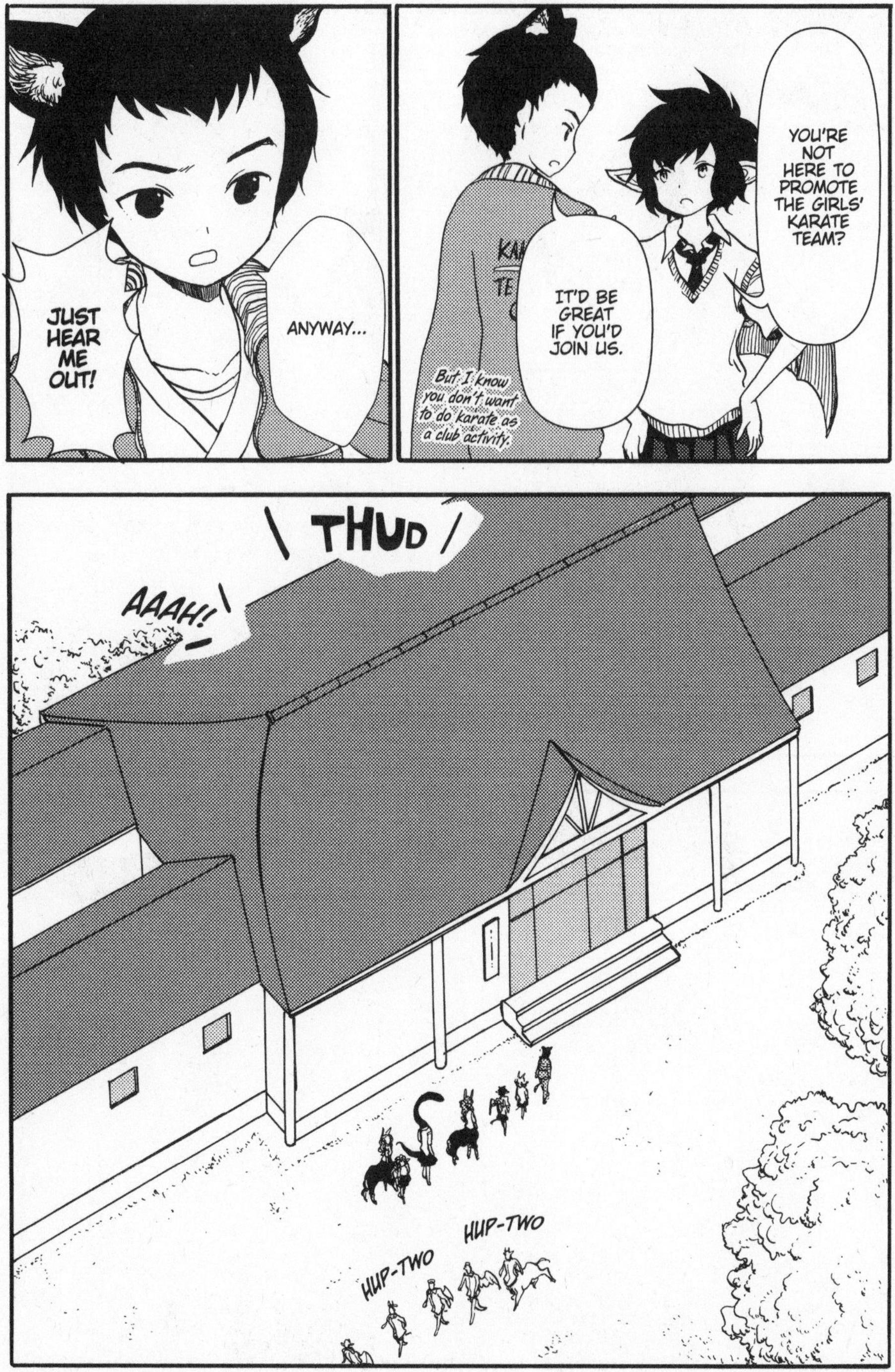
YOU'RE NOT HERE TO PROMOTE THE GIRLS' KARATE TEAM?
IT'D BE GREAT IF YOU'D JOIN US.
But I know you don't want to do karate as a club activity.
ANYWAY...
JUST HEAR ME OUT!
THUD
AAAH!
HUP-TWO
HUP-TWO

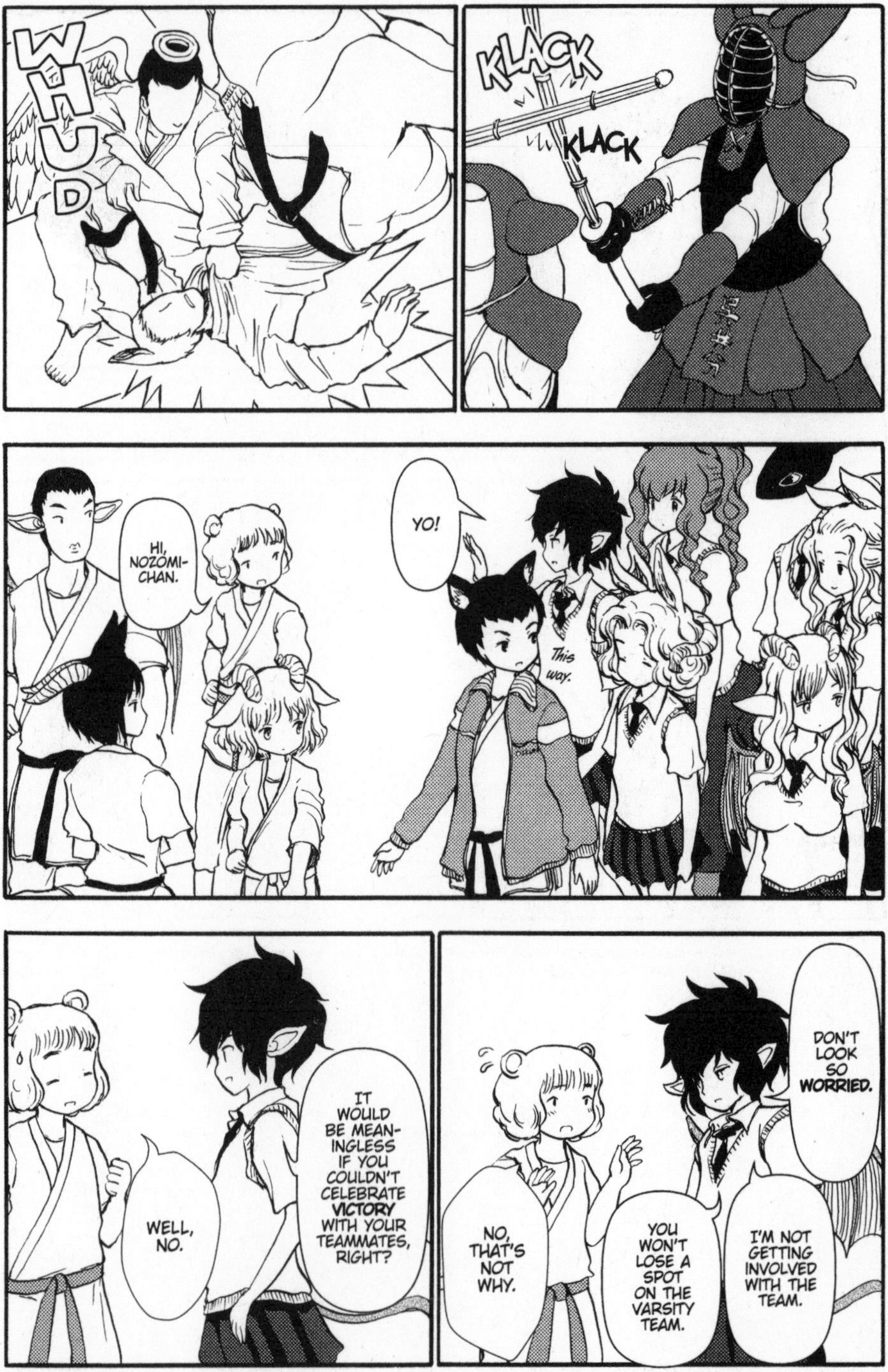
KLACK
KLACK
WHUD
YO!
This way.
HI, NOZOMI-CHAN.
DON'T LOOK SO **WORRIED.**
I'M NOT GETTING INVOLVED WITH THE TEAM.
YOU WON'T LOSE A SPOT ON THE VARSITY TEAM.
NO, THAT'S NOT WHY.
IT WOULD BE MEANINGLESS IF YOU COULDN'T CELEBRATE **VICTORY** WITH YOUR TEAMMATES, RIGHT?
WELL, NO.

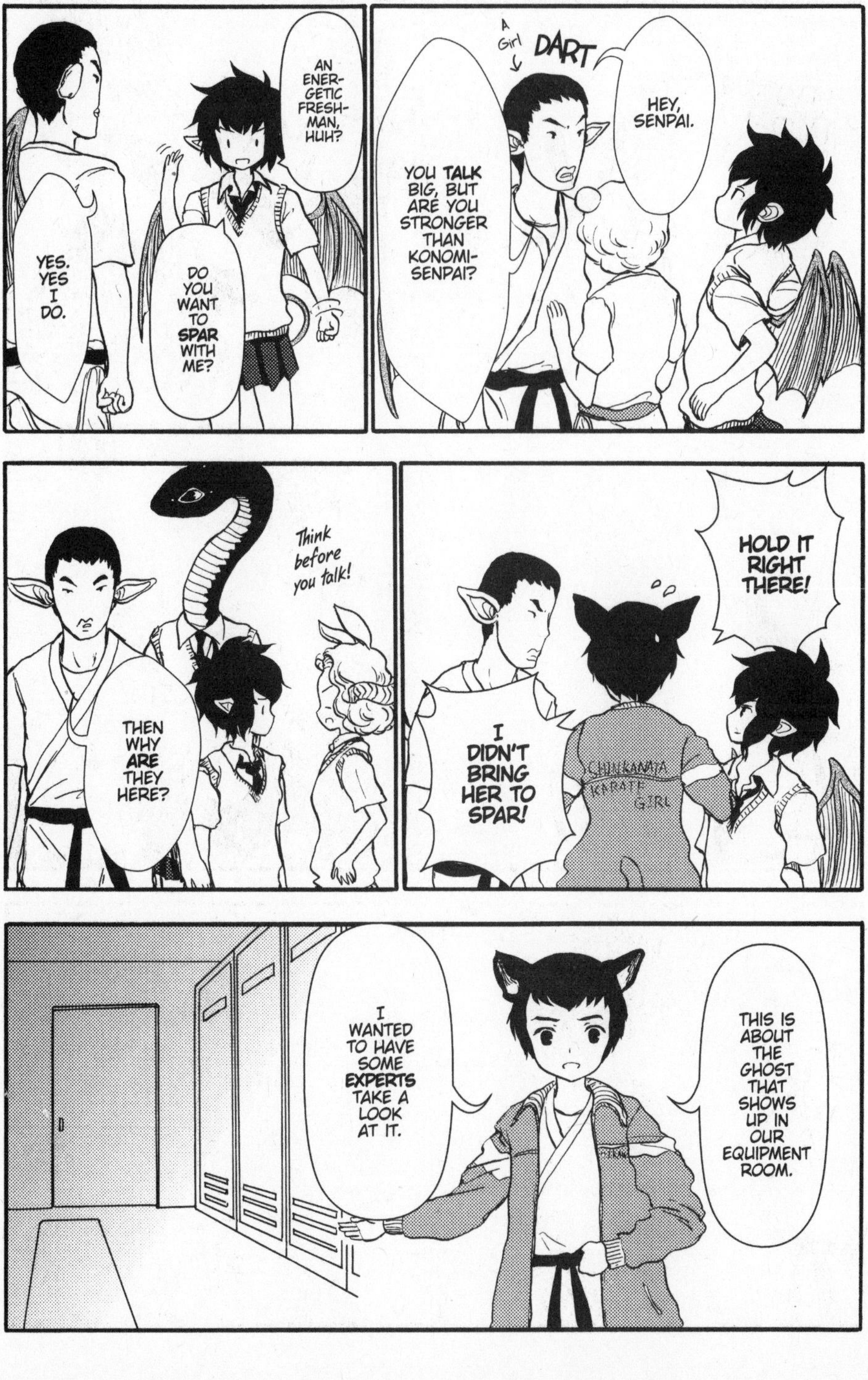
A Girl
DART
HEY, SENPAI.
YOU TALK BIG, BUT ARE YOU STRONGER THAN KONOMI-SENPAI?
AN ENERGETIC FRESHMAN, HUH?
DO YOU WANT TO SPAR WITH ME?
YES. YES I DO.
HOLD IT RIGHT THERE!
I DIDN'T BRING HER TO SPAR!
KARATE GIRL
Think before you talk!
THEN WHY ARE THEY HERE?
THIS IS ABOUT THE GHOST THAT SHOWS UP IN OUR EQUIPMENT ROOM.
I WANTED TO HAVE SOME EXPERTS TAKE A LOOK AT IT.

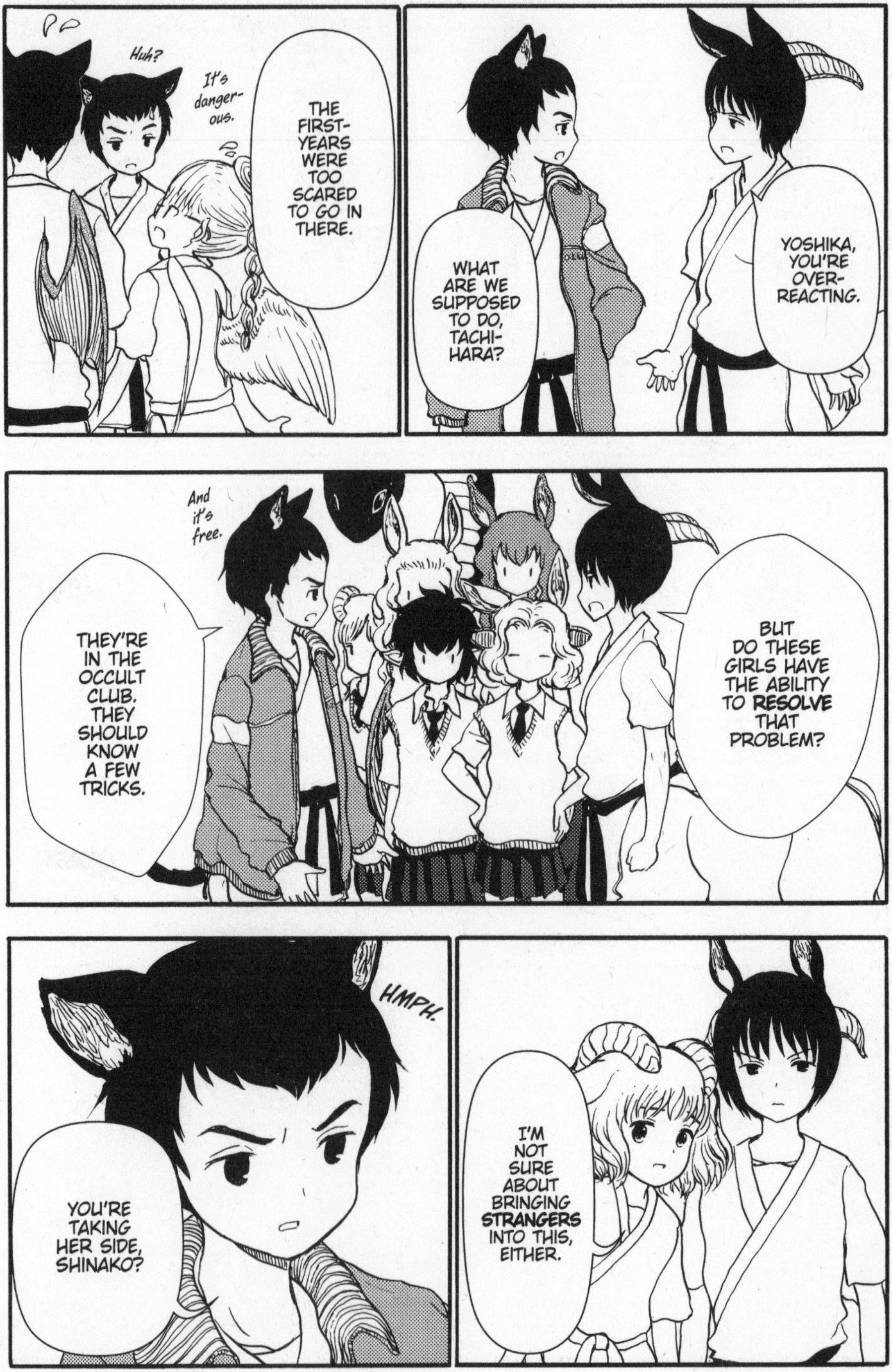
YOSHIKA, YOU'RE OVER-REACTING.
WHAT ARE WE SUPPOSED TO DO, TACHI-HARA?
THE FIRST-YEARS WERE TOO SCARED TO GO IN THERE.
It's danger-ous.
Huh?
BUT DO THESE GIRLS HAVE THE ABILITY TO **RESOLVE** THAT PROBLEM?
THEY'RE IN THE OCCULT CLUB. THEY SHOULD KNOW A FEW TRICKS.
And it's free.
I'M NOT SURE ABOUT BRINGING **STRANGERS** INTO THIS, EITHER.
HMPH.
YOU'RE TAKING HER SIDE, SHINAKO?

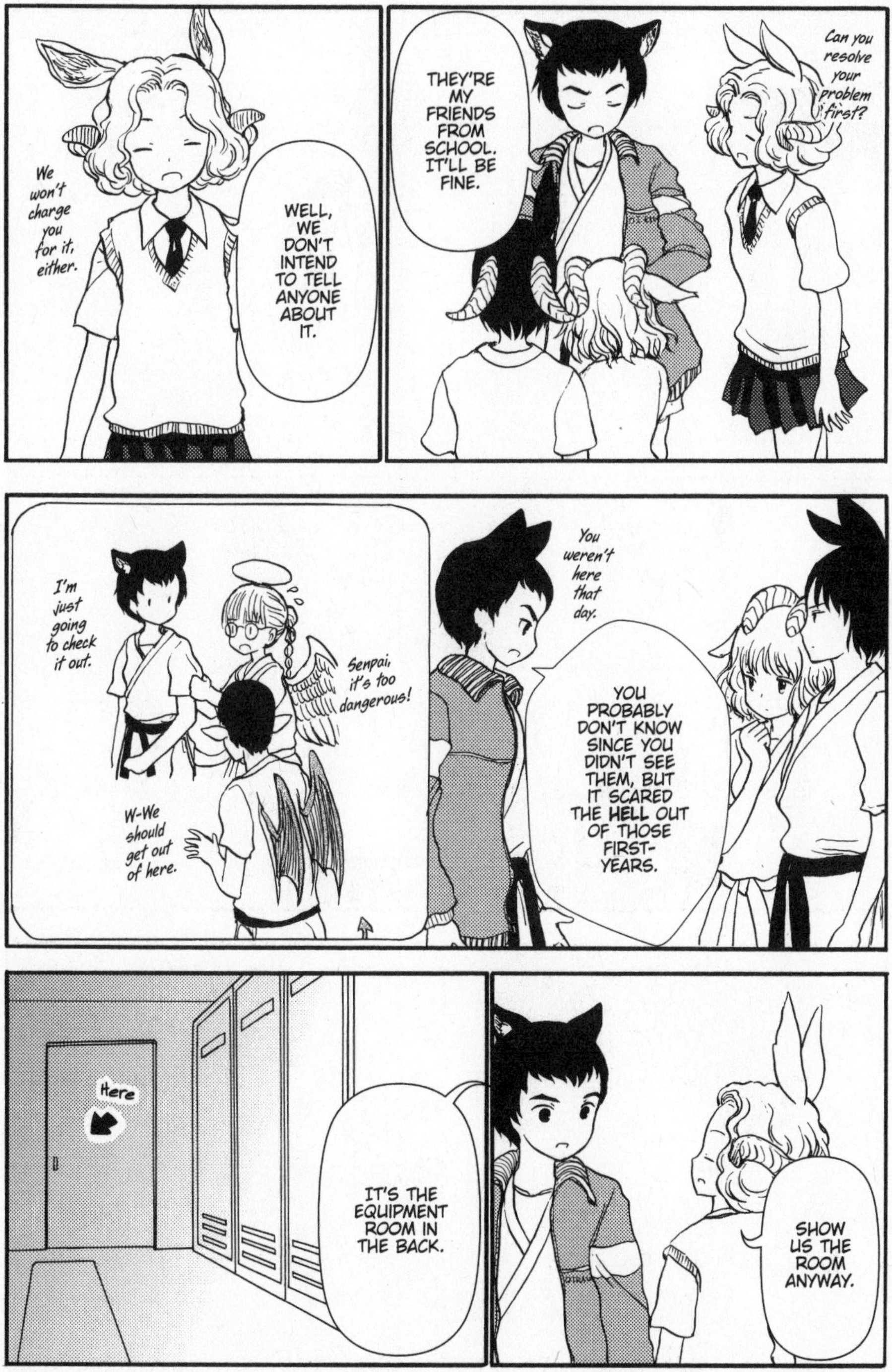
Can you resolve your problem first?
THEY'RE MY FRIENDS FROM SCHOOL. IT'LL BE FINE.
WELL, WE DON'T INTEND TO TELL ANYONE ABOUT IT.
We won't charge you for it, either.
You weren't here that day.
YOU PROBABLY DON'T KNOW SINCE YOU DIDN'T SEE THEM, BUT IT SCARED THE **HELL** OUT OF THOSE FIRST-YEARS.
I'm just going to check it out.
Senpai, it's too dangerous!
W-We should get out of here.
SHOW US THE ROOM ANYWAY.
IT'S THE EQUIPMENT ROOM IN THE BACK.
Here

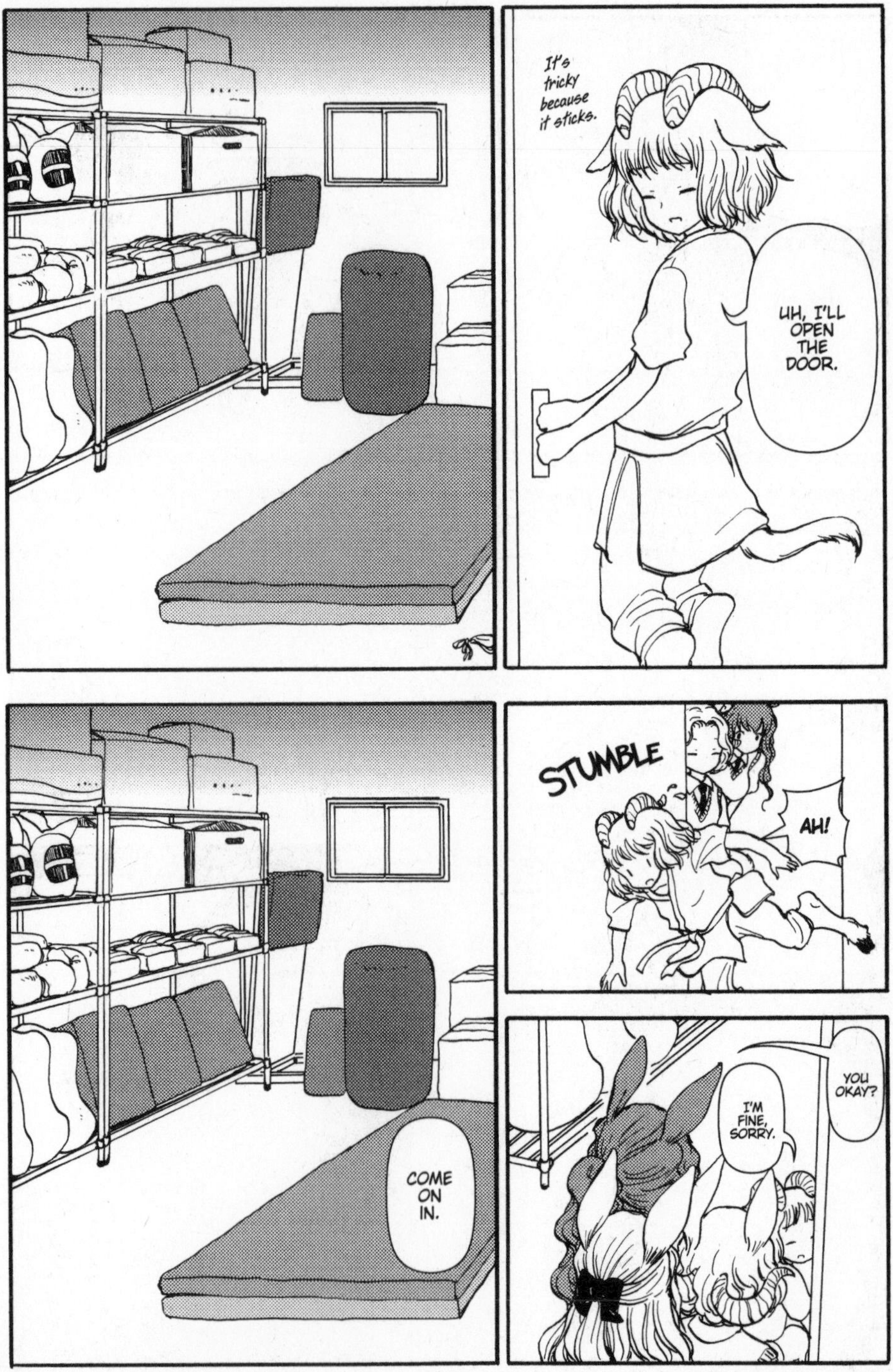
UH, I'LL OPEN THE DOOR.
It's tricky because it sticks.
AH!
STUMBLE
YOU OKAY?
I'M FINE, SORRY.
COME ON IN.

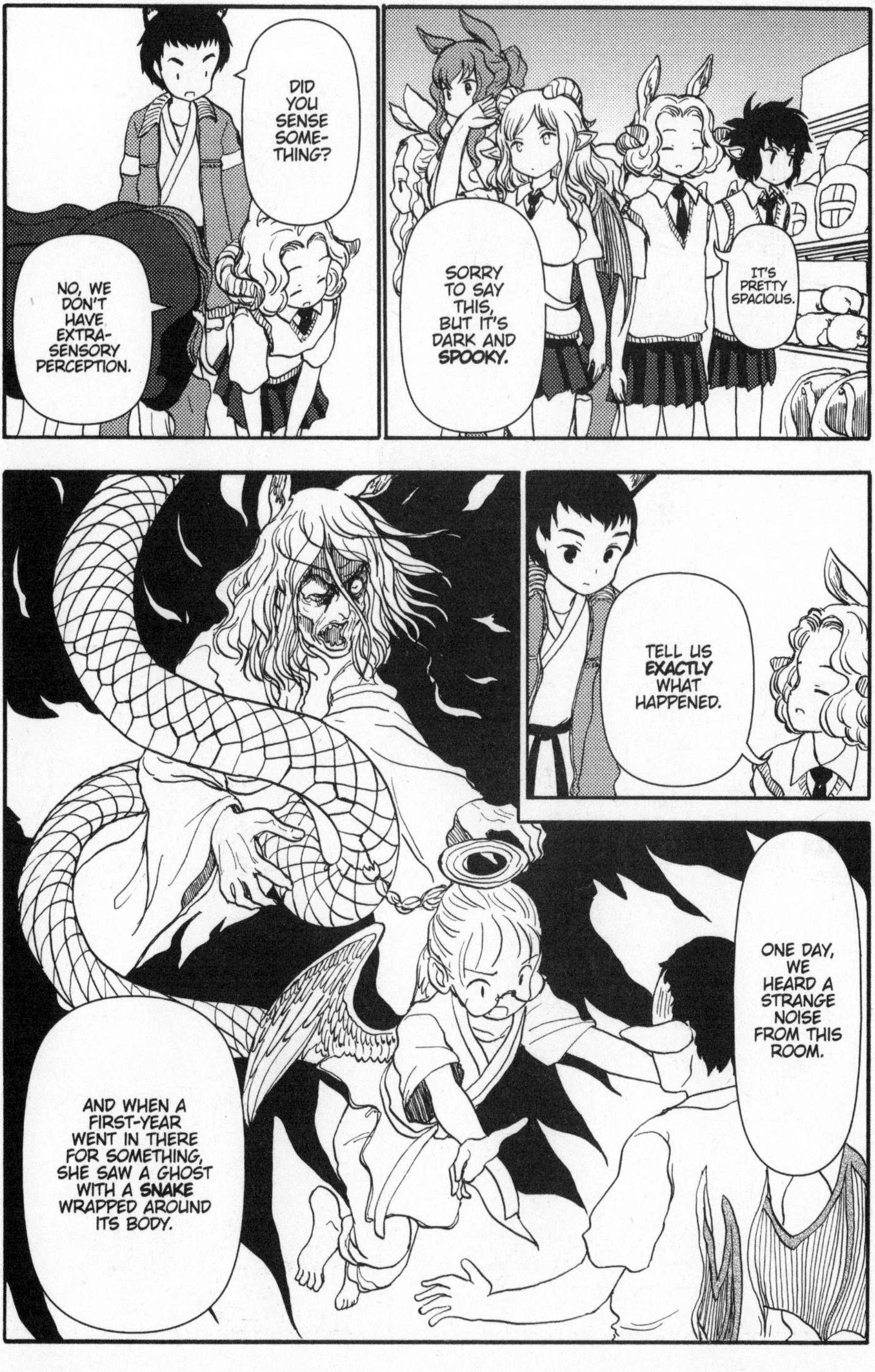
IT'S PRETTY SPACIOUS.
SORRY TO SAY THIS, BUT IT'S DARK AND **SPOOKY.**
DID YOU SENSE SOME-THING?
NO, WE DON'T HAVE EXTRA-SENSORY PERCEPTION.
TELL US **EXACTLY** WHAT HAPPENED.
ONE DAY, WE HEARD A STRANGE NOISE FROM THIS ROOM.
AND WHEN A FIRST-YEAR WENT IN THERE FOR SOMETHING, SHE SAW A GHOST WITH A **SNAKE** WRAPPED AROUND ITS BODY.

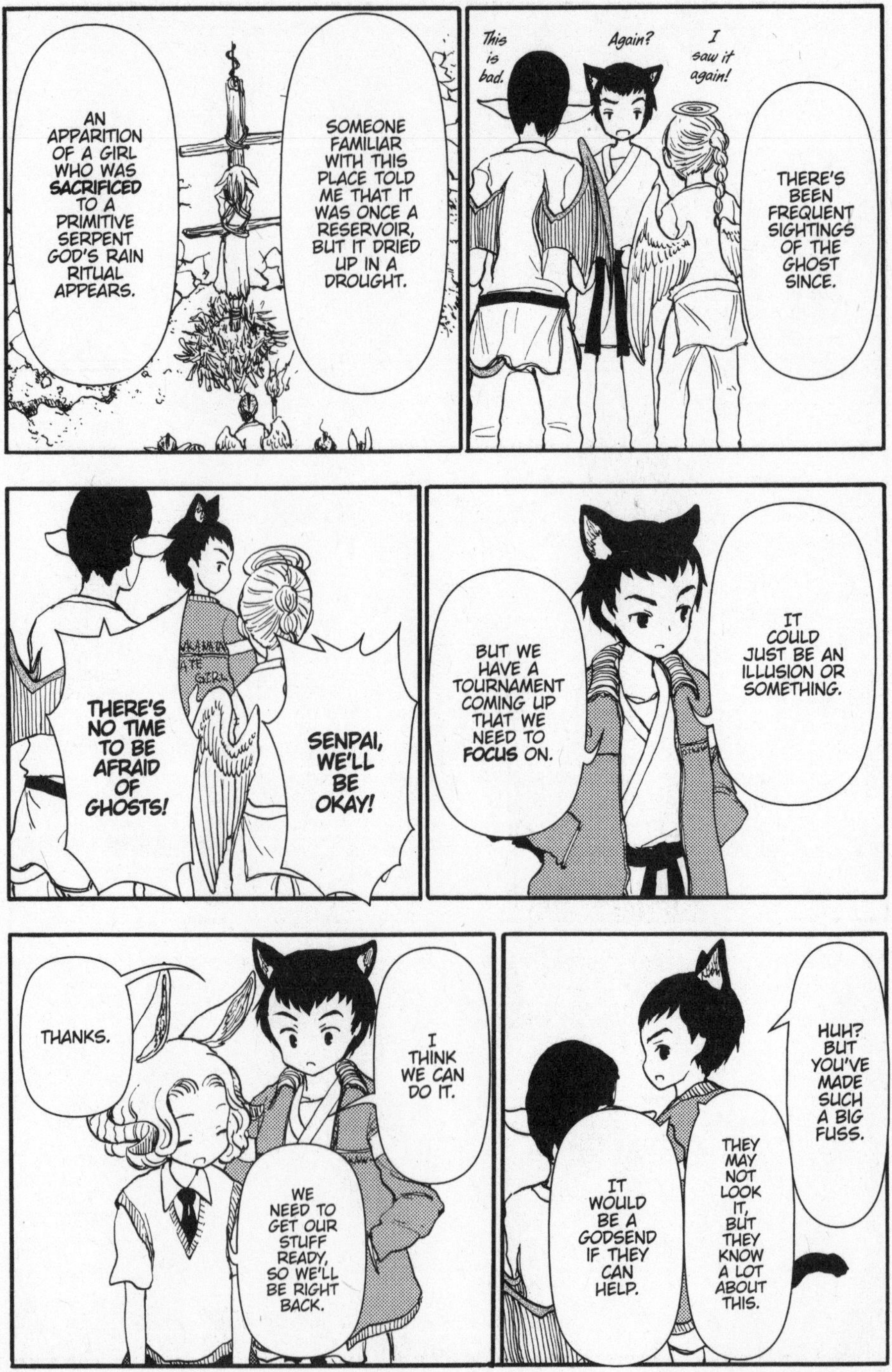
I saw it again!
Again?
This is bad.
THERE'S BEEN FREQUENT SIGHTINGS OF THE GHOST SINCE.
SOMEONE FAMILIAR WITH THIS PLACE TOLD ME THAT IT WAS ONCE A RESERVOIR, BUT IT DRIED UP IN A DROUGHT.
AN APPARITION OF A GIRL WHO WAS **SACRIFICED** TO A PRIMITIVE SERPENT GOD'S RAIN RITUAL APPEARS.
IT COULD JUST BE AN ILLUSION OR SOMETHING.
BUT WE HAVE A TOURNAMENT COMING UP THAT WE NEED TO **FOCUS** ON.
SENPAI, WE'LL BE OKAY!
THERE'S NO TIME TO BE AFRAID OF GHOSTS!
HUH? BUT YOU'VE MADE SUCH A BIG FUSS.
THEY MAY NOT LOOK IT, BUT THEY KNOW A LOT ABOUT THIS.
IT WOULD BE A GODSEND IF THEY CAN HELP.
I THINK WE CAN DO IT.
THANKS.
WE NEED TO GET OUR STUFF READY, SO WE'LL BE RIGHT BACK.

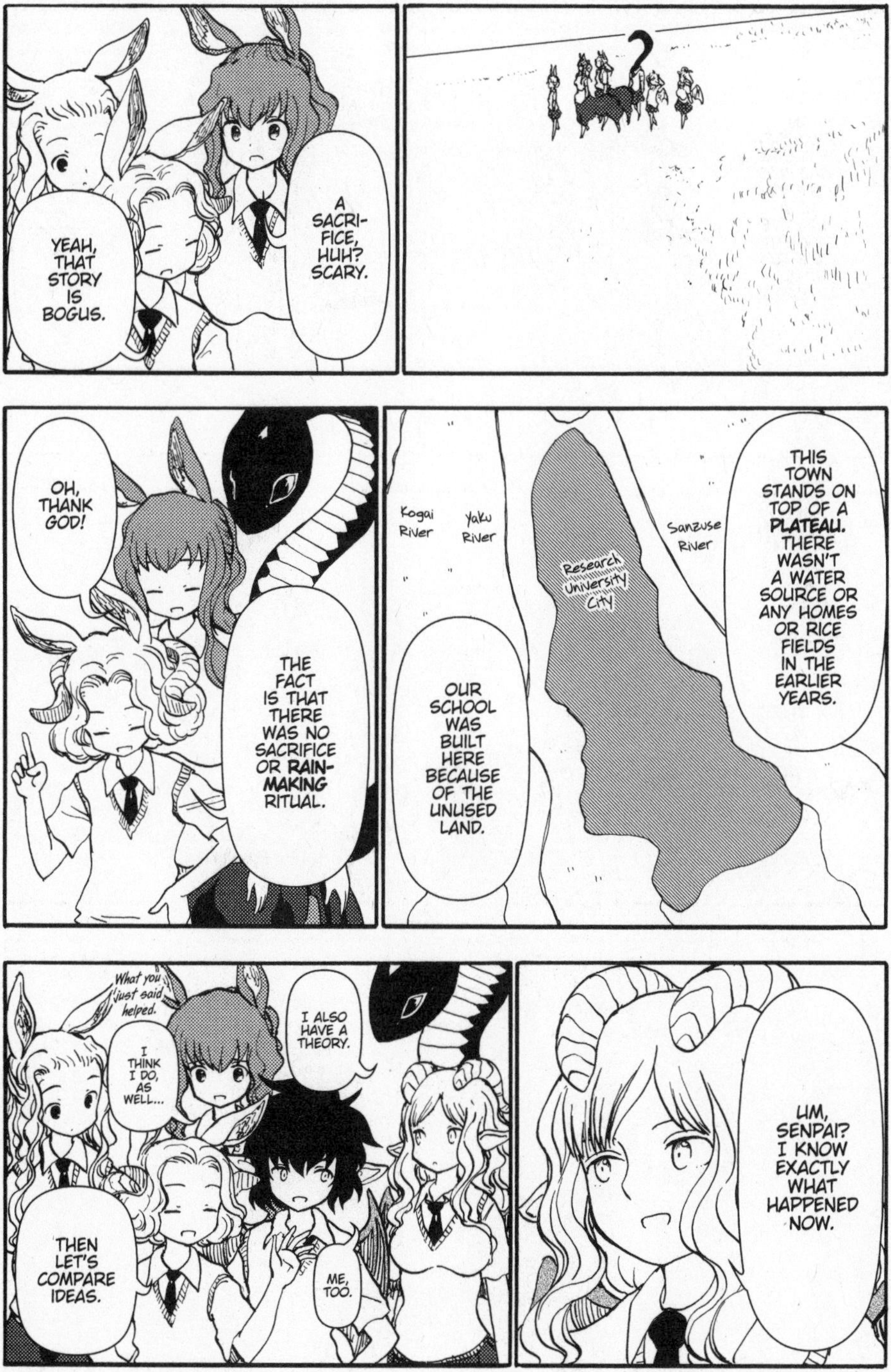
A SACRI-FICE, HUH? SCARY.
YEAH, THAT STORY IS BOGUS.
THIS TOWN STANDS ON TOP OF A **PLATEAU.** THERE WASN'T A WATER SOURCE OR ANY HOMES OR RICE FIELDS IN THE EARLIER YEARS.
Sanzuse River
Research University City
Yaku River
Kogai River
OUR SCHOOL WAS BUILT HERE BECAUSE OF THE UNUSED LAND.
THE FACT IS THAT THERE WAS NO SACRIFICE OR **RAIN-MAKING** RITUAL.
OH, THANK GOD!
UM, SENPAI? I KNOW EXACTLY WHAT HAPPENED NOW.
I ALSO HAVE A THEORY.
What you just said helped.
I THINK I DO, AS WELL...
ME, TOO.
THEN LET'S COMPARE IDEAS.

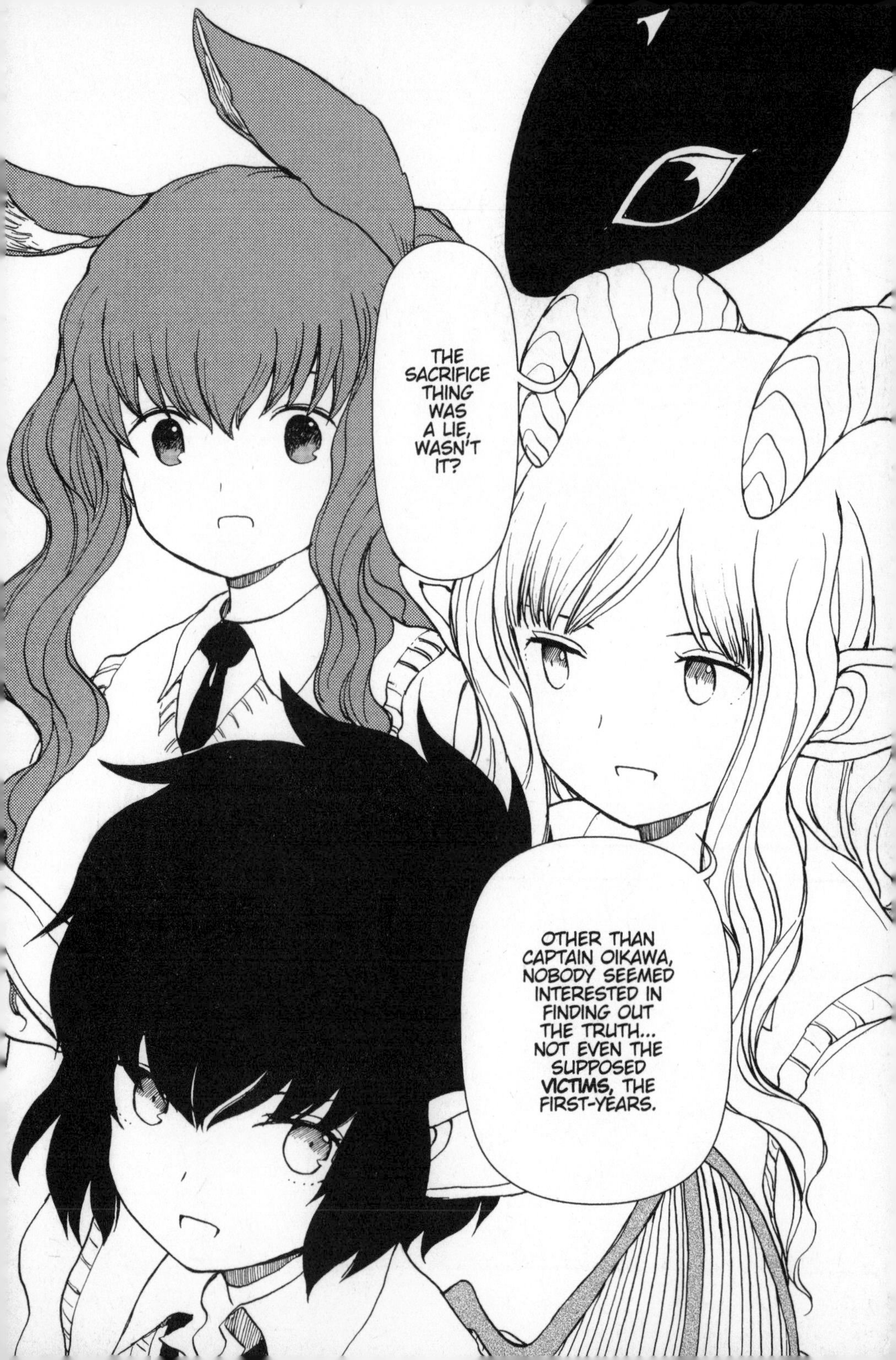
THE SACRIFICE THING WAS A LIE, WASN'T IT?
OTHER THAN CAPTAIN OIKAWA, NOBODY SEEMED INTERESTED IN FINDING OUT THE TRUTH... NOT EVEN THE SUPPOSED **VICTIMS**, THE FIRST-YEARS.

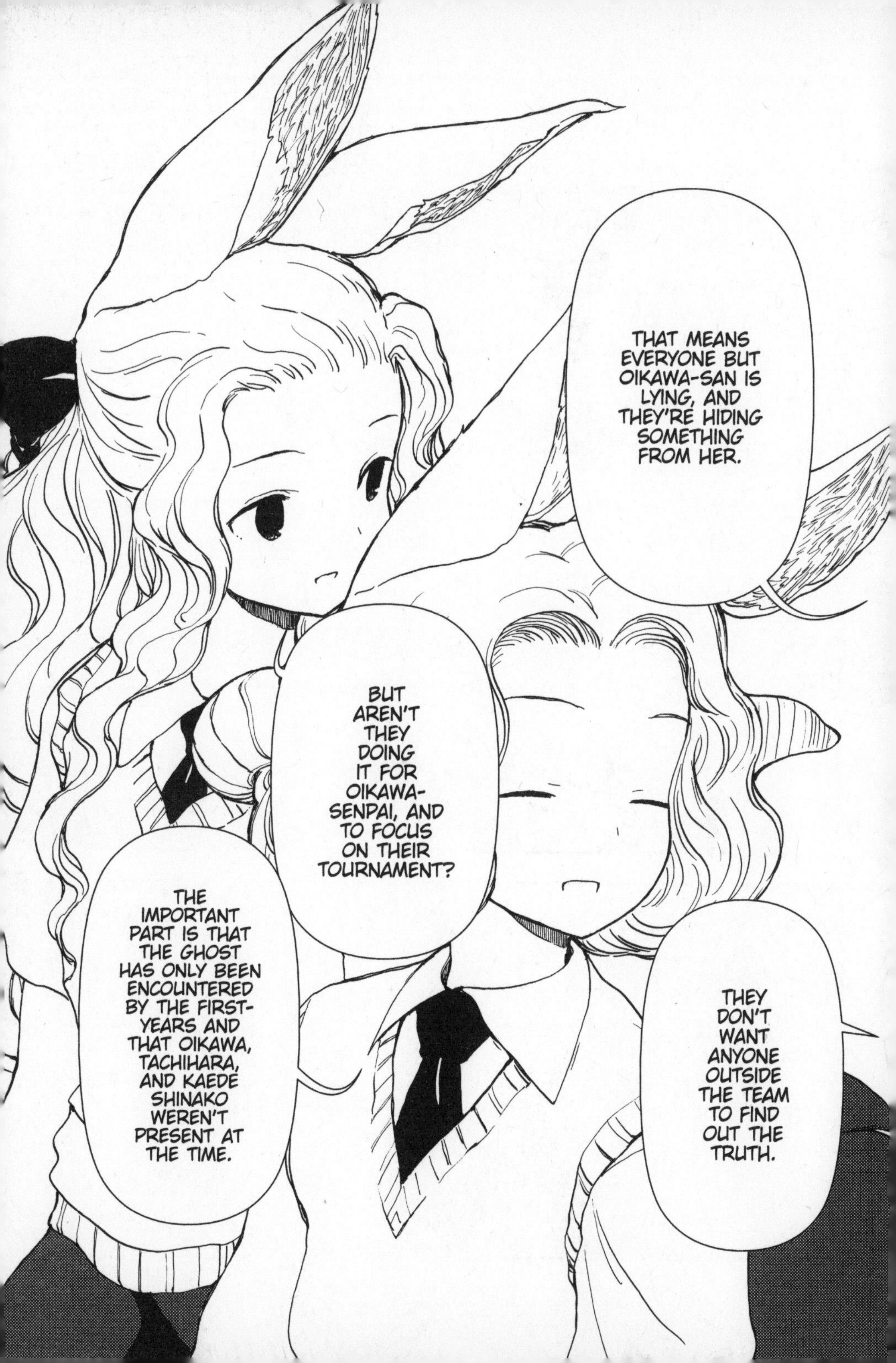
THAT MEANS EVERYONE BUT OIKAWA-SAN IS LYING, AND THEY'RE HIDING SOMETHING FROM HER.
BUT AREN'T THEY DOING IT FOR OIKAWA-SENPAI, AND TO FOCUS ON THEIR TOURNAMENT?
THEY DON'T WANT ANYONE OUTSIDE THE TEAM TO FIND OUT THE TRUTH.
THE IMPORTANT PART IS THAT THE GHOST HAS ONLY BEEN ENCOUNTERED BY THE FIRST-YEARS AND THAT OIKAWA, TACHIHARA, AND KAEDE SHINAKO WEREN'T PRESENT AT THE TIME.

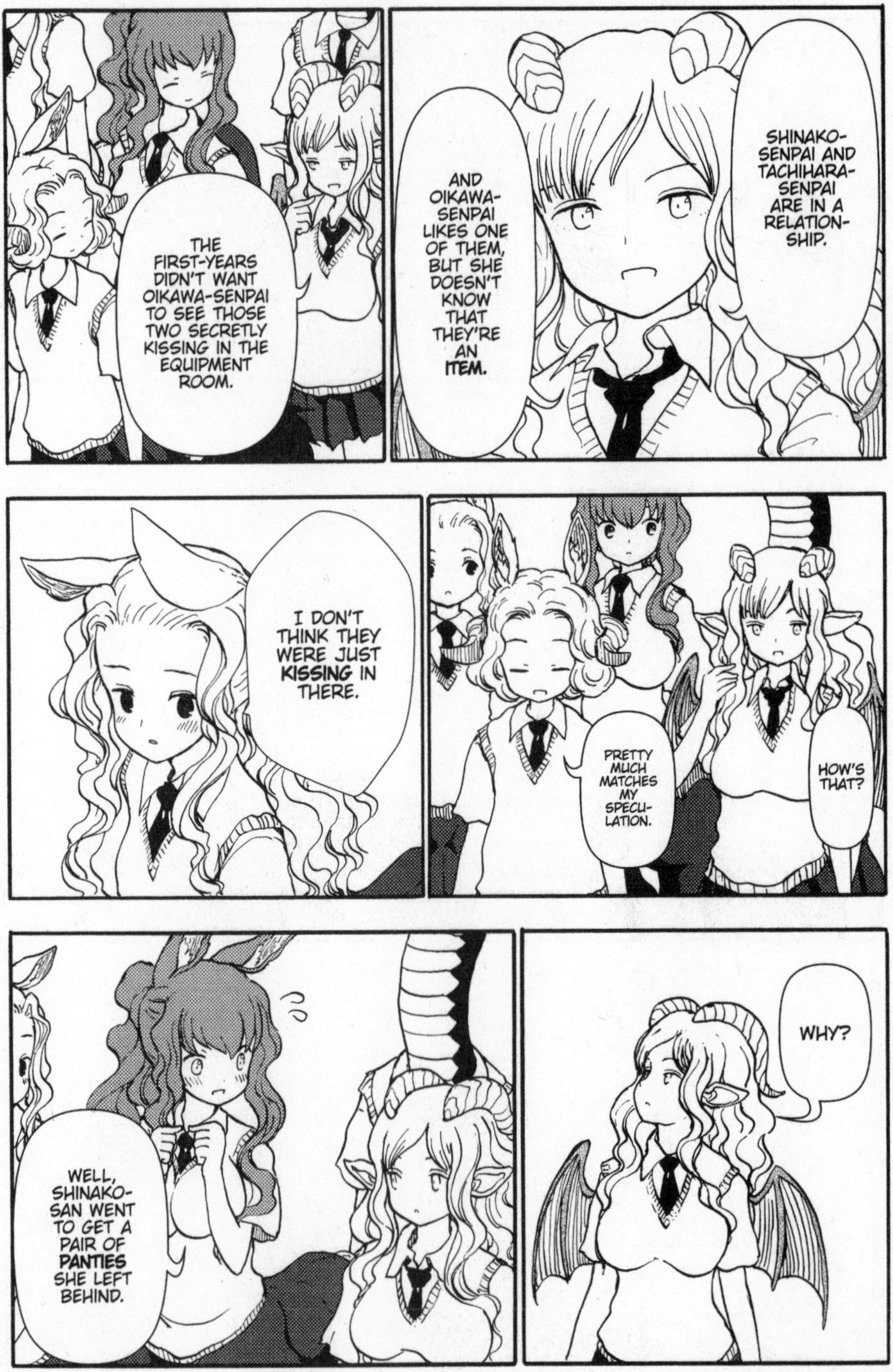
SHINAKO-SENPAI AND TACHIHARA-SENPAI ARE IN A RELATIONSHIP.
AND OIKAWA-SENPAI LIKES ONE OF THEM, BUT SHE DOESN'T KNOW THAT THEY'RE AN **ITEM.**
THE FIRST-YEARS DIDN'T WANT OIKAWA-SENPAI TO SEE THOSE TWO SECRETLY KISSING IN THE EQUIPMENT ROOM.
HOW'S THAT?
PRETTY MUCH MATCHES MY SPECULATION.
I DON'T THINK THEY WERE JUST **KISSING** IN THERE.
WHY?
WELL, SHINAKO-SAN WENT TO GET A PAIR OF **PANTIES** SHE LEFT BEHIND.

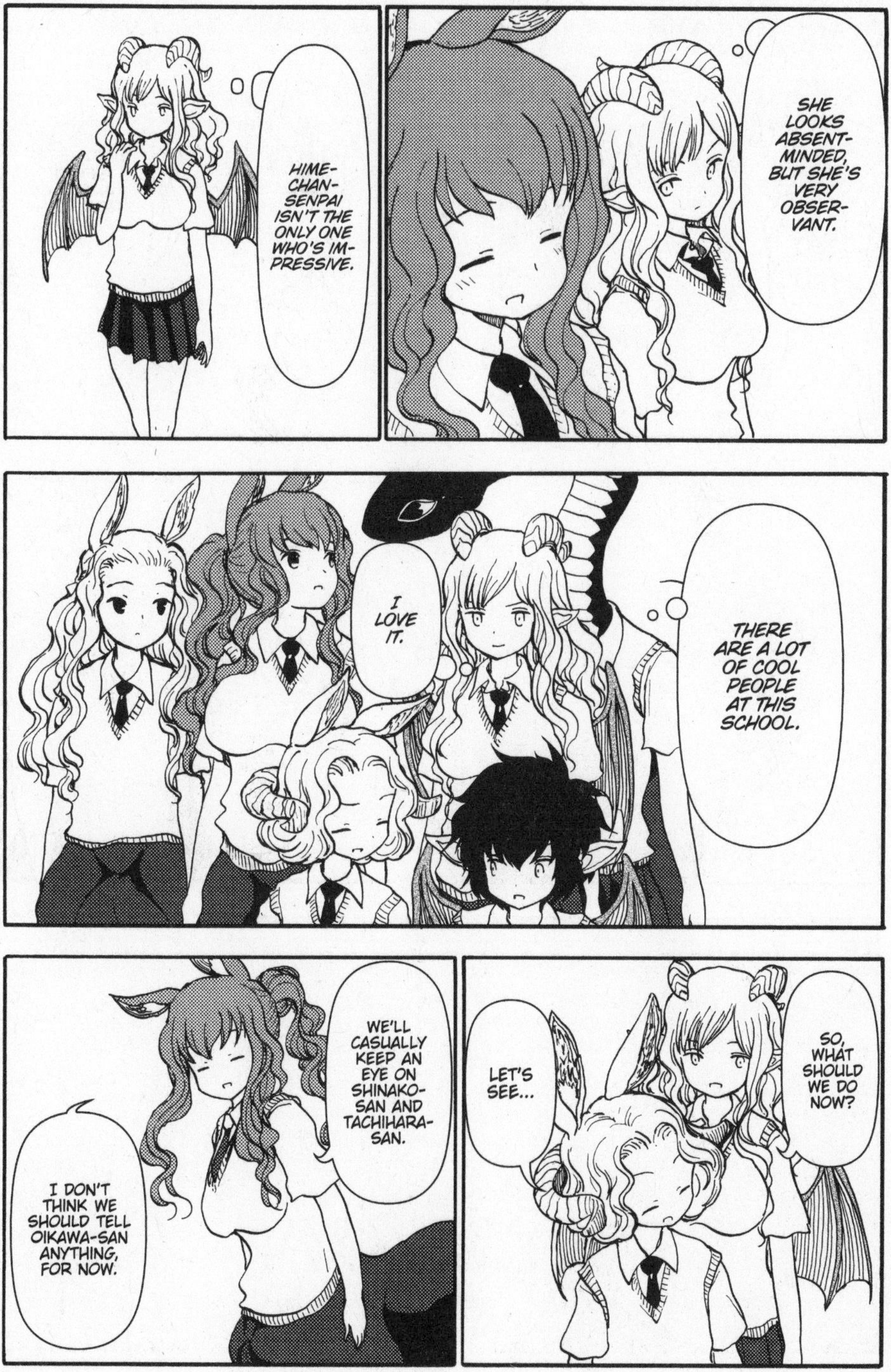
SHE LOOKS ABSENT-MINDED, BUT SHE'S VERY OBSERVANT.
HIME-CHAN-SENPAI ISN'T THE ONLY ONE WHO'S IMPRESSIVE.
THERE ARE A LOT OF COOL PEOPLE AT THIS SCHOOL.
I LOVE IT.
SO, WHAT SHOULD WE DO NOW?
LET'S SEE...
WE'LL CASUALLY KEEP AN EYE ON SHINAKO-SAN AND TACHIHARA-SAN.
I DON'T THINK WE SHOULD TELL OIKAWA-SAN ANYTHING, FOR NOW.

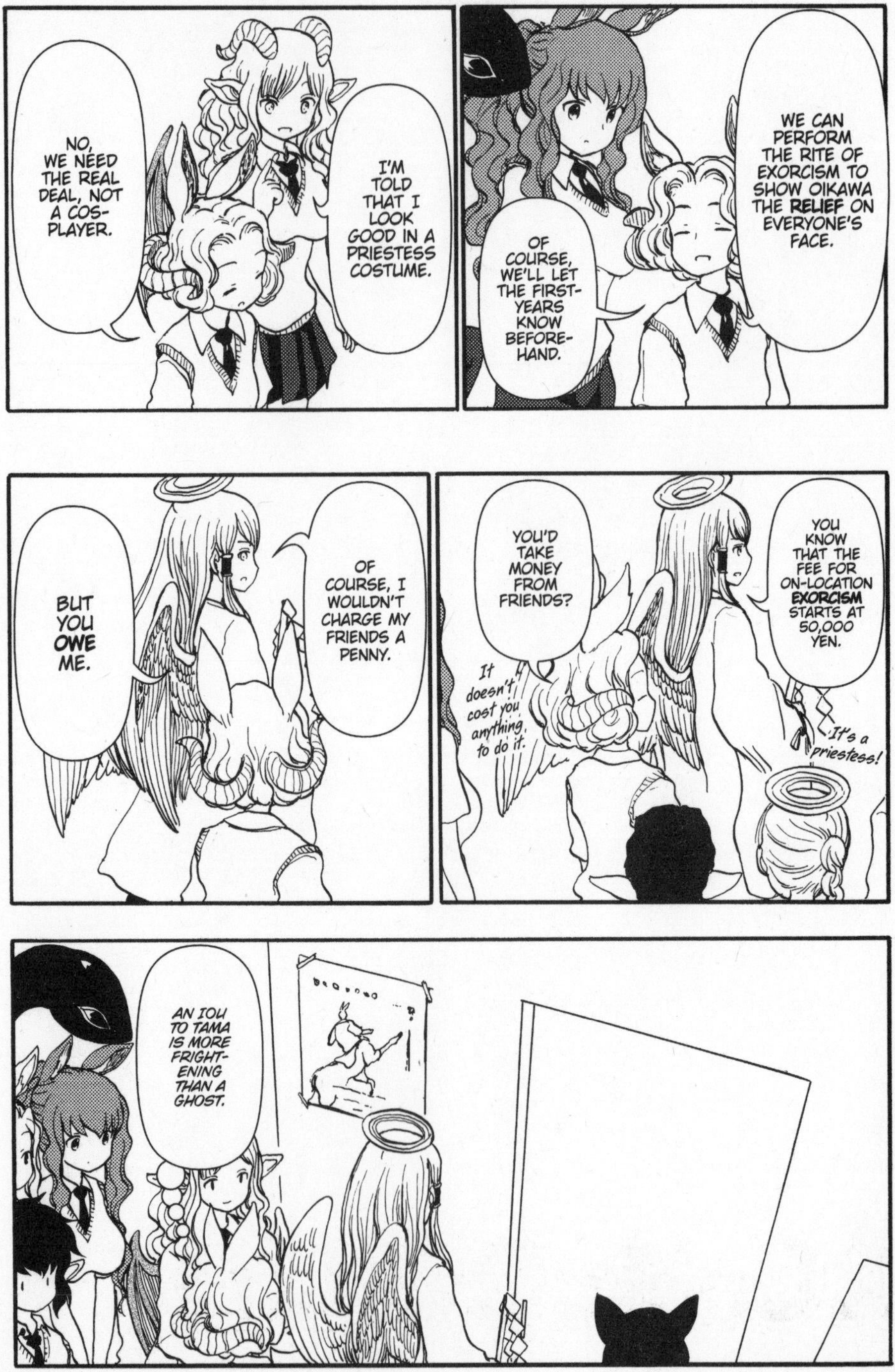
WE CAN PERFORM THE RITE OF EXORCISM TO SHOW OIKAWA THE RELIEF ON EVERYONE'S FACE.
OF COURSE, WE'LL LET THE FIRST-YEARS KNOW BEFOREHAND.
I'M TOLD THAT I LOOK GOOD IN A PRIESTESS COSTUME.
NO, WE NEED THE REAL DEAL, NOT A COSPLAYER.
YOU KNOW THAT THE FEE FOR ON-LOCATION EXORCISM STARTS AT 50,000 YEN.
YOU'D TAKE MONEY FROM FRIENDS?
It's a priestess!
It doesn't cost you anything to do it.
OF COURSE, I WOULDN'T CHARGE MY FRIENDS A PENNY.
BUT YOU OWE ME.
AN IOU TO TAMA IS MORE FRIGHTENING THAN A GHOST.

A Centaur's Life

UNDERSTANDING AMPHIBIANFOLK PART 5: AMPHIBIANFOLK HISTORY

BECAUSE OF THEIR LIFESTYLE, THE HISTORY OF THE AMPHIBIANFOLK IS FULL OF MYSTERY. THEY LACK A WRITTEN LANGUAGE, THOUGH THEY MAY HAVE USED A FORM OF PICTOGRAPHY AS A CODE WITHIN TRIBES OR FAMILIES, AND THEIR RELIANCE ON PLANT-BASED MATERIAL RESOURCES MEANT THAT MOST STRUCTURES, TOOLS, AND ARTIFACTS WERE LOST TO DECOMPOSITION IN THEIR JUNGLE HOME. ONE CIVILIZATION, TAWANTINSUYU, SEEMS TO HAVE HAD CONTACT WITH AMPHIBIANFOLK FOR CENTURIES, BUT BECAUSE THEY WERE A PRE-LITERATE CIVILIZATION UNTIL THE MODERN AGE, THEY WERE UNABLE TO CONTRIBUTE MUCH INFORMATION. THEIR RECORDKEEPING WAS ALL DONE WITH A SYSTEM OF KNOTTED STRINGS CALLED QUIPU, AND THEIR ARTWORK HAD ONLY A HANDFUL OF DEPICTIONS OF AMPHIBIANFOLK. THE MOST NOTEWORTHY DISCOVERY IS THAT OF STONE SCULPTURES RESEMBLING AMPHIBIANFOLK WEARING MAMMALIAN MASKS, KNEELING AND HOLDING MAN-CATCHERS WITH TWO PAIRS OF CROSSED ARMS.

THERE IS SOME EVIDENCE THAT AMPHIBIANFOLK DID INDEED HAVE THEIR OWN CIVILIZATION. IN THE GUALO GUABO RUINS IN THE FORMER RIVER A BASIN, RESEARCHERS DISCOVERED WHAT APPEARS TO BE A MEGALITHIC TEMPLE BUILT OF LARGE STONE SLABS AND A STONE STATUE OF A SNAKE-HEADED DEITY. THE STRUCTURE APPEARS TO HAVE BEEN BUILT ABOUT 5,000 YEARS AGO, AND STONE TOOLS OF EQUIVALENT AGE THAT WERE FOUND IN THE AREA WERE POSSIBLY USED IN THE CONSTRUCTION OF THE TEMPLE. THE STRUCTURE ITSELF LACKED THE REFINEMENT OF THOSE BUILT BY TAWANTINSUYU; THE TOOLS DISCOVERED WERE MORE SUITED TO AMPHIBIANFOLK HANDS THAN THOSE OF MAMMALIANS; THE SYMBOLS ENGRAVED IN THE GOD STATUE WERE SIMILAR TO THOSE FORMERLY USED BY THE CTLOLOCTOL AMPHIBIANFOLK TRIBE; THESE STRONG PIECES OF EVIDENCE SUGGEST THAT THESE RUINS WERE LIKELY BUILT BY AMPHIBIANFOLK. WHETHER THIS CIVILIZATION WAS ABANDONED OR SIMPLY MOVED ELSEWHERE REMAINS AN UNSOLVED RIDDLE.

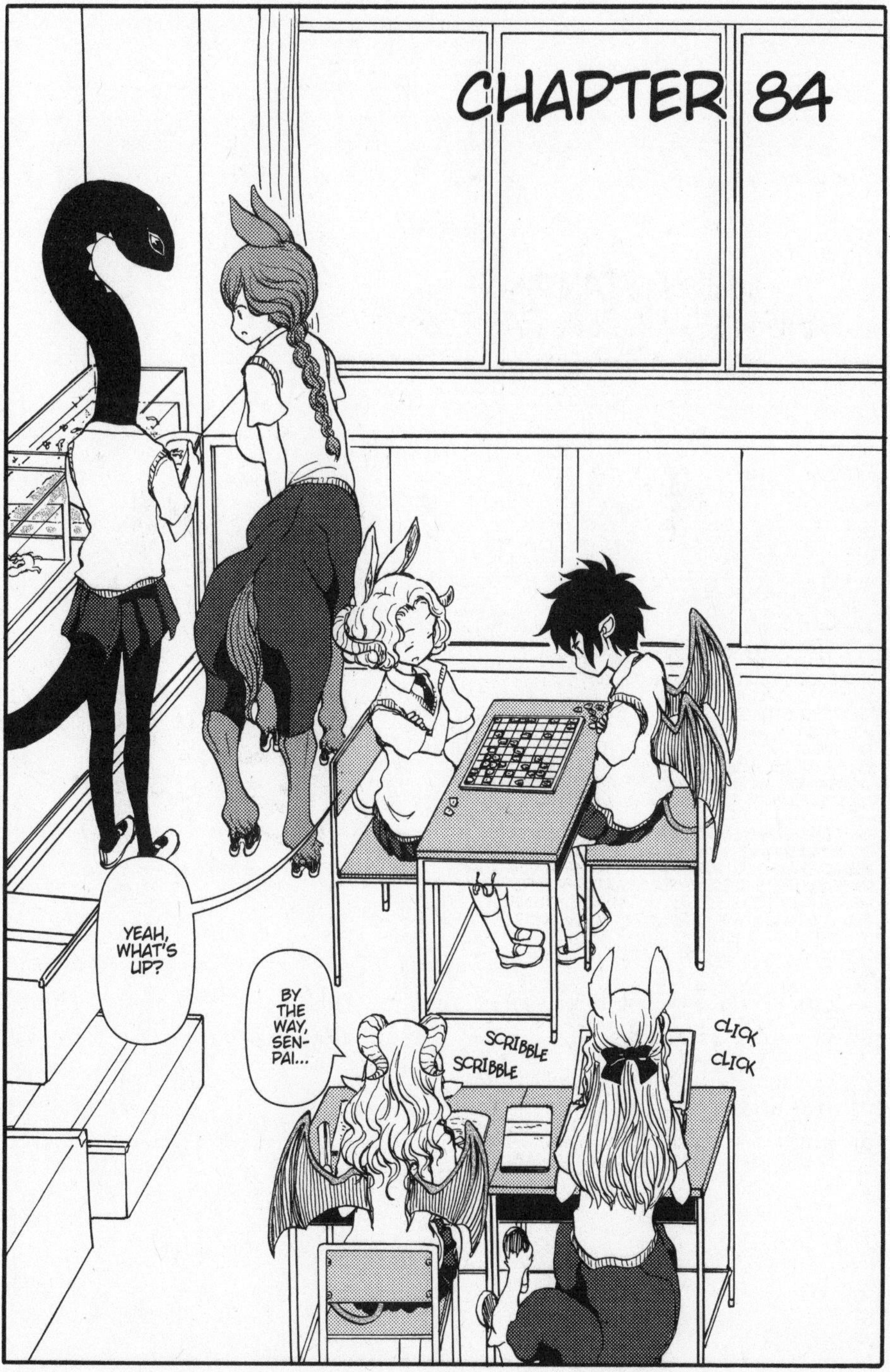
CHAPTER 84
CLICK CLICK
SCRIBBLE SCRIBBLE
BY THE WAY, SEN-PAI...
YEAH, WHAT'S UP?

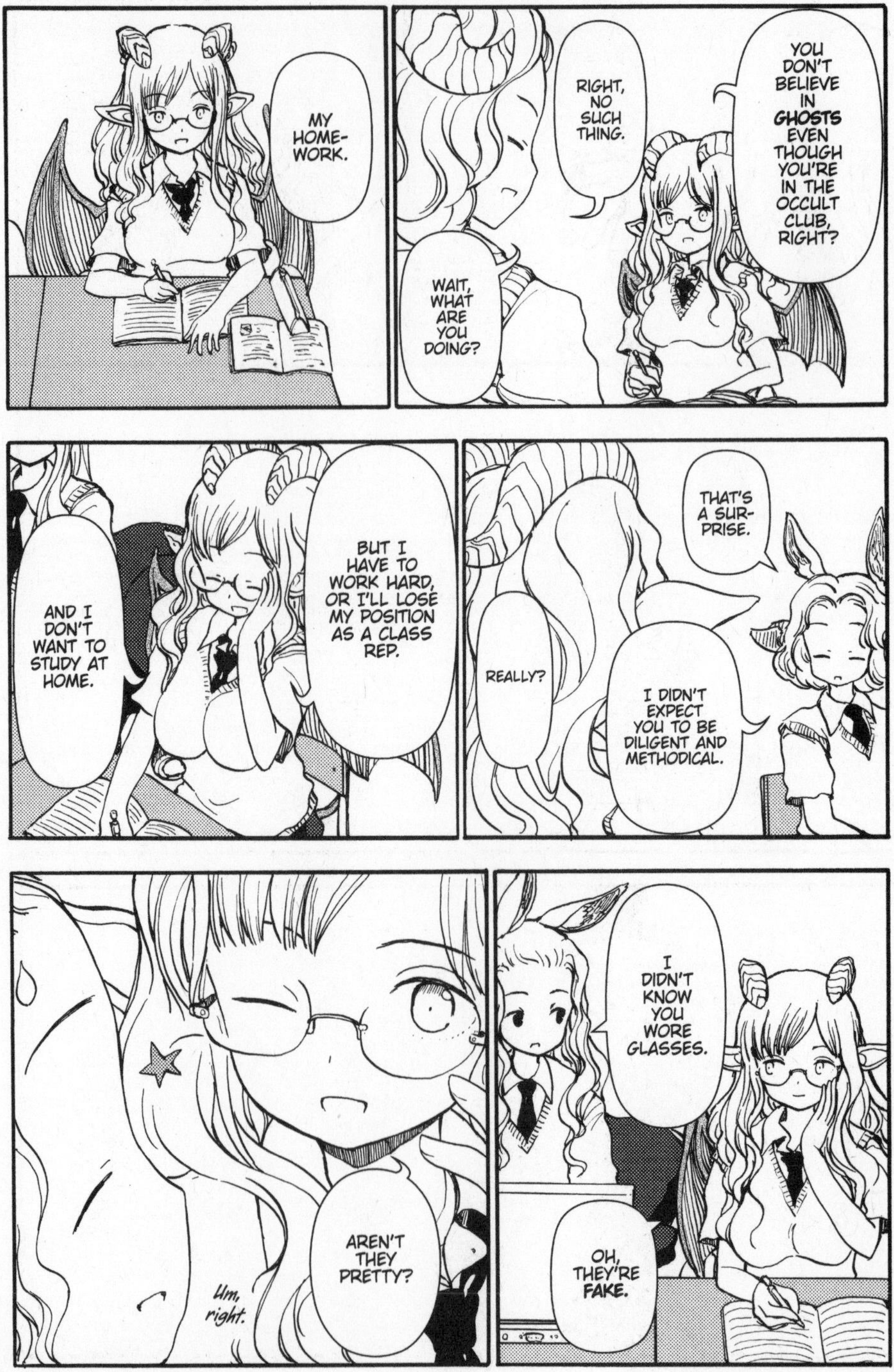
YOU DON'T BELIEVE IN **GHOSTS** EVEN THOUGH YOU'RE IN THE OCCULT CLUB, RIGHT?
RIGHT, NO SUCH THING.
WAIT, WHAT ARE YOU DOING?
MY HOME-WORK.
THAT'S A SUR-PRISE.
I DIDN'T EXPECT YOU TO BE DILIGENT AND METHODICAL.
REALLY?
BUT I HAVE TO WORK HARD, OR I'LL LOSE MY POSITION AS A CLASS REP.
AND I DON'T WANT TO STUDY AT HOME.
I DIDN'T KNOW YOU WORE GLASSES.
OH, THEY'RE **FAKE.**
AREN'T THEY PRETTY?
Um, right.

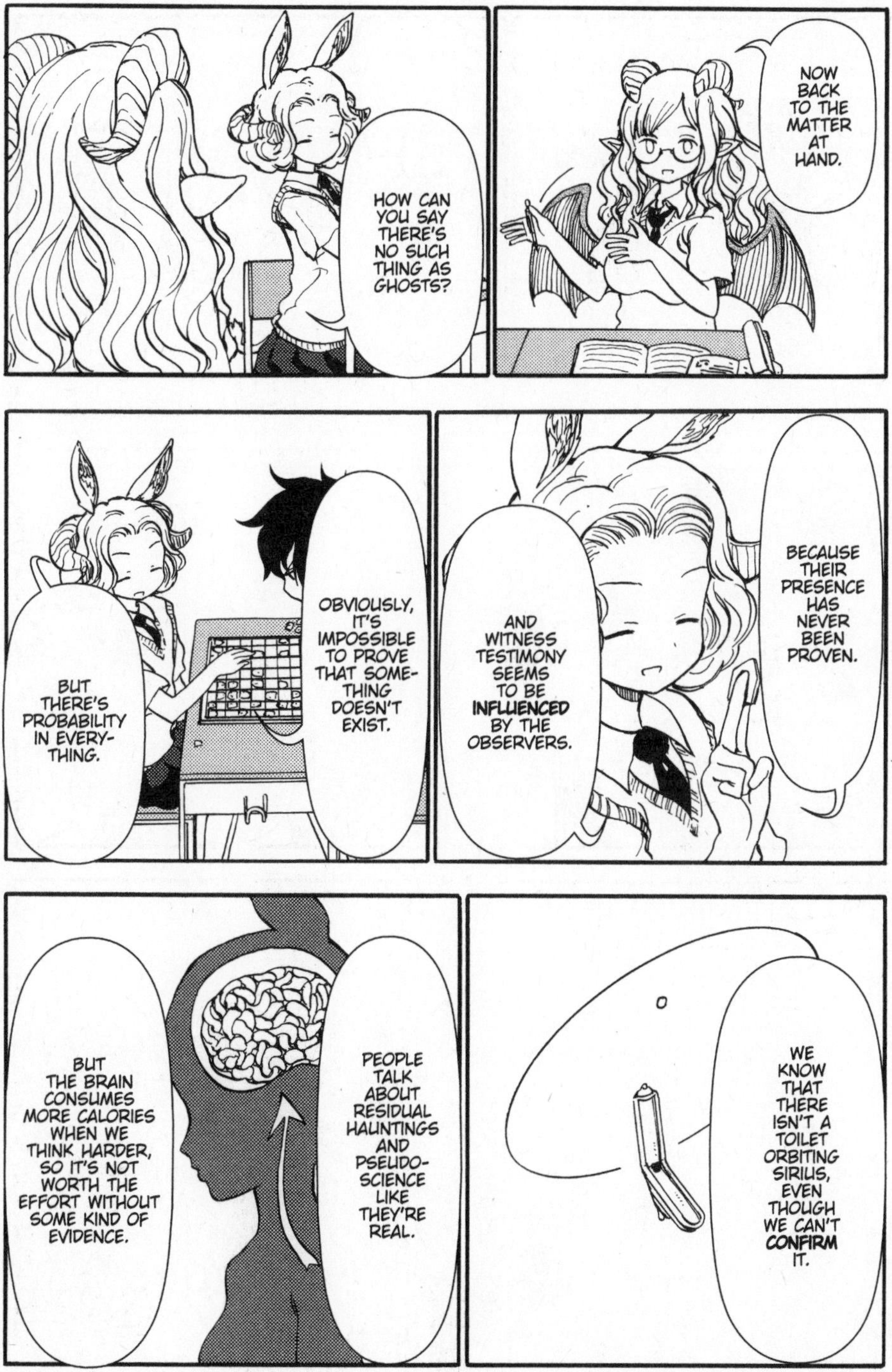
NOW BACK TO THE MATTER AT HAND.
HOW CAN YOU SAY THERE'S NO SUCH THING AS GHOSTS?
BECAUSE THEIR PRESENCE HAS NEVER BEEN PROVEN.
AND WITNESS TESTIMONY SEEMS TO BE **INFLUENCED** BY THE OBSERVERS.
OBVIOUSLY, IT'S IMPOSSIBLE TO PROVE THAT SOME-THING DOESN'T EXIST.
BUT THERE'S PROBABILITY IN EVERY-THING.
WE KNOW THAT THERE ISN'T A TOILET ORBITING SIRIUS, EVEN THOUGH WE CAN'T **CONFIRM** IT.
PEOPLE TALK ABOUT RESIDUAL HAUNTINGS AND PSEUDO-SCIENCE LIKE THEY'RE REAL.
BUT THE BRAIN CONSUMES MORE CALORIES WHEN WE THINK HARDER, SO IT'S NOT WORTH THE EFFORT WITHOUT SOME KIND OF EVIDENCE.

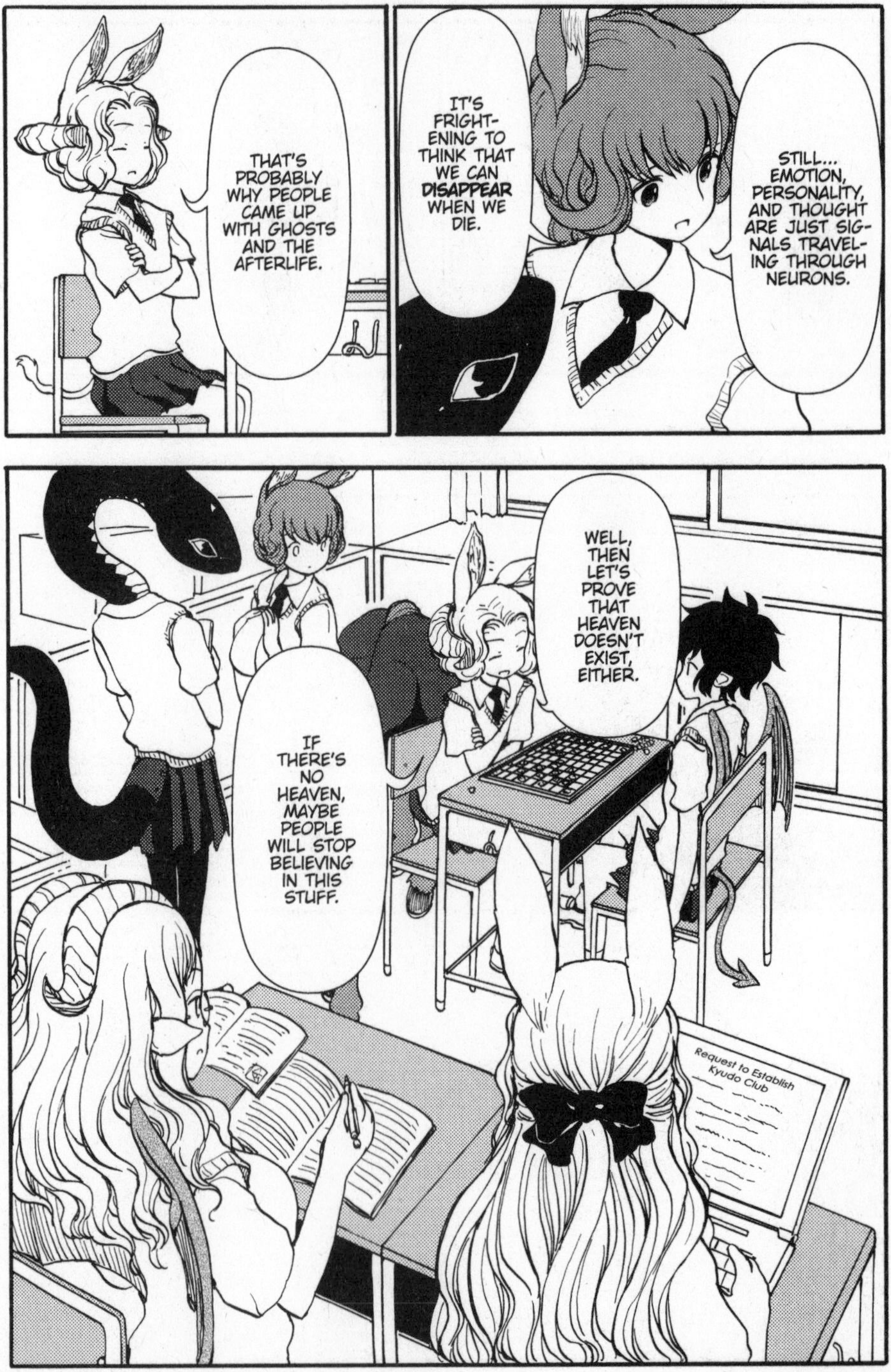
STILL... EMOTION, PERSONALITY, AND THOUGHT ARE JUST SIGNALS TRAVELING THROUGH NEURONS.
IT'S FRIGHTENING TO THINK THAT WE CAN **DISAPPEAR** WHEN WE DIE.
THAT'S PROBABLY WHY PEOPLE CAME UP WITH GHOSTS AND THE AFTERLIFE.
WELL, THEN LET'S PROVE THAT HEAVEN DOESN'T EXIST, EITHER.
IF THERE'S NO HEAVEN, MAYBE PEOPLE WILL STOP BELIEVING IN THIS STUFF.
Request to Establish Kyudo Club

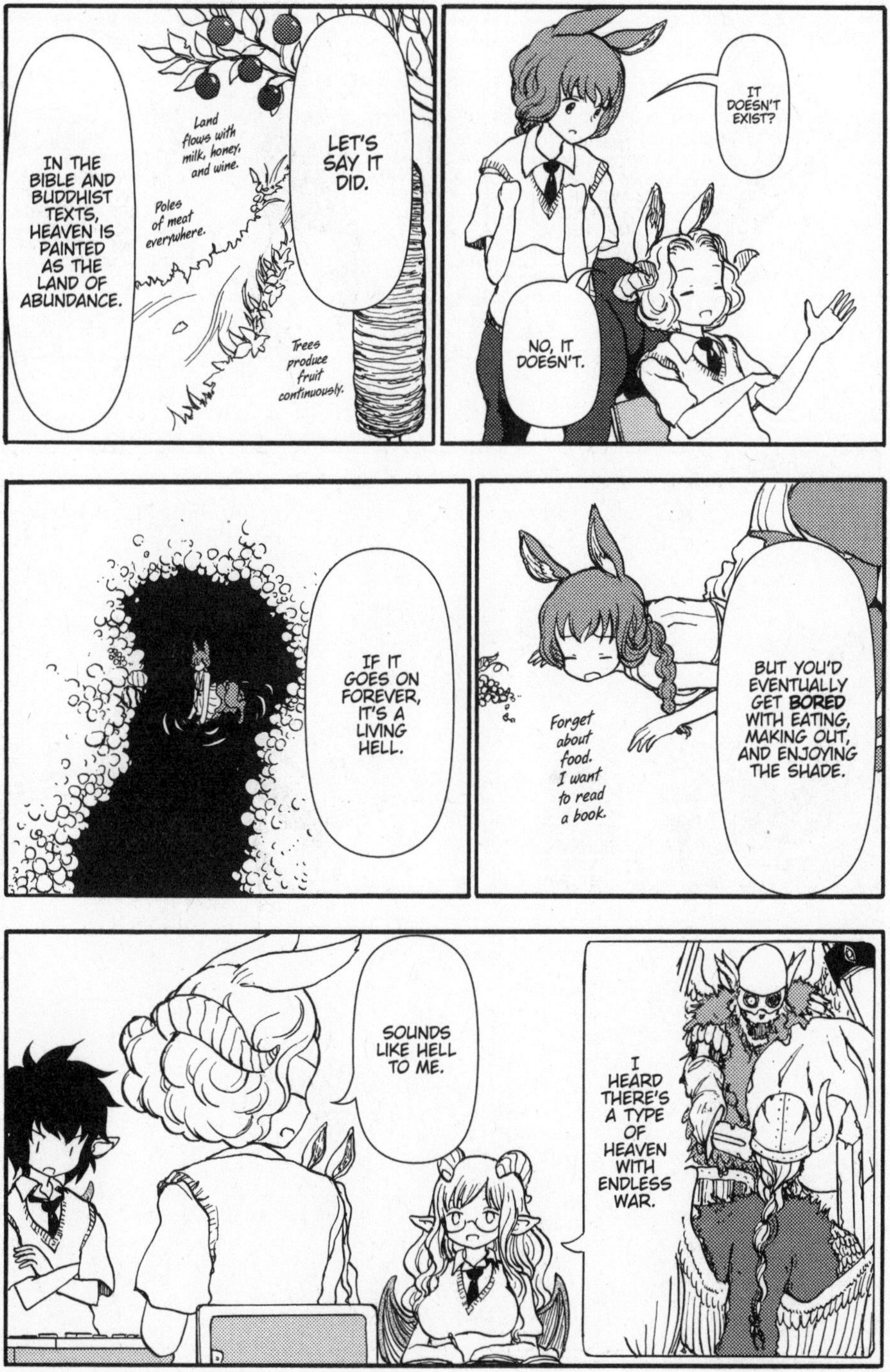
IT DOESN'T EXIST?
NO, IT DOESN'T.
LET'S SAY IT DID.
Land flows with milk, honey, and wine.
Poles of meat everywhere.
Trees produce fruit continuously.
IN THE BIBLE AND BUDDHIST TEXTS, HEAVEN IS PAINTED AS THE LAND OF ABUNDANCE.
BUT YOU'D EVENTUALLY GET **BORED** WITH EATING, MAKING OUT, AND ENJOYING THE SHADE.
Forget about food. I want to read a book.
IF IT GOES ON FOREVER, IT'S A LIVING HELL.
I HEARD THERE'S A TYPE OF HEAVEN WITH ENDLESS WAR.
SOUNDS LIKE HELL TO ME.

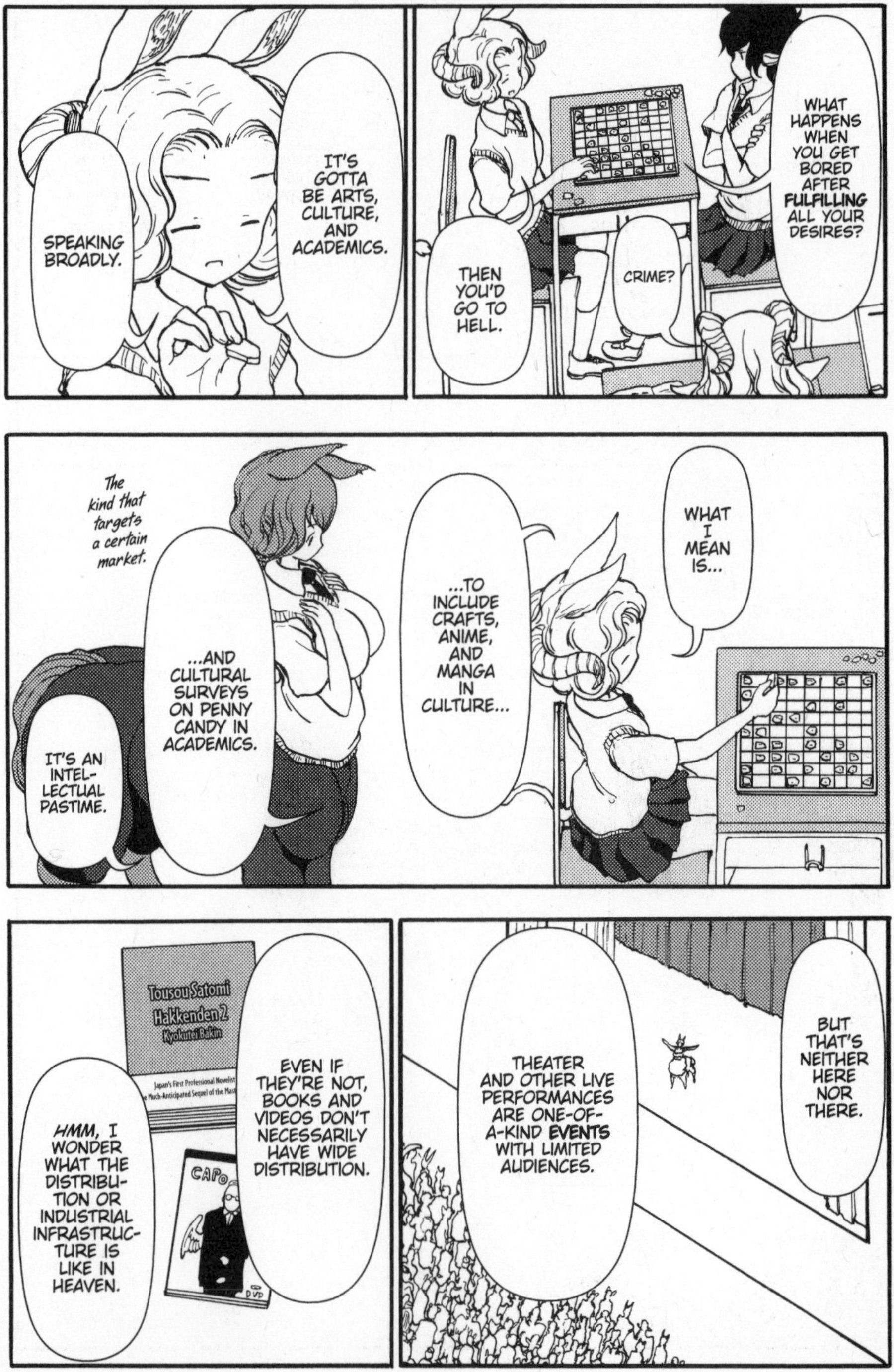
WHAT HAPPENS WHEN YOU GET BORED AFTER **FULFILLING** ALL YOUR DESIRES?
CRIME?
THEN YOU'D GO TO HELL.
IT'S GOTTA BE ARTS, CULTURE, AND ACADEMICS.
SPEAKING BROADLY.
WHAT I MEAN IS...
...TO INCLUDE CRAFTS, ANIME, AND MANGA IN CULTURE...
...AND CULTURAL SURVEYS ON PENNY CANDY IN ACADEMICS.
The kind that targets a certain market.
IT'S AN INTEL-LECTUAL PASTIME.
BUT THAT'S NEITHER HERE NOR THERE.
THEATER AND OTHER LIVE PERFORMANCES ARE ONE-OF-A-KIND **EVENTS** WITH LIMITED AUDIENCES.
EVEN IF THEY'RE NOT, BOOKS AND VIDEOS DON'T NECESSARILY HAVE WIDE DISTRIBUTION.
Tousou Satomi Hakkenden 2
Kyokutei Bakin
Japan's First Professional Novelist
CAPO
DVD
HMM, I WONDER WHAT THE DISTRIBU-TION OR INDUSTRIAL INFRASTRUC-TURE IS LIKE IN HEAVEN.

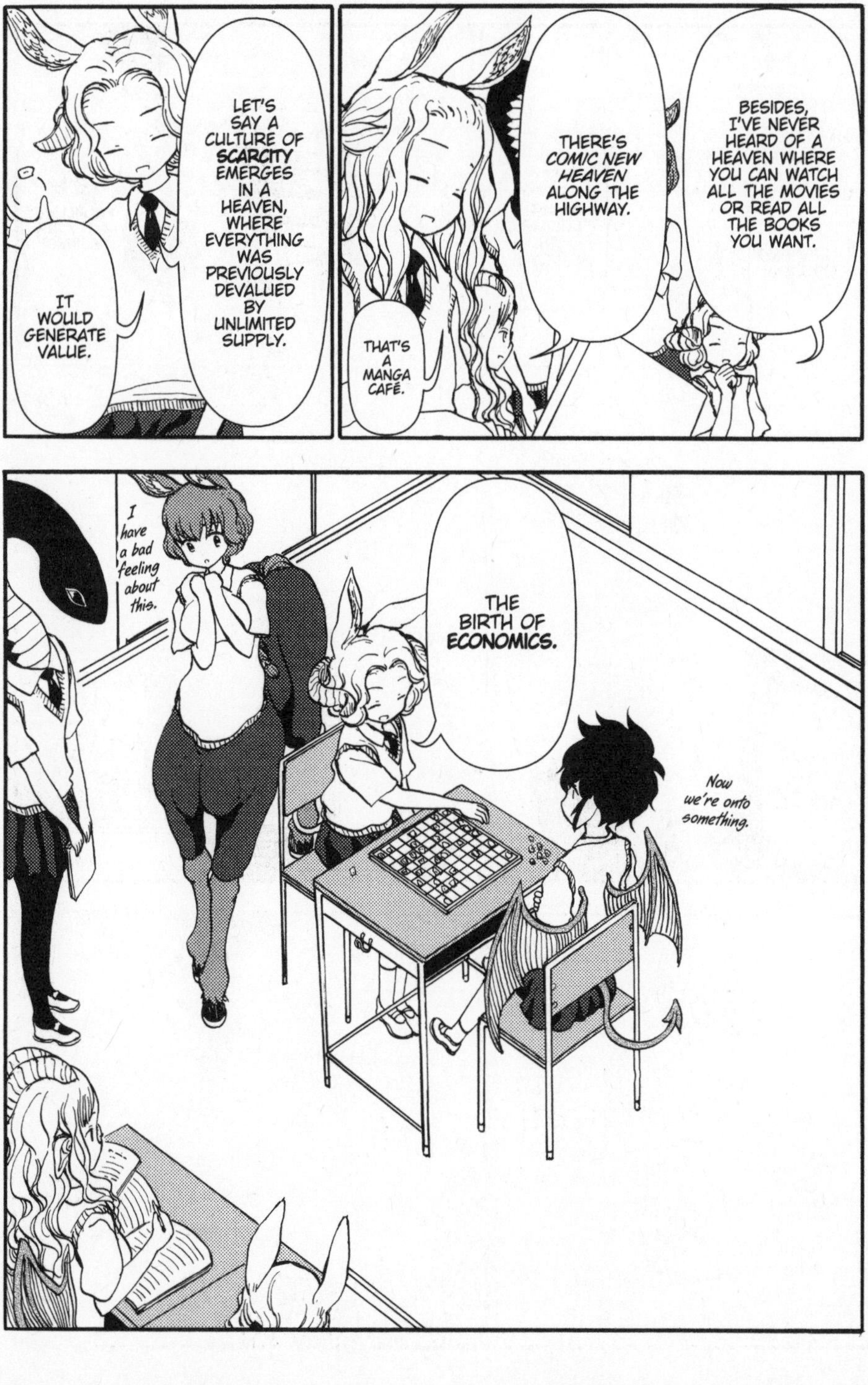
BESIDES, I'VE NEVER HEARD OF A HEAVEN WHERE YOU CAN WATCH ALL THE MOVIES OR READ ALL THE BOOKS YOU WANT.
THERE'S *COMIC NEW HEAVEN* ALONG THE HIGHWAY.
THAT'S A MANGA CAFÉ.
LET'S SAY A CULTURE OF **SCARCITY** EMERGES IN A HEAVEN, WHERE EVERYTHING WAS PREVIOUSLY DEVALUED BY UNLIMITED SUPPLY.
IT WOULD GENERATE VALUE.
THE BIRTH OF **ECONOMICS.**
Now we're onto something.
I have a bad feeling about this.

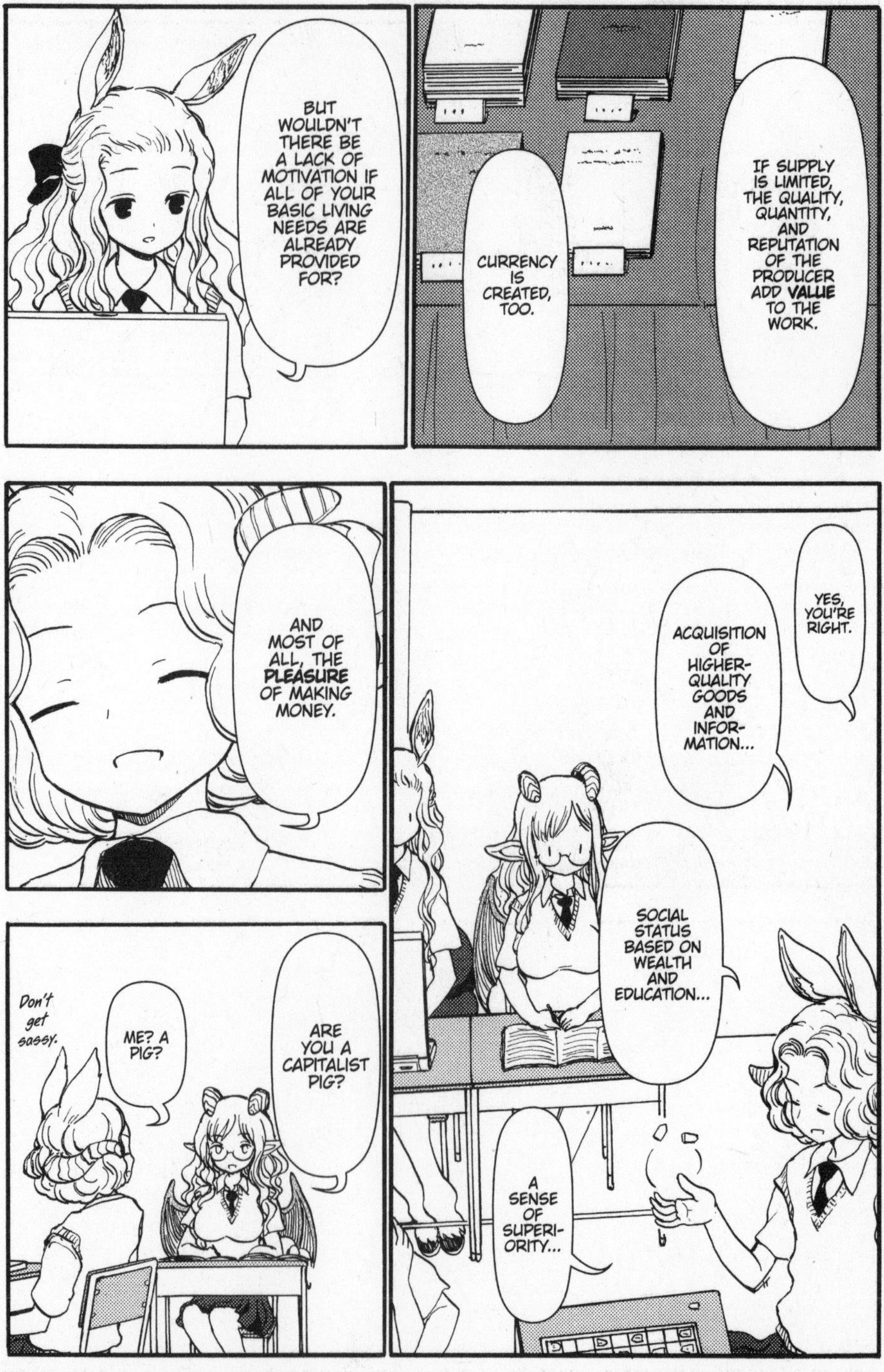
IF SUPPLY IS LIMITED, THE QUALITY, QUANTITY, AND REPUTATION OF THE PRODUCER ADD VALUE TO THE WORK.
CURRENCY IS CREATED, TOO.
BUT WOULDN'T THERE BE A LACK OF MOTIVATION IF ALL OF YOUR BASIC LIVING NEEDS ARE ALREADY PROVIDED FOR?
YES, YOU'RE RIGHT.
ACQUISITION OF HIGHER-QUALITY GOODS AND INFOR-MATION...
SOCIAL STATUS BASED ON WEALTH AND EDUCATION...
A SENSE OF SUPERI-ORITY...
AND MOST OF ALL, THE PLEASURE OF MAKING MONEY.
ARE YOU A CAPITALIST PIG?
ME? A PIG?
Don't get sassy.

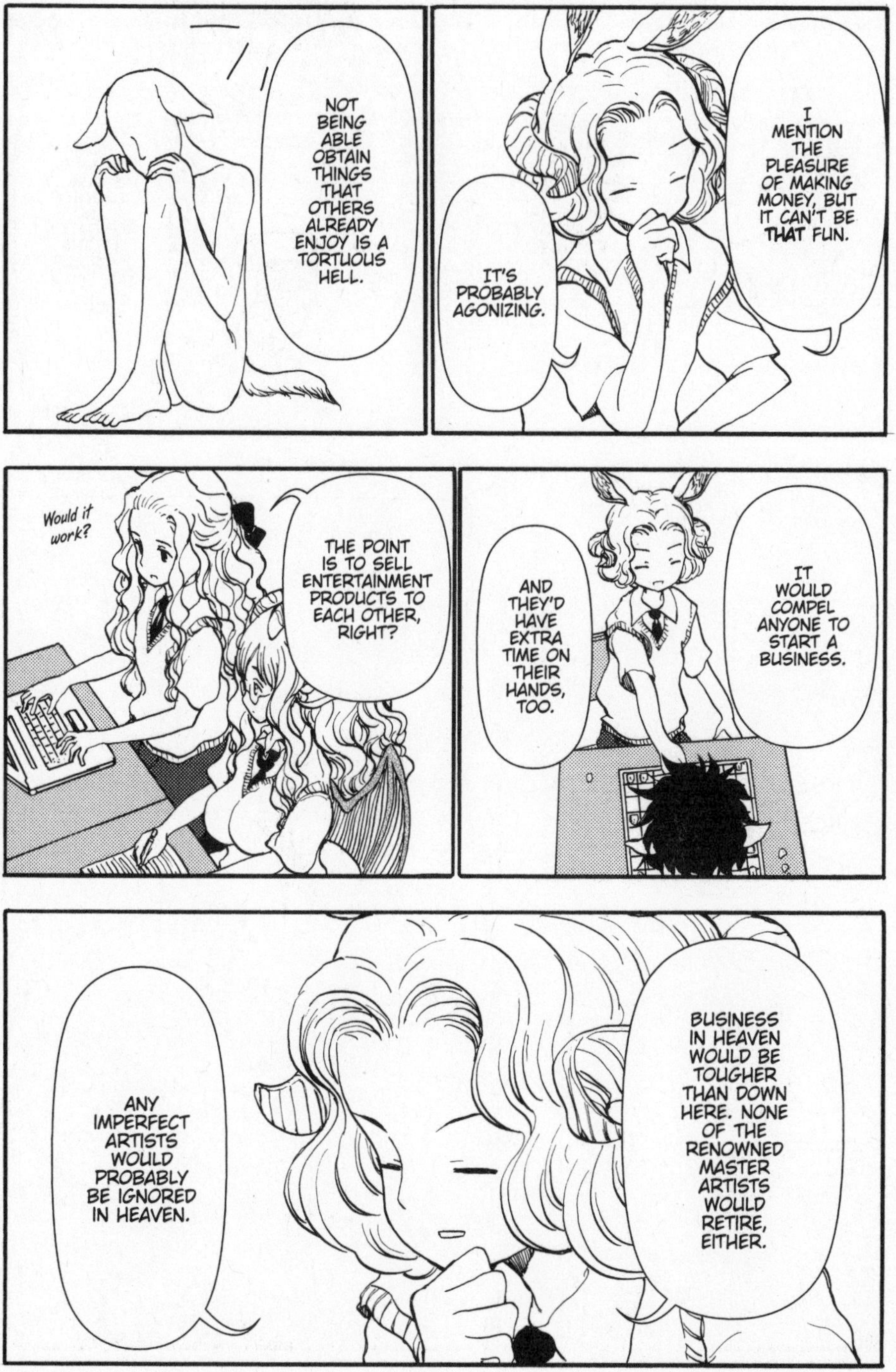
I MENTION THE PLEASURE OF MAKING MONEY, BUT IT CAN'T BE **THAT** FUN.
IT'S PROBABLY AGONIZING.
NOT BEING ABLE OBTAIN THINGS THAT OTHERS ALREADY ENJOY IS A TORTUOUS HELL.
IT WOULD COMPEL ANYONE TO START A BUSINESS.
AND THEY'D HAVE EXTRA TIME ON THEIR HANDS, TOO.
THE POINT IS TO SELL ENTERTAINMENT PRODUCTS TO EACH OTHER, RIGHT?
Would it work?
BUSINESS IN HEAVEN WOULD BE TOUGHER THAN DOWN HERE. NONE OF THE RENOWNED MASTER ARTISTS WOULD RETIRE, EITHER.
ANY IMPERFECT ARTISTS WOULD PROBABLY BE IGNORED IN HEAVEN.

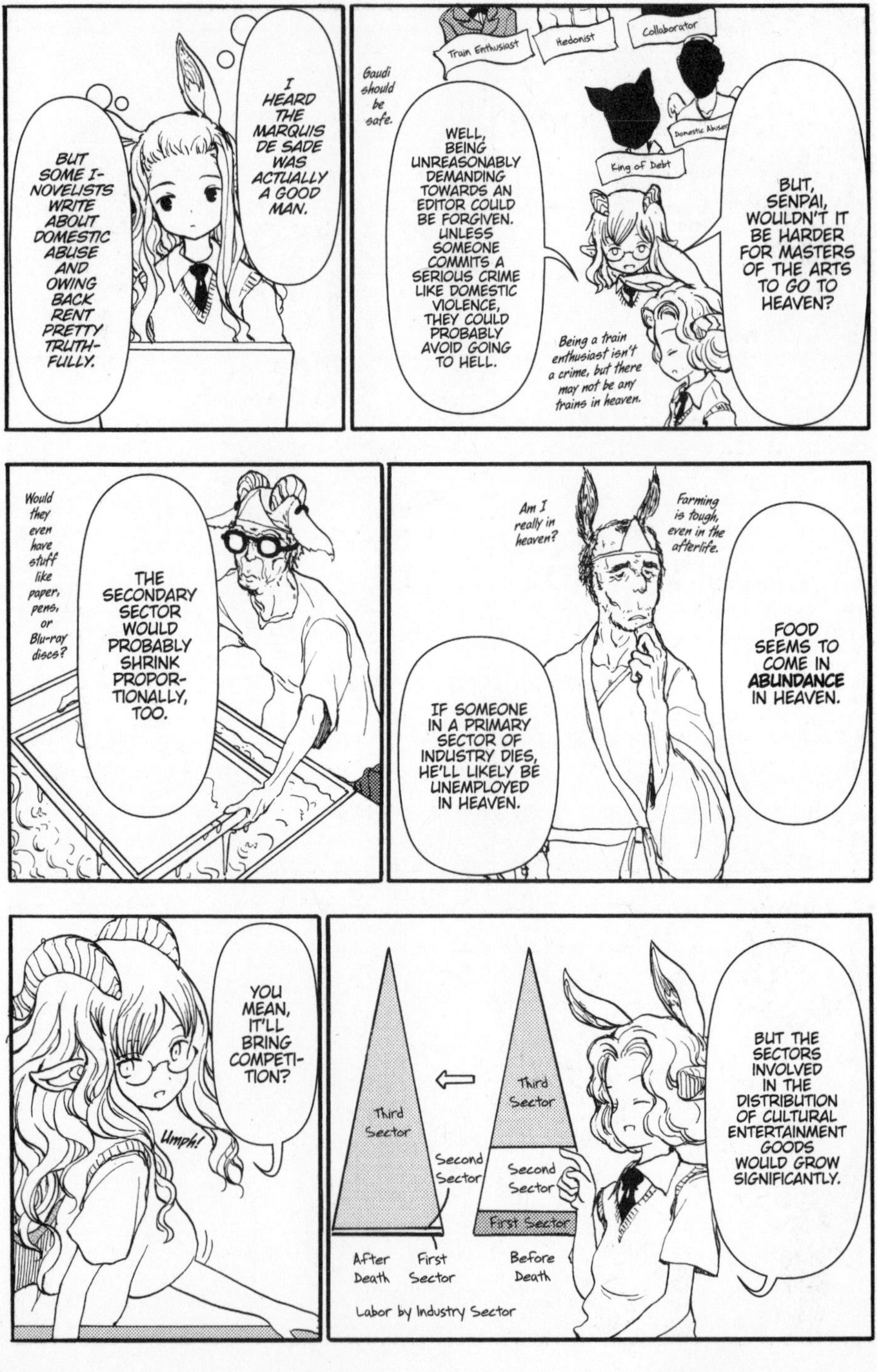
Train Enthusiast
Hedonist
Collaborator
Domestic Abuser
King of Debt
BUT, SENPAI, WOULDN'T IT BE HARDER FOR MASTERS OF THE ARTS TO GO TO HEAVEN?
WELL, BEING UNREASONABLY DEMANDING TOWARDS AN EDITOR COULD BE FORGIVEN. UNLESS SOMEONE COMMITS A SERIOUS CRIME LIKE DOMESTIC VIOLENCE, THEY COULD PROBABLY AVOID GOING TO HELL.
Gaudi should be safe.
Being a train enthusiast isn't a crime, but there may not be any trains in heaven.
I HEARD THE MARQUIS DE SADE WAS ACTUALLY A GOOD MAN.
BUT SOME I-NOVELISTS WRITE ABOUT DOMESTIC ABUSE AND OWING BACK RENT PRETTY TRUTH-FULLY.
Farming is tough, even in the afterlife.
FOOD SEEMS TO COME IN **ABUNDANCE** IN HEAVEN.
Am I really in heaven?
IF SOMEONE IN A PRIMARY SECTOR OF INDUSTRY DIES, HE'LL LIKELY BE UNEMPLOYED IN HEAVEN.
THE SECONDARY SECTOR WOULD PROBABLY SHRINK PROPOR-TIONALLY, TOO.
Would they even have stuff like paper, pens, or Blu-ray discs?
BUT THE SECTORS INVOLVED IN THE DISTRIBUTION OF CULTURAL ENTERTAINMENT GOODS WOULD GROW SIGNIFICANTLY.
Third Sector
Second Sector
First Sector
Before Death
Third Sector
Second Sector
After Death
First Sector
Labor by Industry Sector
YOU MEAN, IT'LL BRING COMPETITION?
Umph!

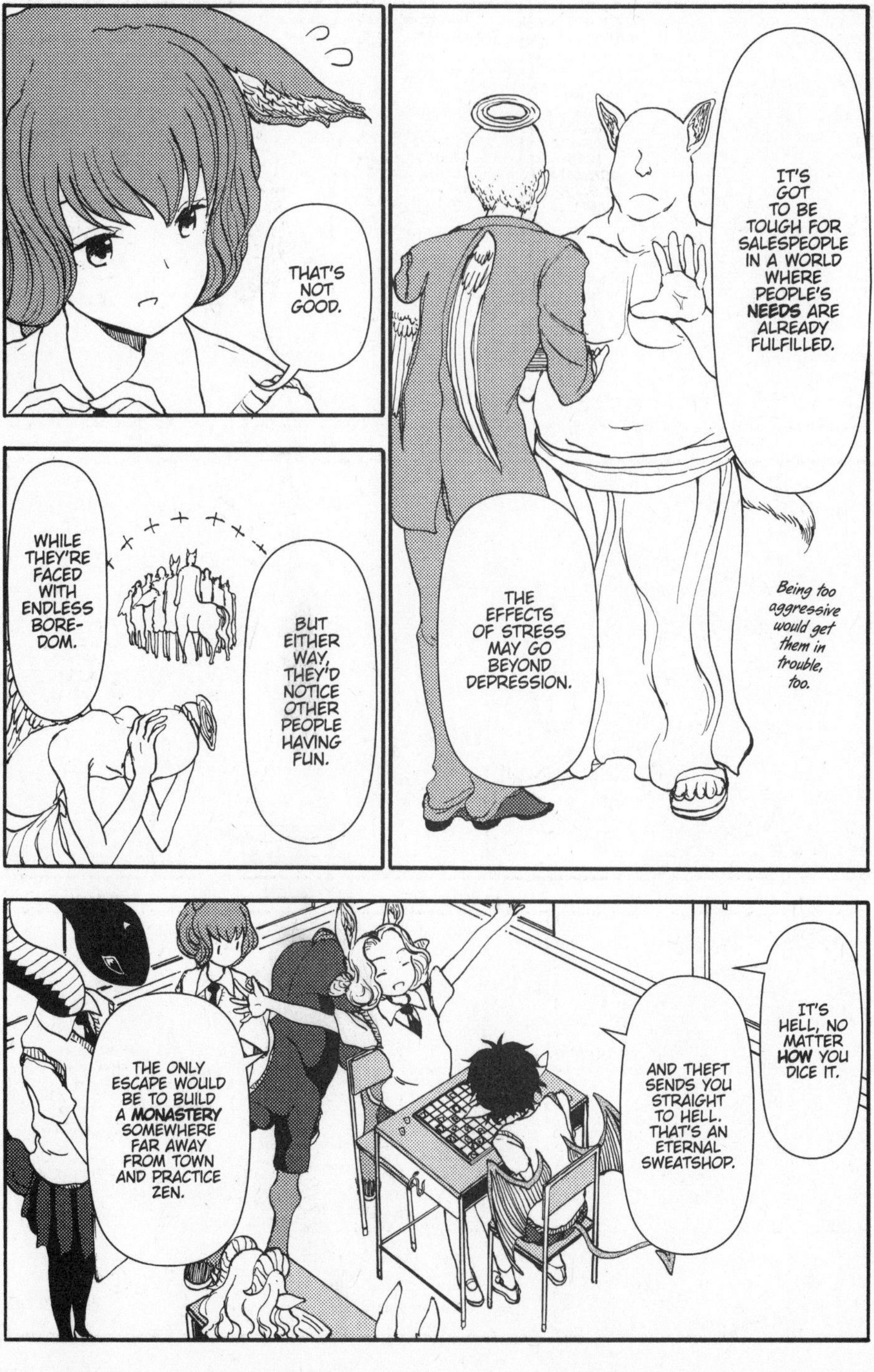
IT'S GOT TO BE TOUGH FOR SALESPEOPLE IN A WORLD WHERE PEOPLE'S NEEDS ARE ALREADY FULFILLED.
Being too aggressive would get them in trouble, too.
THE EFFECTS OF STRESS MAY GO BEYOND DEPRESSION.
THAT'S NOT GOOD.
BUT EITHER WAY, THEY'D NOTICE OTHER PEOPLE HAVING FUN.
WHILE THEY'RE FACED WITH ENDLESS BORE-DOM.
IT'S HELL, NO MATTER HOW YOU DICE IT.
AND THEFT SENDS YOU STRAIGHT TO HELL. THAT'S AN ETERNAL SWEATSHOP.
THE ONLY ESCAPE WOULD BE TO BUILD A MONASTERY SOMEWHERE FAR AWAY FROM TOWN AND PRACTICE ZEN.

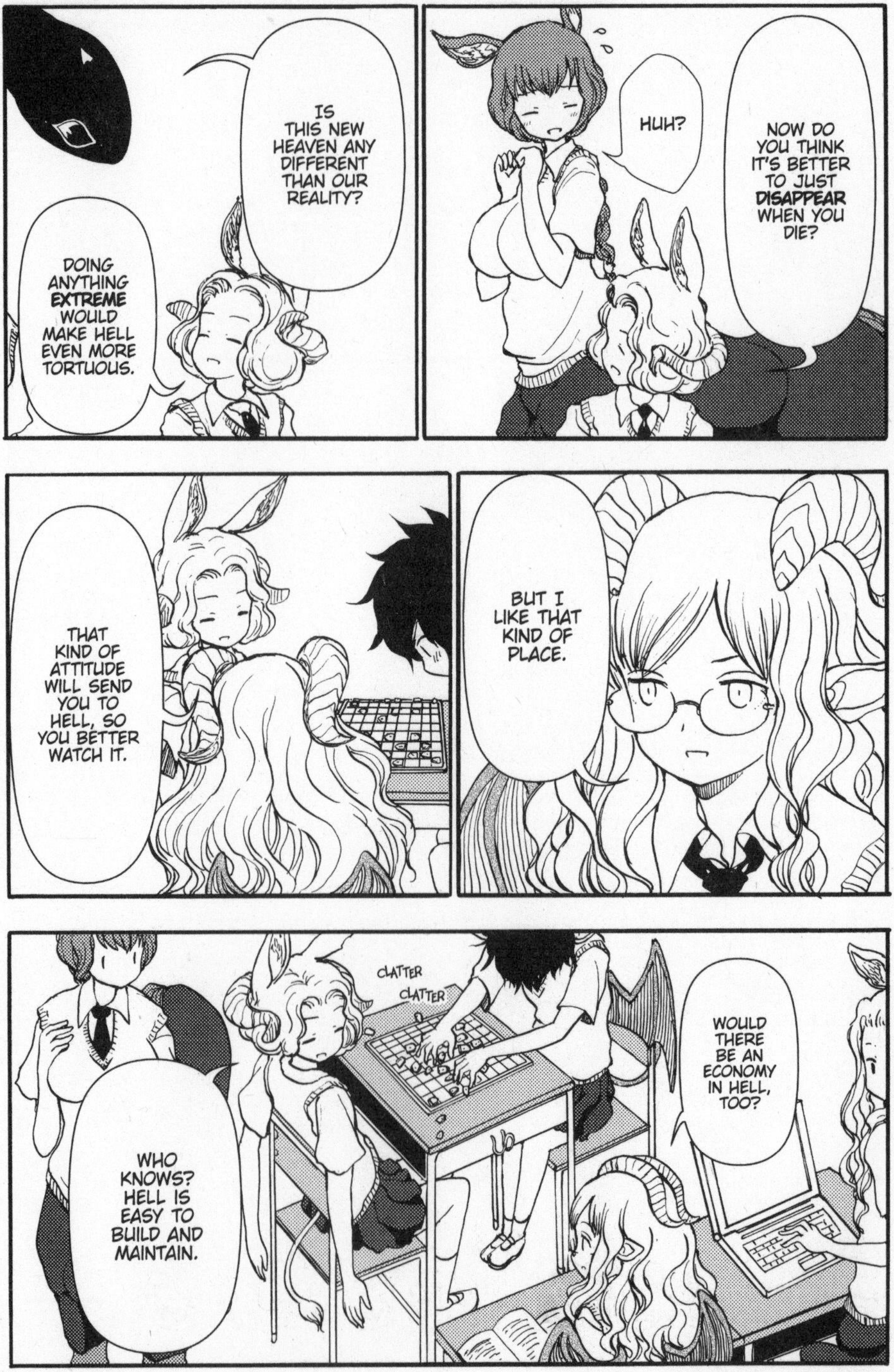
NOW DO YOU THINK IT'S BETTER TO JUST **DISAPPEAR** WHEN YOU DIE?
HUH?
IS THIS NEW HEAVEN ANY DIFFERENT THAN OUR REALITY?
DOING ANYTHING **EXTREME** WOULD MAKE HELL EVEN MORE TORTUOUS.
BUT I LIKE THAT KIND OF PLACE.
THAT KIND OF ATTITUDE WILL SEND YOU TO HELL, SO YOU BETTER WATCH IT.
WOULD THERE BE AN ECONOMY IN HELL, TOO?
CLATTER
CLATTER
WHO KNOWS? HELL IS EASY TO BUILD AND MAINTAIN.

A CentaUr's Life

UNDERSTANDING AMPHIBIANFOLK PART 6: THE EVOLUTION OF AMPHIBIANFOLK

JUST AS MAMMALIANS SLOWLY EVOLVED FROM AMPHIBIANS, AMPHIBIANFOLK WENT THROUGH MANY STAGES PRIOR TO REACHING THEIR PRESENT FORM. UNFORTUNATELY, WE HAVEN'T FOUND MUCH EVIDENCE OF THESE TRANSITIONAL STAGES, PARTIALLY BECAUSE ONE OF THEIR EVOLUTIONARY FORMS IS BELIEVED TO HAVE LIVED IN AREAS OF DEEP JUNGLE THAT ARE STILL UNEXPLORED. DUE TO THE ENVIRONMENT OF THIS LOCATION AND TIME PERIOD, FOSSILIZATION WAS QUITE RARE, AND ONGOING REGIONAL CONFLICTS CREATED DIFFICULTIES FOR SCIENTISTS ATTEMPTING TO INVESTIGATE THE FEW SPECIMENS THAT WERE FOUND. EVENTUALLY, BETWEEN THOSE VERY FEW RECOVERED FOSSILS AND DETAILED INFORMATION ON THE FORM OF THE MODERN SPECIES, SCIENTISTS WERE ABLE TO FILL IN THE GAPS.

DINOSALAMANDERS:

BIPEDAL AMPHIBIANS THAT APPEARED ON GONDWANA IN THE LATE CRETACEOUS PERIOD. THEY WERE INDEED AMPHIBIANS, DESPITE THE FACT THAT THEY HAD THE PHYSIQUE OF A TERRESTRIAL ANIMAL, THE HEIGHT OF A LARGE DOG, AND THE ELONGATED FACE AND ERECT HIND LIMBS OF A DINOSAUR. BECAUSE THEIR OFFSPRING WERE STILL RAISED IN THE WATER, THE SPECIES REMAINED AMPHIBIAN. THEY WENT EXTINCT AT THE END OF THE CRETACEOUS PERIOD.

MONKEY FROGS:

EVOLUTIONARY FORM OF MODERN ARBOREAL AMPHIBIANS STILL LIVING IN THE JUNGLES OF THE RIVER A BASIN. ALTHOUGH THEY'RE CALLED FROGS, THEY HAVE LITTLE IN COMMON WITH THE MODERN FROGS IN ORDER ANURA, INSTEAD RELATING MUCH MORE CLOSELY TO THE PRIMITIVE AMPHIBIANS OF ORDER TEMNOSPONDYLI. THEIR ADHESIVE DISC, WHICH DID LITTLE TO CARRY THEIR 20-40 KG BODY WEIGHT, WAS PRONE TO DEGENERATION DUE TO SPINAL COMPRESSION. THEY USED THEIR OPPOSABLE THUMBS AND FINGERS TO GRASP TWIGS AND VINES. THEY WERE SKILLFUL IN SWIMMING AND CATCHING PREY UNDERWATER, AND THEY LIVED IN TREES WHERE FEWER PREDATORS EXISTED.

DINOSALAMANDER   MONKEY FROG

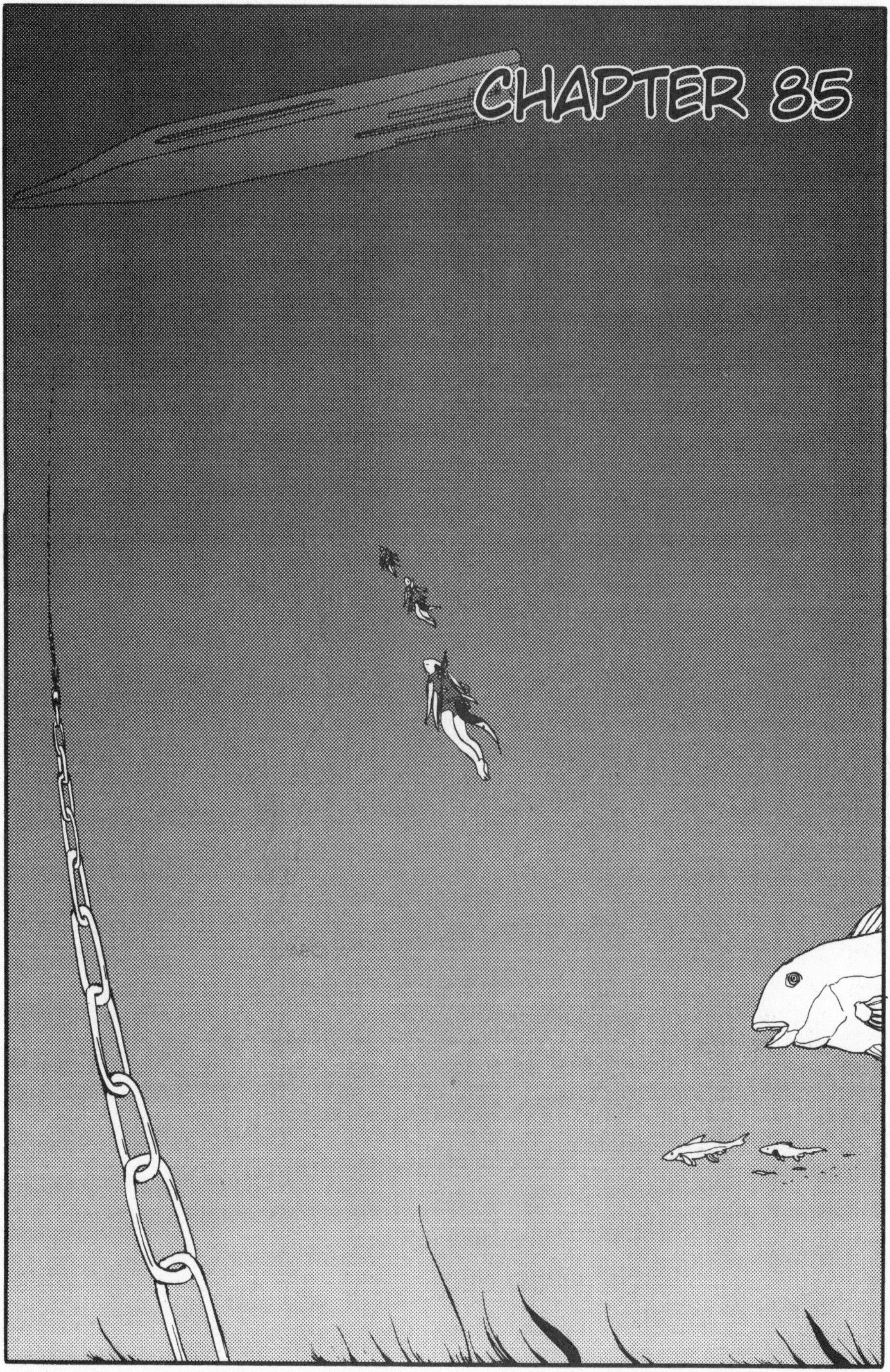
CHAPTER 85

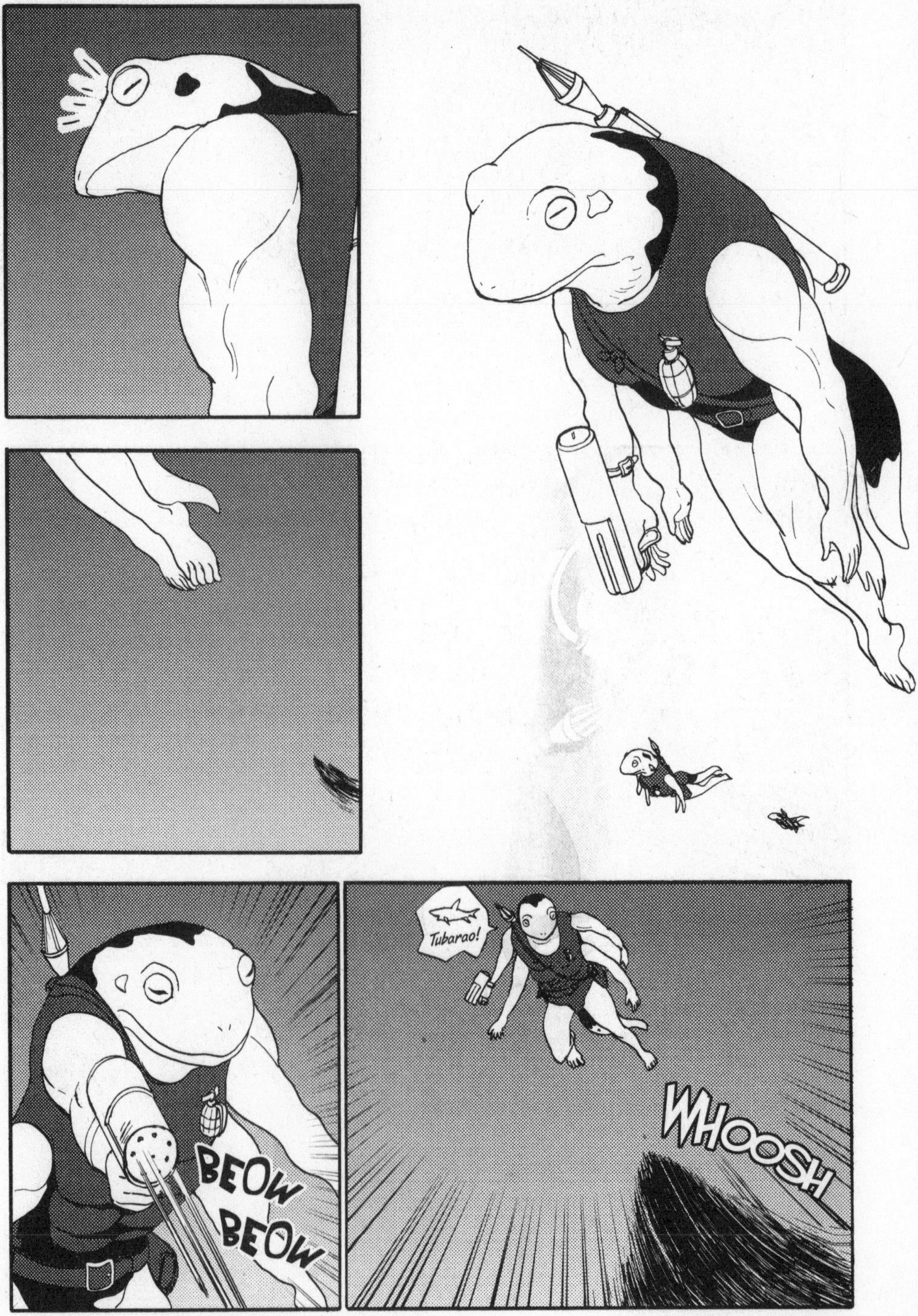
Tubarao!
WHOOSH
BEOW
BEOW

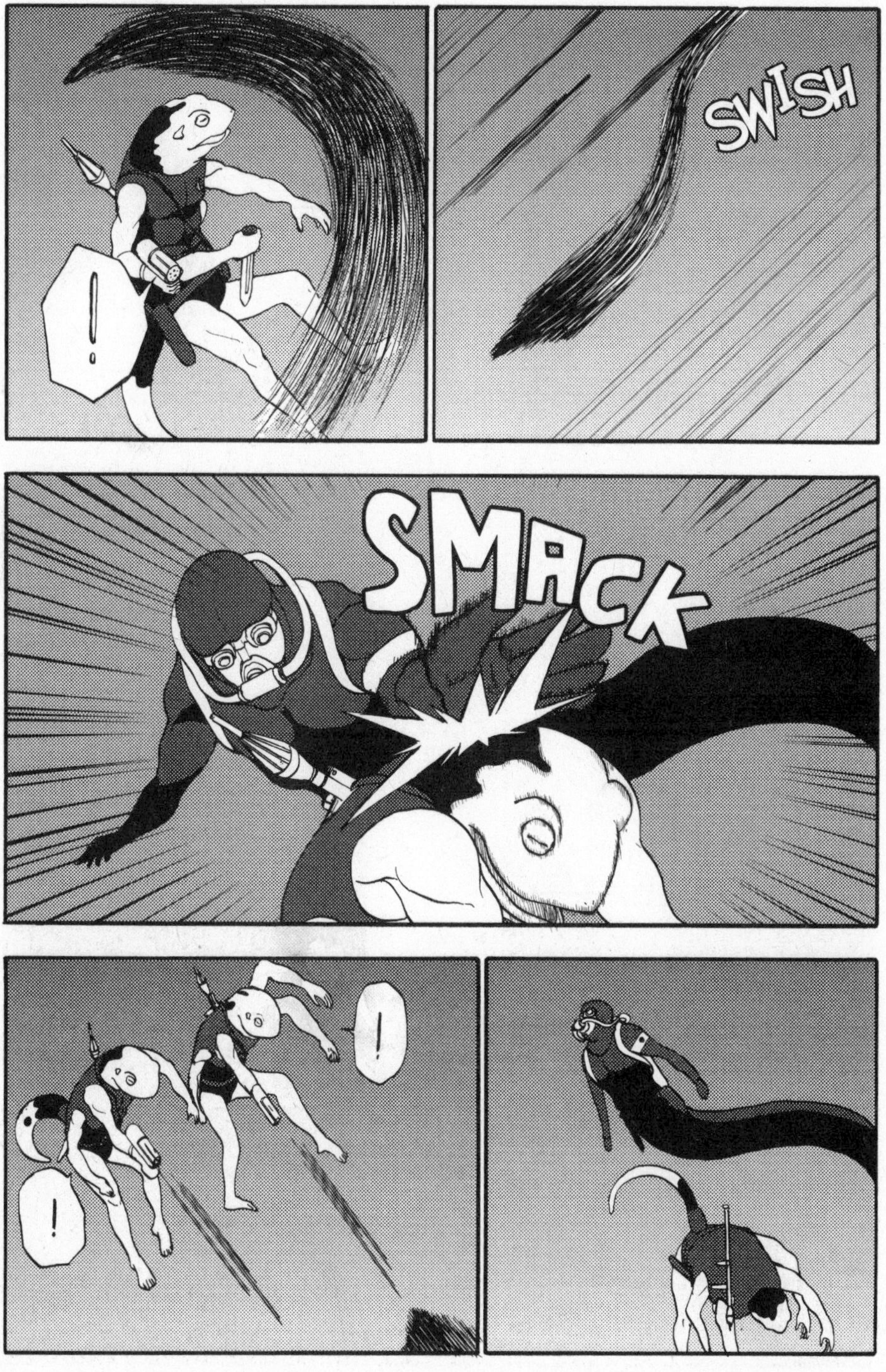
SWISH
!
SMACK
!
!

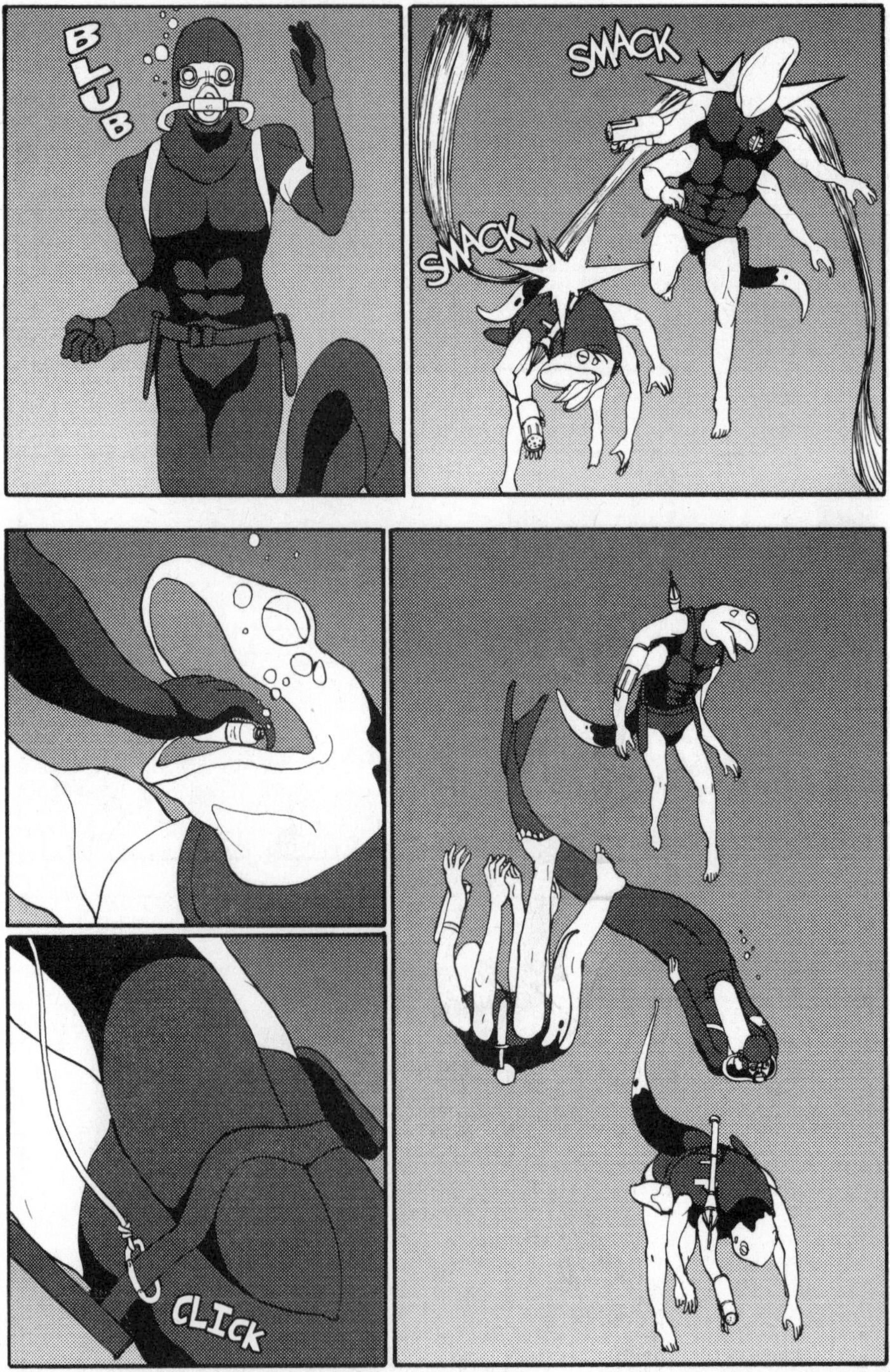
SMACK
SMACK
BLUB
CLICK

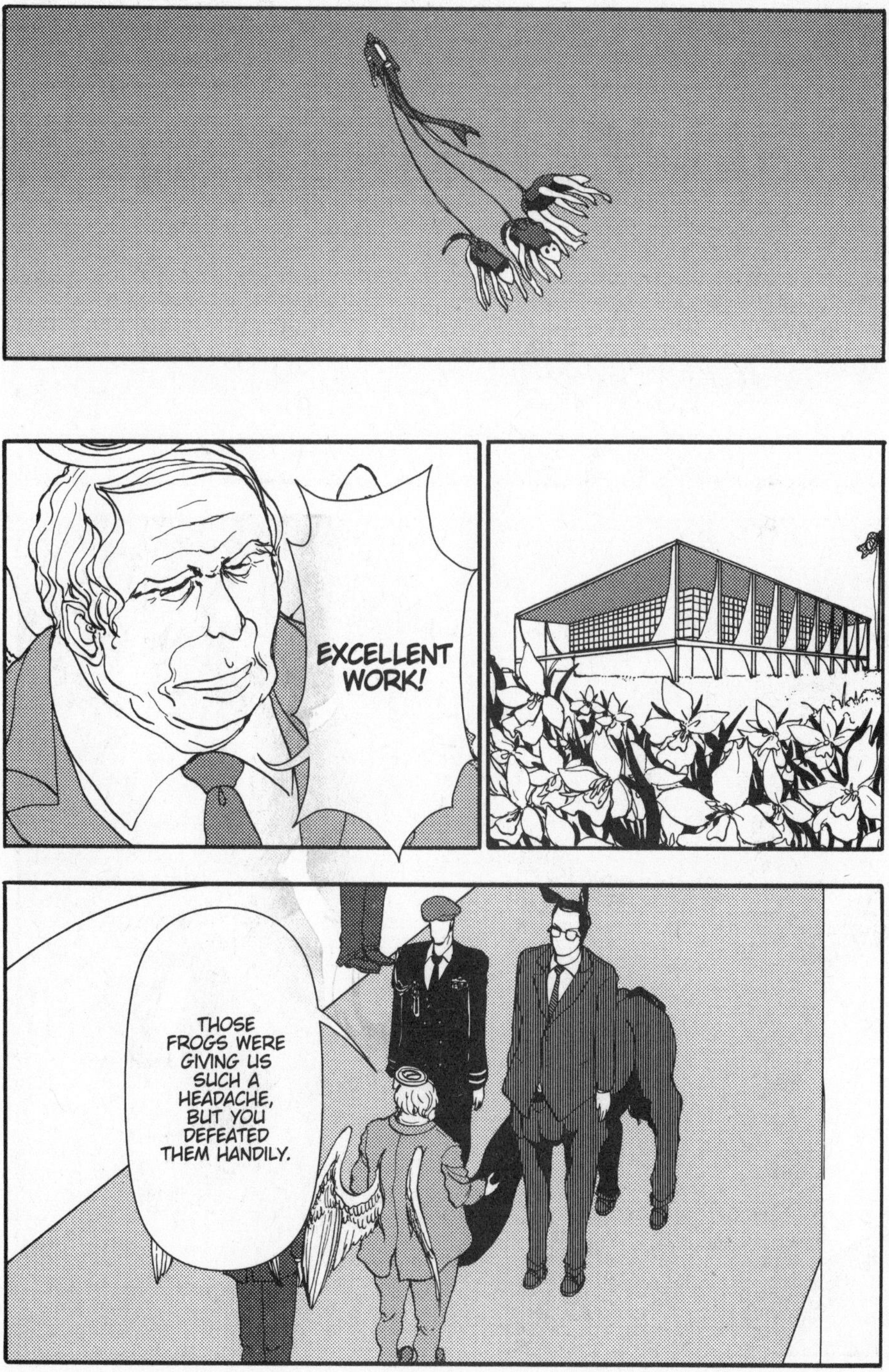
EXCELLENT WORK!
THOSE FROGS WERE GIVING US SUCH A HEADACHE, BUT YOU DEFEATED THEM HANDILY.

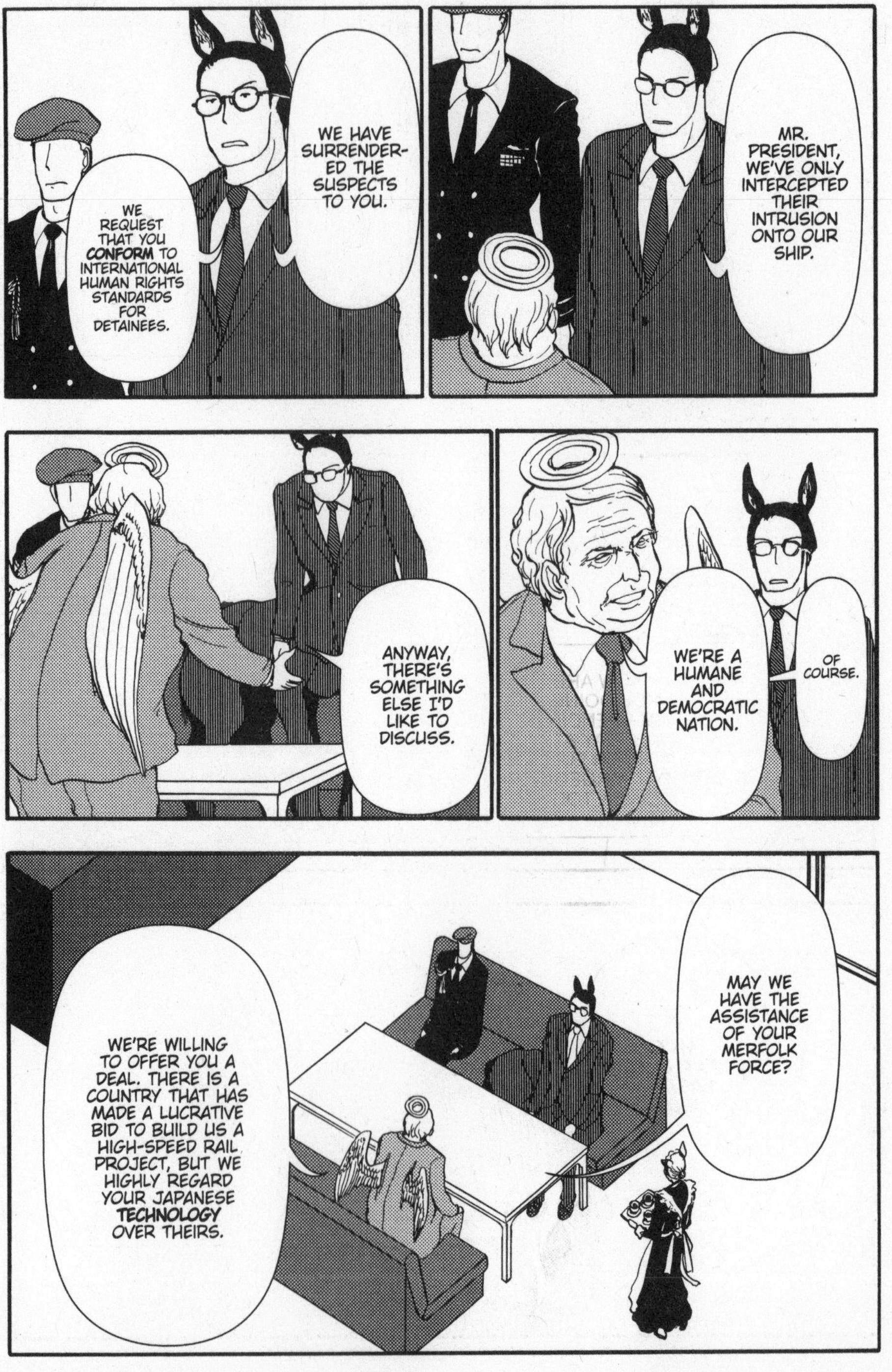
MR. PRESIDENT, WE'VE ONLY INTERCEPTED THEIR INTRUSION ONTO OUR SHIP.
WE HAVE SURRENDER-ED THE SUSPECTS TO YOU.
WE REQUEST THAT YOU **CONFORM** TO INTERNATIONAL HUMAN RIGHTS STANDARDS FOR DETAINEES.
OF COURSE.
WE'RE A HUMANE AND DEMOCRATIC NATION.
ANYWAY, THERE'S SOMETHING ELSE I'D LIKE TO DISCUSS.
MAY WE HAVE THE ASSISTANCE OF YOUR MERFOLK FORCE?
WE'RE WILLING TO OFFER YOU A DEAL. THERE IS A COUNTRY THAT HAS MADE A LUCRATIVE BID TO BUILD US A HIGH-SPEED RAIL PROJECT, BUT WE HIGHLY REGARD YOUR JAPANESE **TECHNOLOGY** OVER THEIRS.

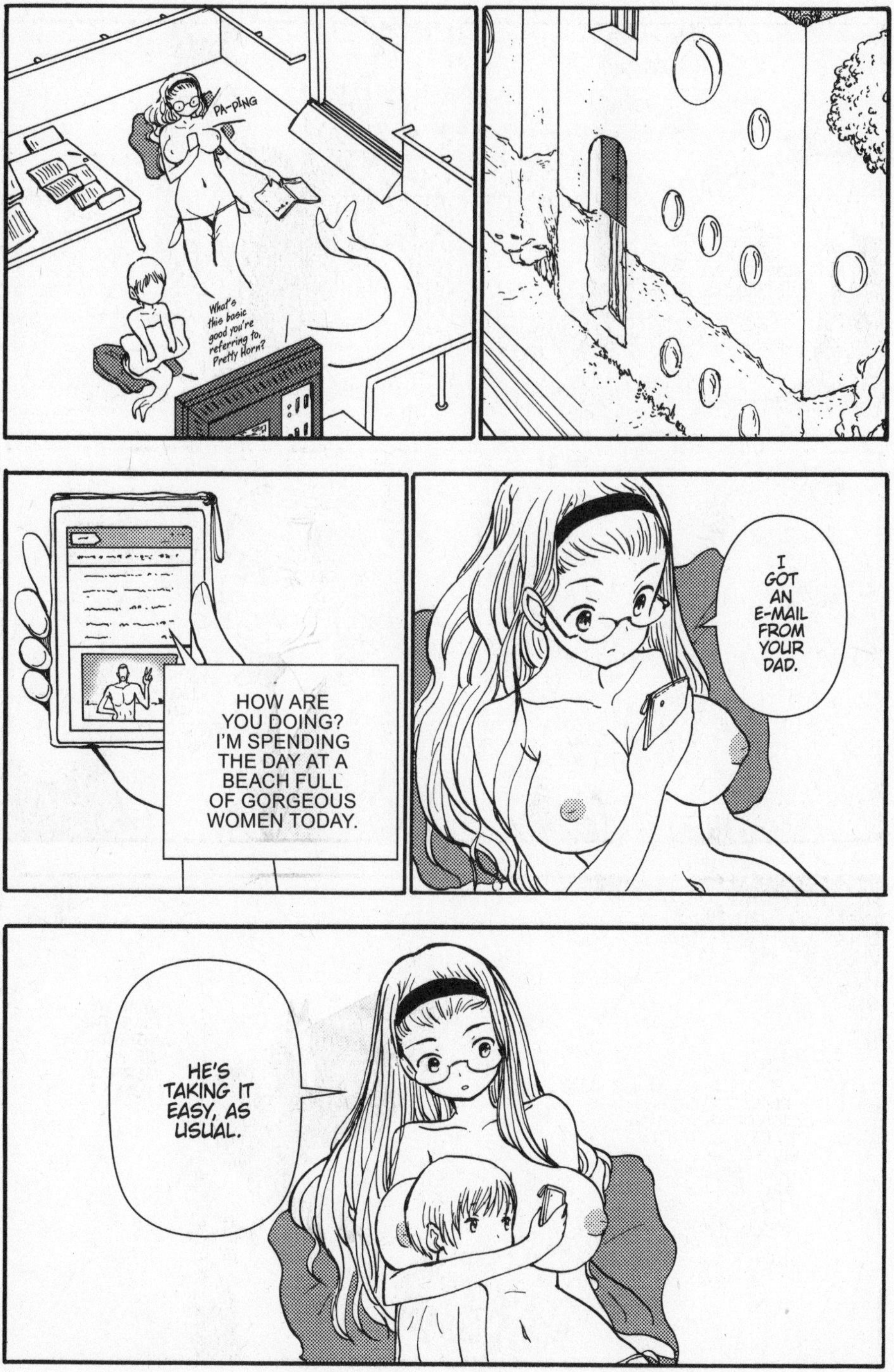
PA-PING
What's this basic good you're referring to, Pretty Horn?
I GOT AN E-MAIL FROM YOUR DAD.
HOW ARE YOU DOING? I'M SPENDING THE DAY AT A BEACH FULL OF GORGEOUS WOMEN TODAY.
HE'S TAKING IT EASY, AS USUAL.

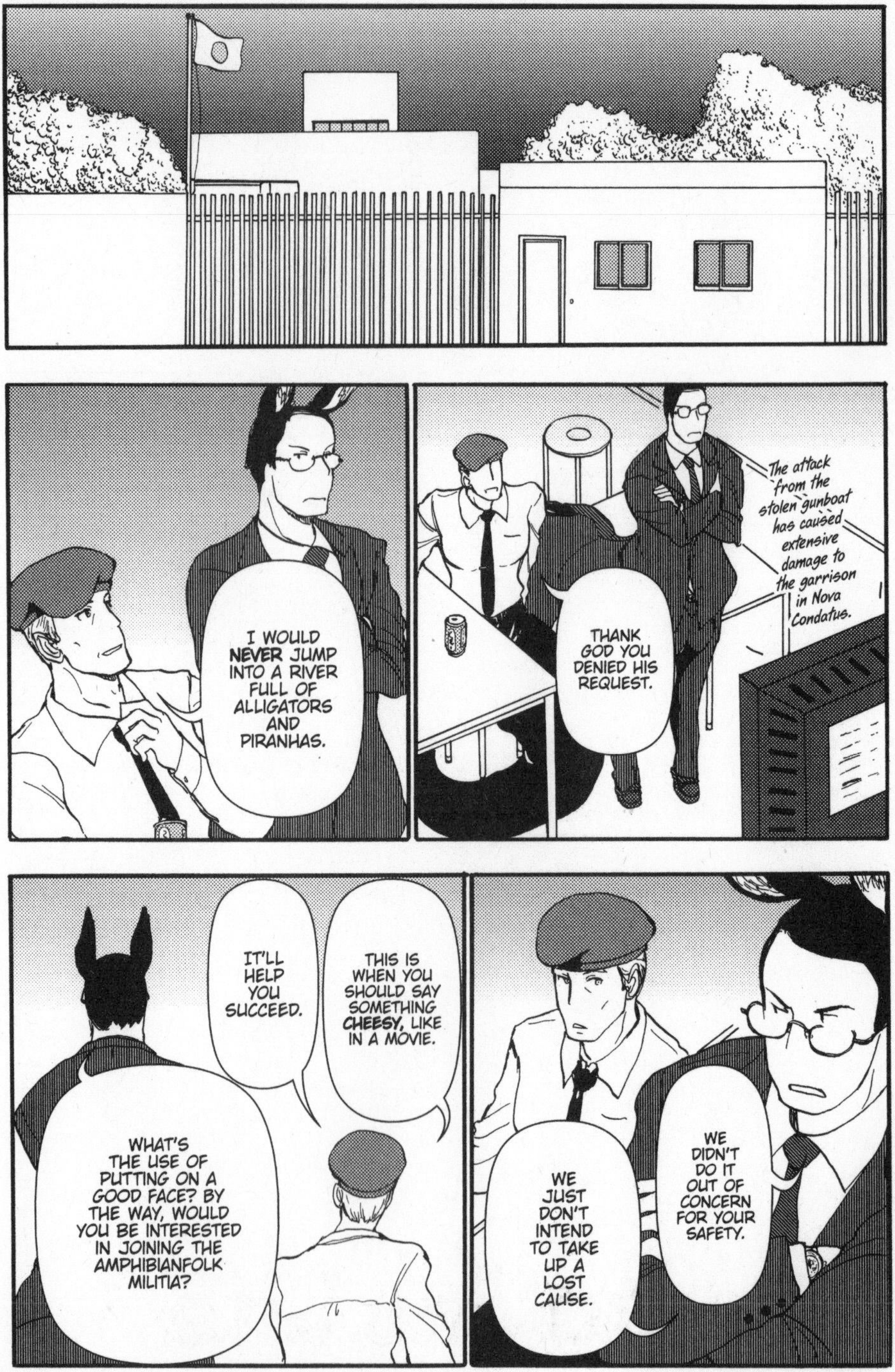
The attack from the stolen gunboat has caused extensive damage to the garrison in Nova Condatus.
THANK GOD YOU DENIED HIS REQUEST.
I WOULD **NEVER** JUMP INTO A RIVER FULL OF ALLIGATORS AND PIRANHAS.
WE DIDN'T DO IT OUT OF CONCERN FOR YOUR SAFETY.
WE JUST DON'T INTEND TO TAKE UP A LOST CAUSE.
THIS IS WHEN YOU SHOULD SAY SOMETHING **CHEESY,** LIKE IN A MOVIE.
IT'LL HELP YOU SUCCEED.
WHAT'S THE USE OF PUTTING ON A GOOD FACE? BY THE WAY, WOULD YOU BE INTERESTED IN JOINING THE AMPHIBIANFOLK MILITIA?

A Centaur's Life

UNDERSTANDING AMPHIBIANFOLK PART 7: BIOLOGICAL CHARACTERISTICS OF AMPHIBIANFOLK

AS MENTIONED BEFORE, AMPHIBIANFOLK HAVE LOST SOME OF THEIR AMPHIBIAN CHARACTERISTICS AND CAN NO LONGER BE TECHNICALLY CLASSIFIED AS AMPHIBIANS. THIS IS THE REASON WHY WE USE THE TERM "EVOLUTIONARY AMPHIBIAN" TO REFER TO THEM, BUT BIOLOGISTS MAY DISAGREE WITH THAT CLASSIFICATION AS WELL. IT'S DIFFICULT TO OBTAIN GENETIC SAMPLES FOR THEIR STUDIES FROM INTELLIGENT SPECIES, AND THE POOR CONDITIONS IN AMPHIBIANFOLK NEIGHBORHOODS ARE DELAYING THE WORK AS WELL.

WHAT WE HAVE BEEN ABLE TO ASCERTAIN IS THAT AMPHIBIANFOLK SKIN ISN'T A MUCUS MEMBRANE, WHICH ENABLES THEM TO TOLERATE DRY CONDITIONS FAR BETTER THAN TYPICAL AMPHIBIANS. HOWEVER, PROLONGED EXPOSURE TO AN EXTREMELY DRY ENVIRONMENT, SUCH AS A DESERT, CAN CAUSE BURN-LIKE SYMPTOMS THAT COULD POTENTIALLY LEAD TO DEATH. THIS IS WHY AMPHIBIANFOLK TEND TO REMAIN IN THE JUNGLE, AND IS PERHAPS WHAT PREVENTED THEM FROM DEVELOPING THEIR CIVILIZATION IN THE WAY THAT MAMMALIANS DID. BECAUSE THEY'RE ESSENTIALLY CONFINED TO THEIR HABITABLE ZONE, THEY HAVE LIMITED RESOURCES.

THE AMPHIBIANFOLK ARE WELL-BUILT AND ATHLETIC COMPARED TO MAMMALIAN HUMANS. THEY HAVE FOUR ARMS THAT ARE ALL EXCEPTIONALLY STRONG, MOST LIKELY DEVELOPED BY THEIR HUNTING AND VIGOROUS SWIMMING HABITS. RESEARCH ON THE INDIGENOUS FISHERMEN IN THE RUSSIAN FAR EAST REVEALED THAT THEIR ARMS AND MUSCLE ATTACHMENTS WERE TWICE AS LARGE AS THOSE OF AN ORDINARY MAMMALIAN HUMAN, POSSIBLY DUE TO ROWING BOATS THROUGH ROUGH SEAS. THEIR EXCELLENT DYNAMIC VISUAL ACUITY AND REFLEXES MAY ALSO COME FROM BEING NATURAL HUNTERS. AMPHIBIANFOLK ATHLETIC PERFORMANCE SEEMS LACKLUSTER WHEN RUNNING ON A TRACK, BUT THEY MOVE VERY QUICKLY IN THE JUNGLE ENVIRONMENTS TO WHICH THEY ARE ACCUSTOMED. THEIR COGNITIVE FUNCTION AND PROCESSING SPEED IS ROUGHLY EQUIVALENT TO THAT EXHIBITED BY THE MAMMALIAN HUMAN BRAIN.

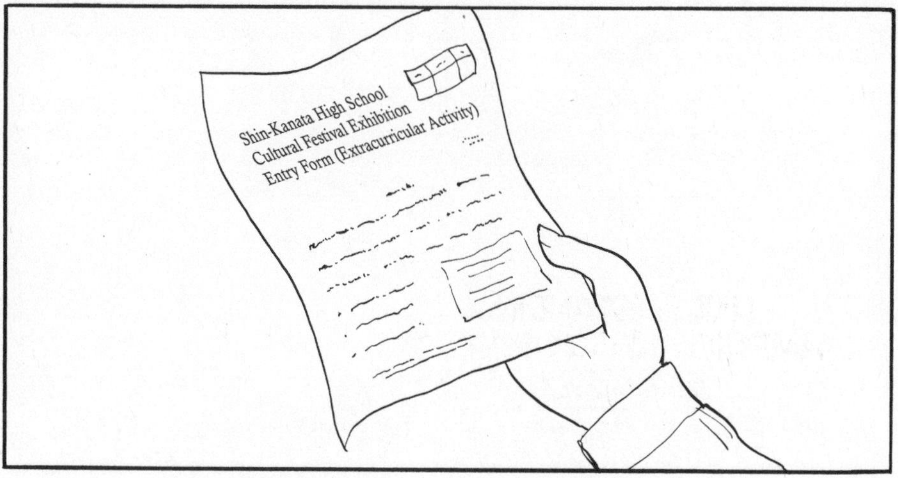
Shin-Kanata High School
Cultural Festival Exhibition
Entry Form (Extracurricular Activity)

CHAPTER 86

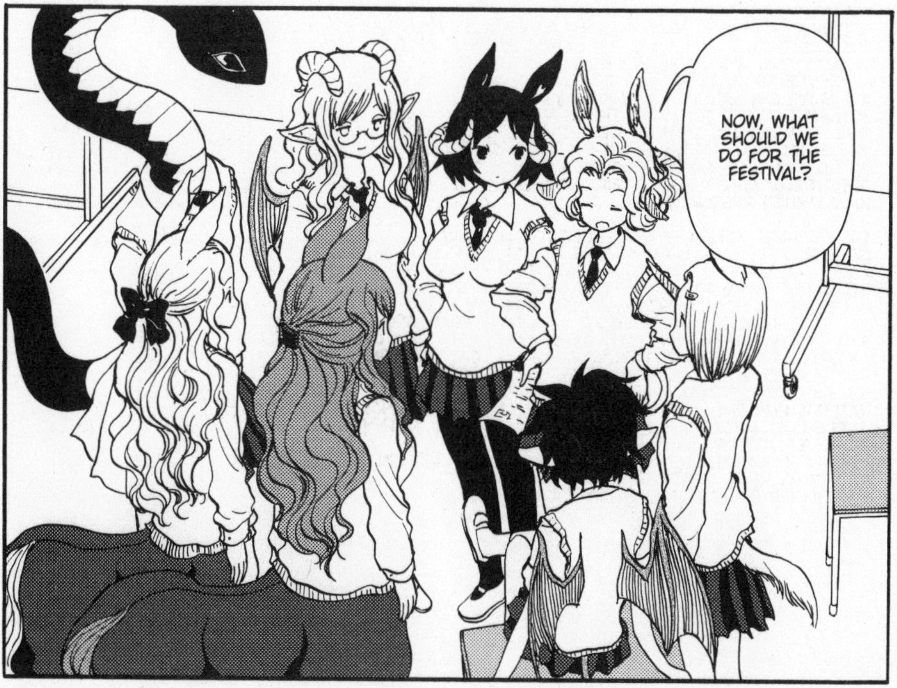
NOW, WHAT SHOULD WE DO FOR THE FESTIVAL?

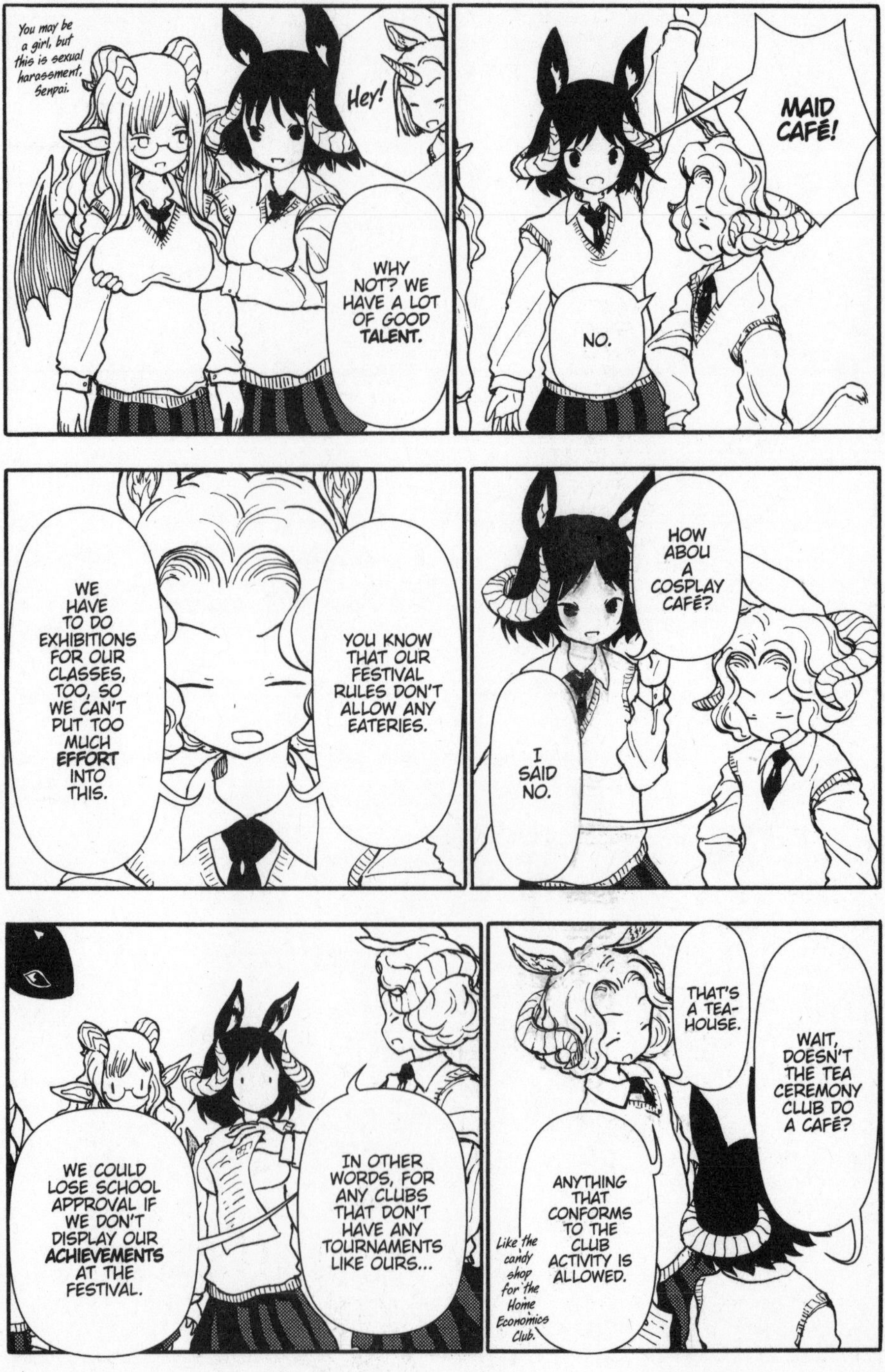
MAID CAFÉ!
NO.
Hey!
WHY NOT? WE HAVE A LOT OF GOOD TALENT.
You may be a girl, but this is sexual harassment, Senpai.
HOW ABOU A COSPLAY CAFÉ?
I SAID NO.
YOU KNOW THAT OUR FESTIVAL RULES DON'T ALLOW ANY EATERIES.
WE HAVE TO DO EXHIBITIONS FOR OUR CLASSES, TOO, SO WE CAN'T PUT TOO MUCH EFFORT INTO THIS.
WAIT, DOESN'T THE TEA CEREMONY CLUB DO A CAFÉ?
THAT'S A TEA-HOUSE.
ANYTHING THAT CONFORMS TO THE CLUB ACTIVITY IS ALLOWED.
Like the candy shop for the Home Economics Club.
IN OTHER WORDS, FOR ANY CLUBS THAT DON'T HAVE ANY TOURNAMENTS LIKE OURS...
WE COULD LOSE SCHOOL APPROVAL IF WE DON'T DISPLAY OUR ACHIEVEMENTS AT THE FESTIVAL.

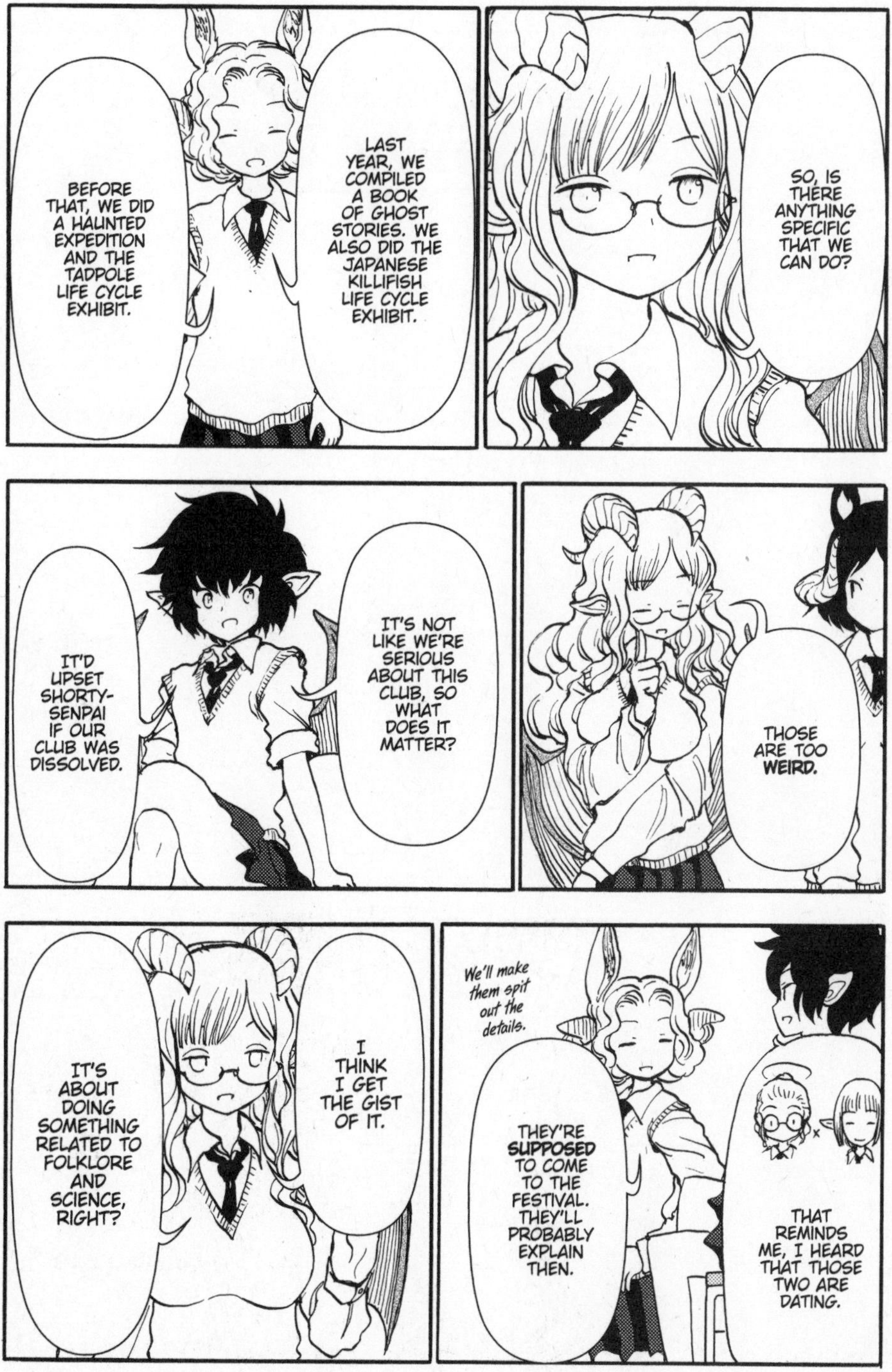
SO, IS THERE ANYTHING SPECIFIC THAT WE CAN DO?
LAST YEAR, WE COMPILED A BOOK OF GHOST STORIES. WE ALSO DID THE JAPANESE KILLIFISH LIFE CYCLE EXHIBIT.
BEFORE THAT, WE DID A HAUNTED EXPEDITION AND THE TADPOLE LIFE CYCLE EXHIBIT.
THOSE ARE TOO **WEIRD.**
IT'S NOT LIKE WE'RE SERIOUS ABOUT THIS CLUB, SO WHAT DOES IT MATTER?
IT'D UPSET SHORTY-SENPAI IF OUR CLUB WAS DISSOLVED.
THAT REMINDS ME, I HEARD THAT THOSE TWO ARE DATING.
THEY'RE **SUPPOSED** TO COME TO THE FESTIVAL. THEY'LL PROBABLY EXPLAIN THEN.
We'll make them spit out the details.
I THINK I GET THE GIST OF IT.
IT'S ABOUT DOING SOMETHING RELATED TO FOLKLORE AND SCIENCE, RIGHT?

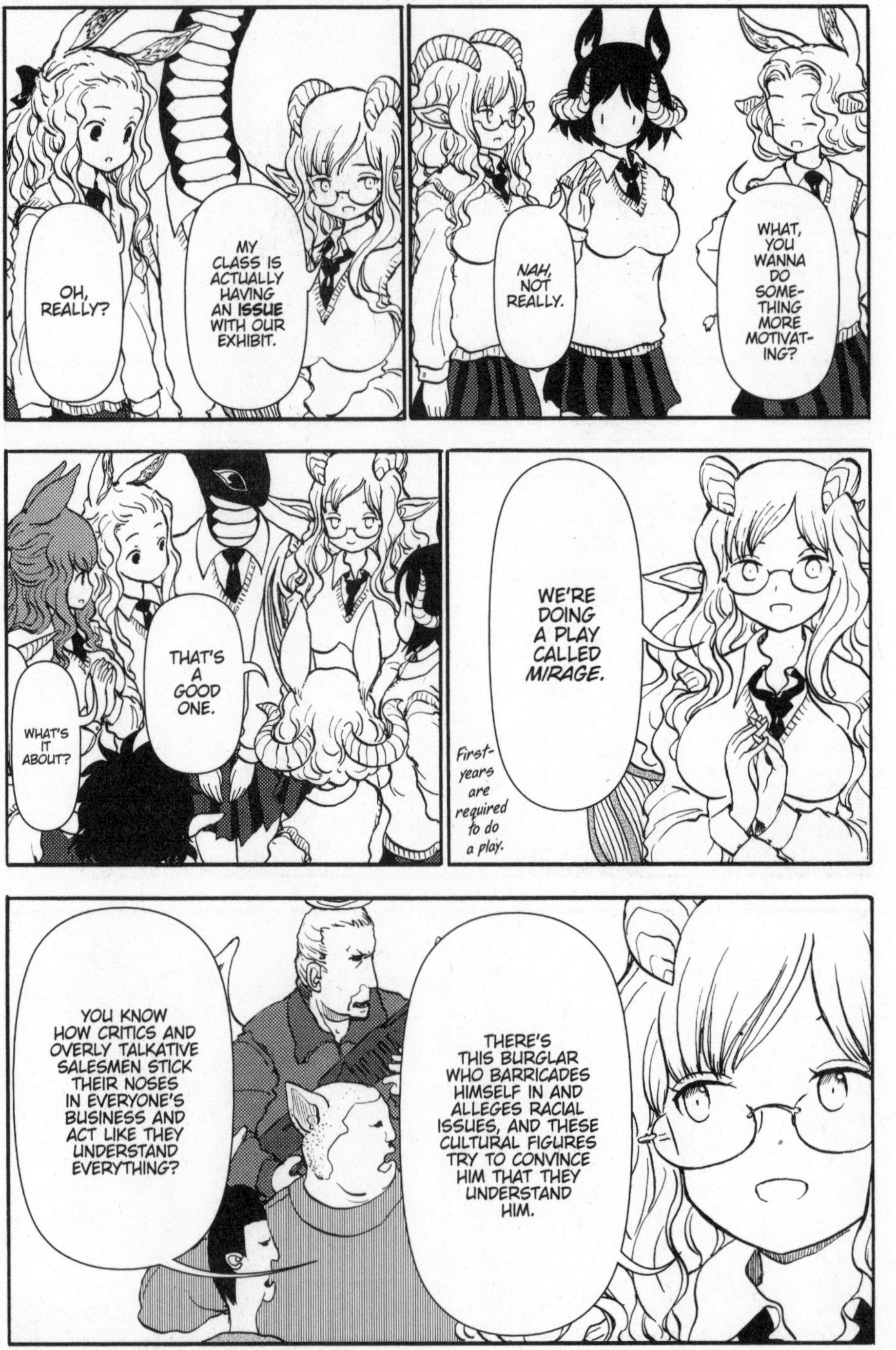
WHAT, YOU WANNA DO SOMETHING MORE MOTIVATING?
NAH, NOT REALLY.
MY CLASS IS ACTUALLY HAVING AN ISSUE WITH OUR EXHIBIT.
OH, REALLY?
WE'RE DOING A PLAY CALLED MIRAGE.
First-years are required to do a play.
THAT'S A GOOD ONE.
WHAT'S IT ABOUT?
THERE'S THIS BURGLAR WHO BARRICADES HIMSELF IN AND ALLEGES RACIAL ISSUES, AND THESE CULTURAL FIGURES TRY TO CONVINCE HIM THAT THEY UNDERSTAND HIM.
YOU KNOW HOW CRITICS AND OVERLY TALKATIVE SALESMEN STICK THEIR NOSES IN EVERYONE'S BUSINESS AND ACT LIKE THEY UNDERSTAND EVERYTHING?

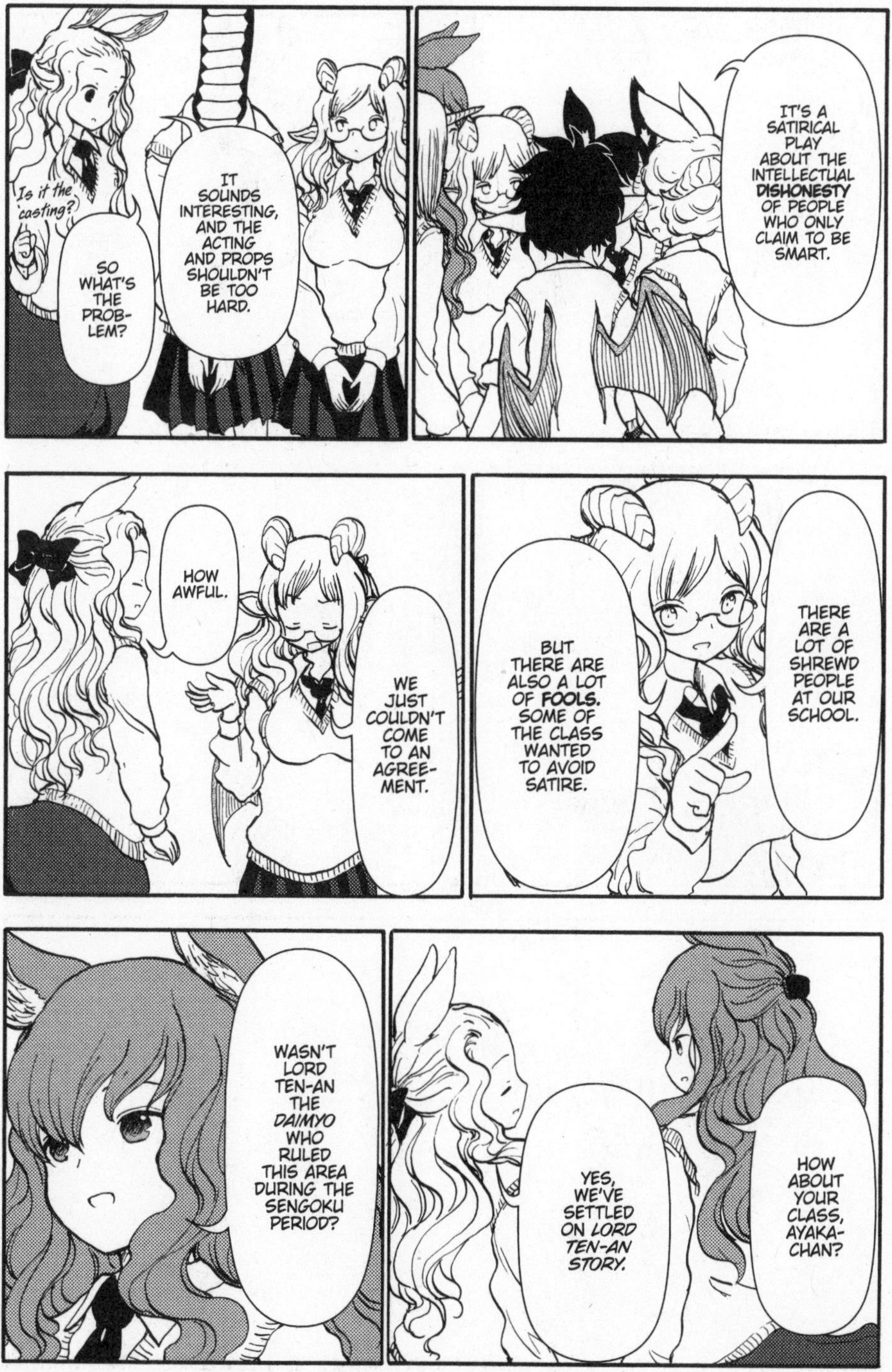
IT'S A SATIRICAL PLAY ABOUT THE INTELLECTUAL **DISHONESTY** OF PEOPLE WHO ONLY CLAIM TO BE SMART.
IT SOUNDS INTERESTING, AND THE ACTING AND PROPS SHOULDN'T BE TOO HARD.
SO WHAT'S THE PROBLEM?
Is it the casting?
THERE ARE A LOT OF SHREWD PEOPLE AT OUR SCHOOL.
BUT THERE ARE ALSO A LOT OF **FOOLS**. SOME OF THE CLASS WANTED TO AVOID SATIRE.
WE JUST COULDN'T COME TO AN AGREEMENT.
HOW AWFUL.
HOW ABOUT YOUR CLASS, AYAKA-CHAN?
YES, WE'VE SETTLED ON *LORD TEN-AN STORY.*
WASN'T LORD TEN-AN THE *DAIMYO* WHO RULED THIS AREA DURING THE SENGOKU PERIOD?

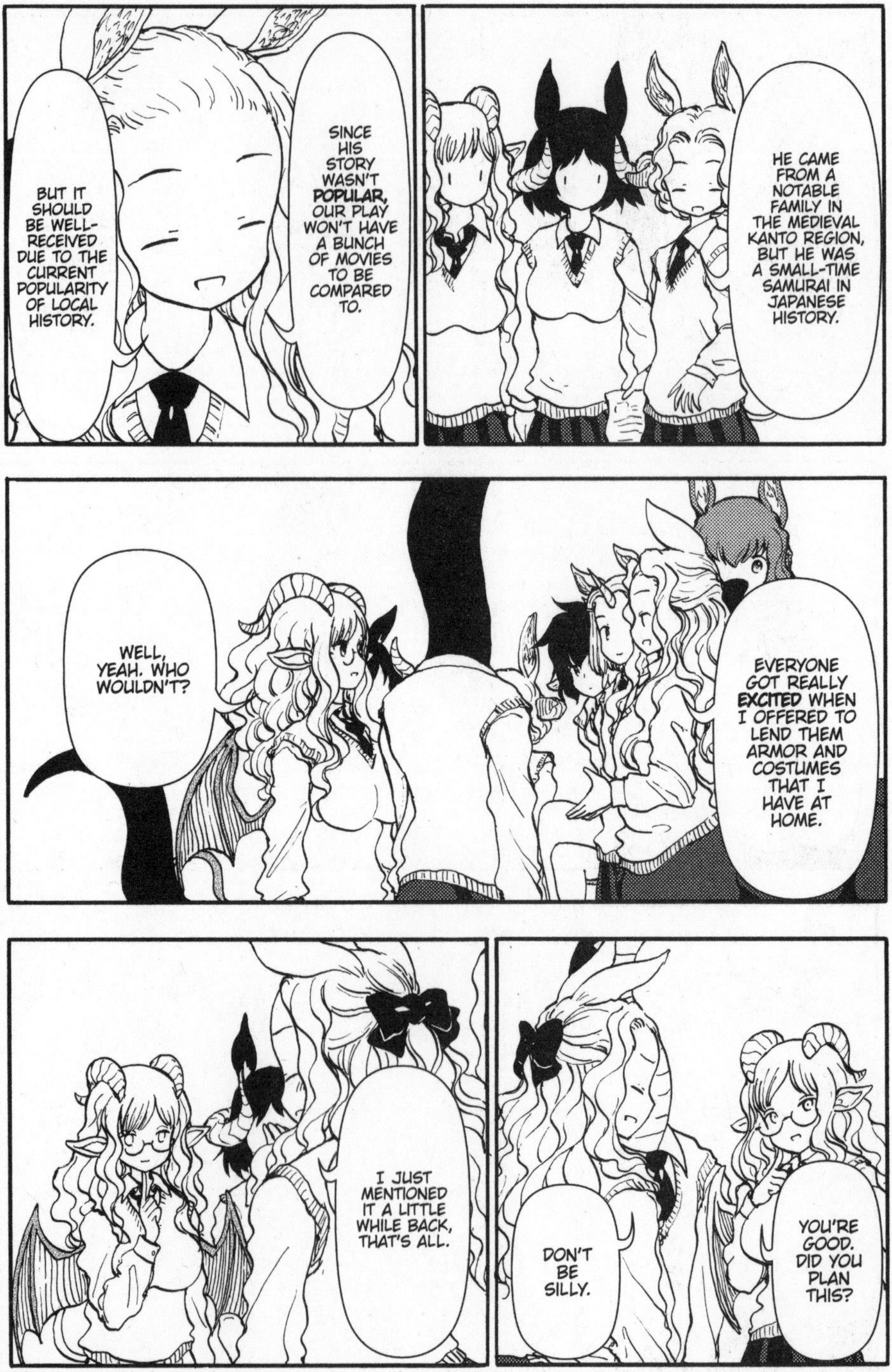
HE CAME FROM A NOTABLE FAMILY IN THE MEDIEVAL KANTO REGION, BUT HE WAS A SMALL-TIME SAMURAI IN JAPANESE HISTORY.
SINCE HIS STORY WASN'T **POPULAR,** OUR PLAY WON'T HAVE A BUNCH OF MOVIES TO BE COMPARED TO.
BUT IT SHOULD BE WELL-RECEIVED DUE TO THE CURRENT POPULARITY OF LOCAL HISTORY.
EVERYONE GOT REALLY **EXCITED** WHEN I OFFERED TO LEND THEM ARMOR AND COSTUMES THAT I HAVE AT HOME.
WELL, YEAH. WHO WOULDN'T?
YOU'RE GOOD. DID YOU PLAN THIS?
DON'T BE SILLY.
I JUST MENTIONED IT A LITTLE WHILE BACK, THAT'S ALL.

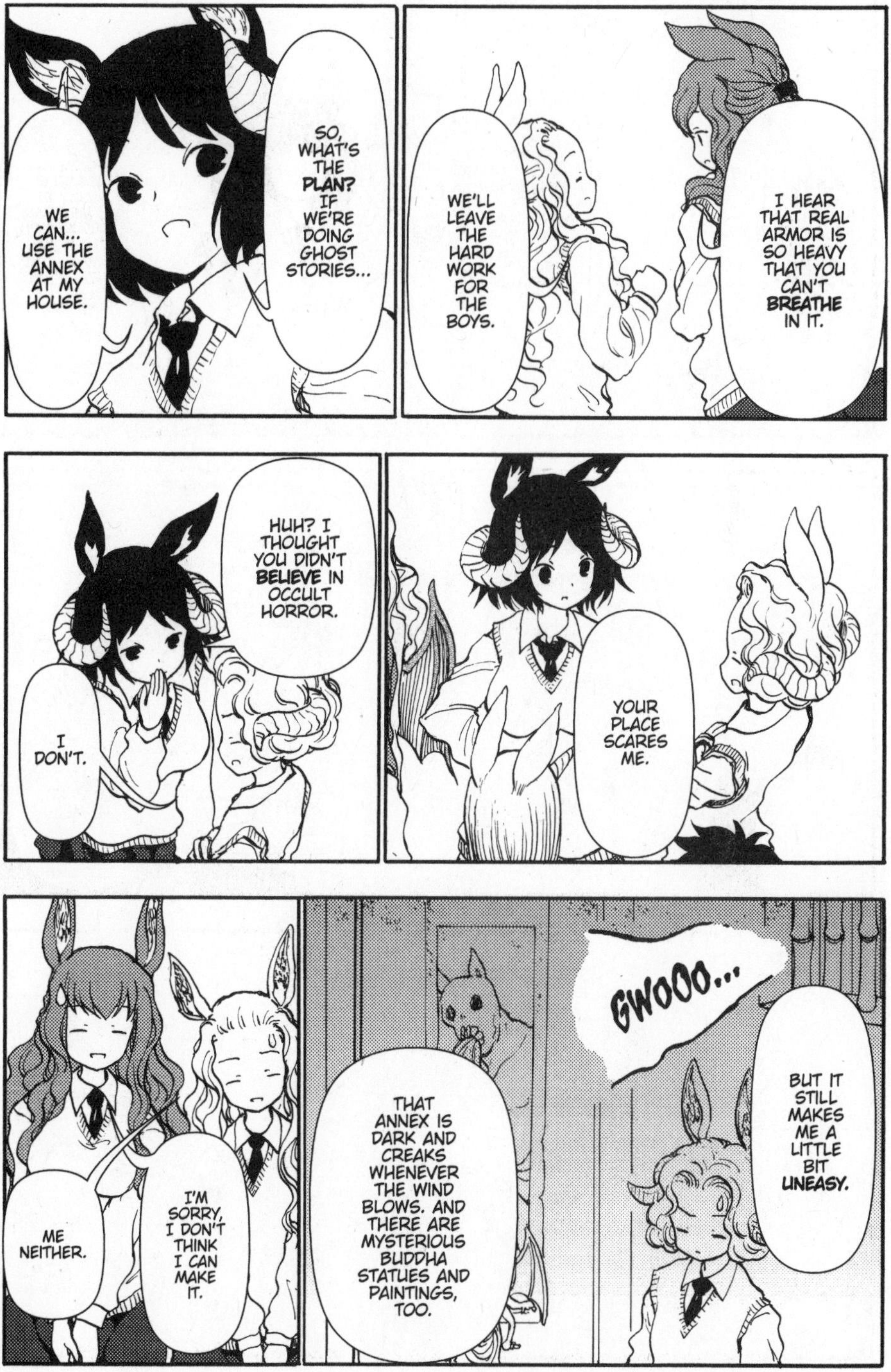
I HEAR THAT REAL ARMOR IS SO HEAVY THAT YOU CAN'T BREATHE IN IT.
WE'LL LEAVE THE HARD WORK FOR THE BOYS.
SO, WHAT'S THE PLAN? IF WE'RE DOING GHOST STORIES...
WE CAN... USE THE ANNEX AT MY HOUSE.
YOUR PLACE SCARES ME.
HUH? I THOUGHT YOU DIDN'T BELIEVE IN OCCULT HORROR.
I DON'T.
GWOOO...
BUT IT STILL MAKES ME A LITTLE BIT UNEASY.
THAT ANNEX IS DARK AND CREAKS WHENEVER THE WIND BLOWS. AND THERE ARE MYSTERIOUS BUDDHA STATUES AND PAINTINGS, TOO.
I'M SORRY, I DON'T THINK I CAN MAKE IT.
ME NEITHER.

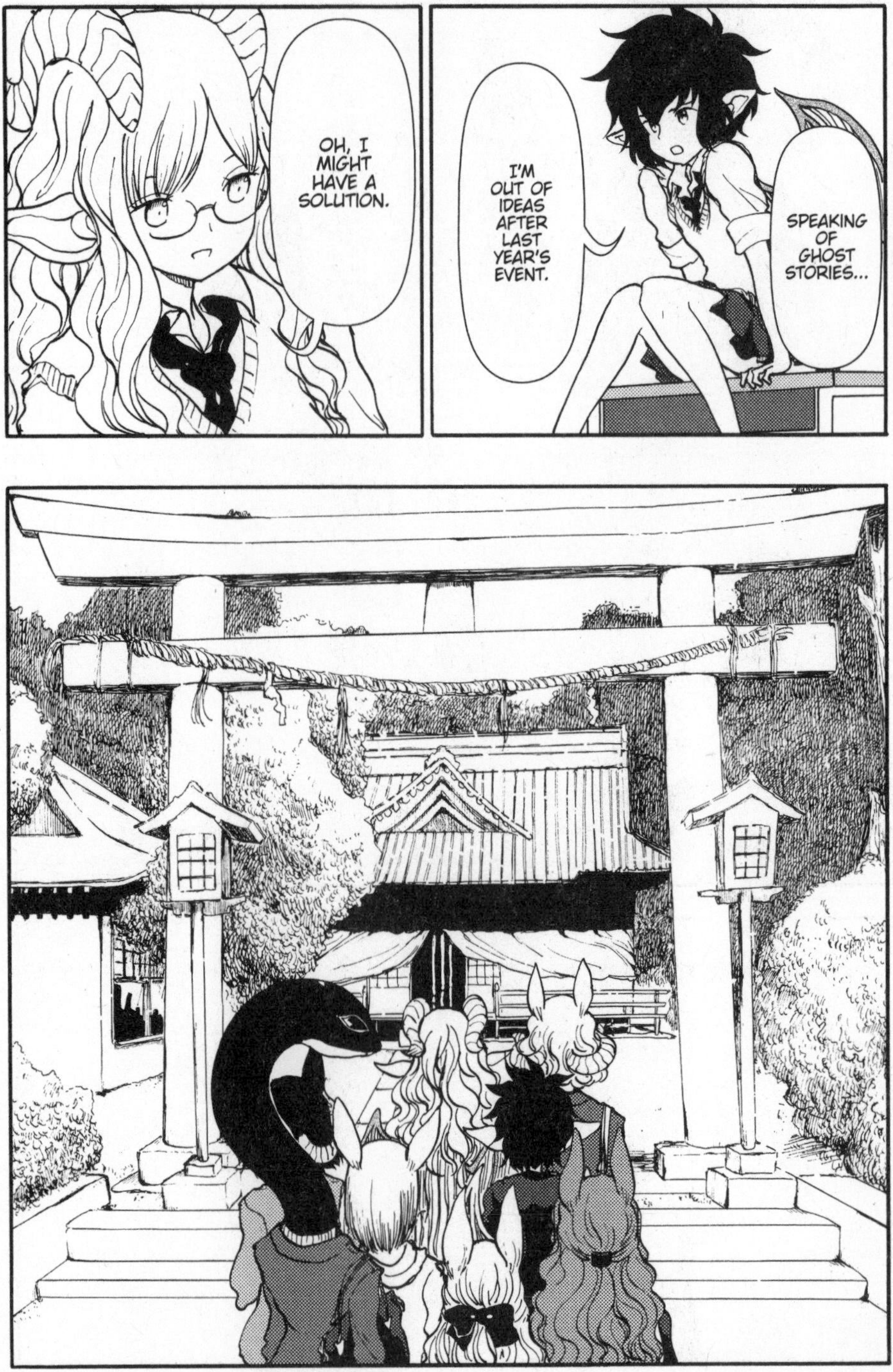
SPEAKING OF GHOST STORIES...
I'M OUT OF IDEAS AFTER LAST YEAR'S EVENT.
OH, I MIGHT HAVE A SOLUTION.

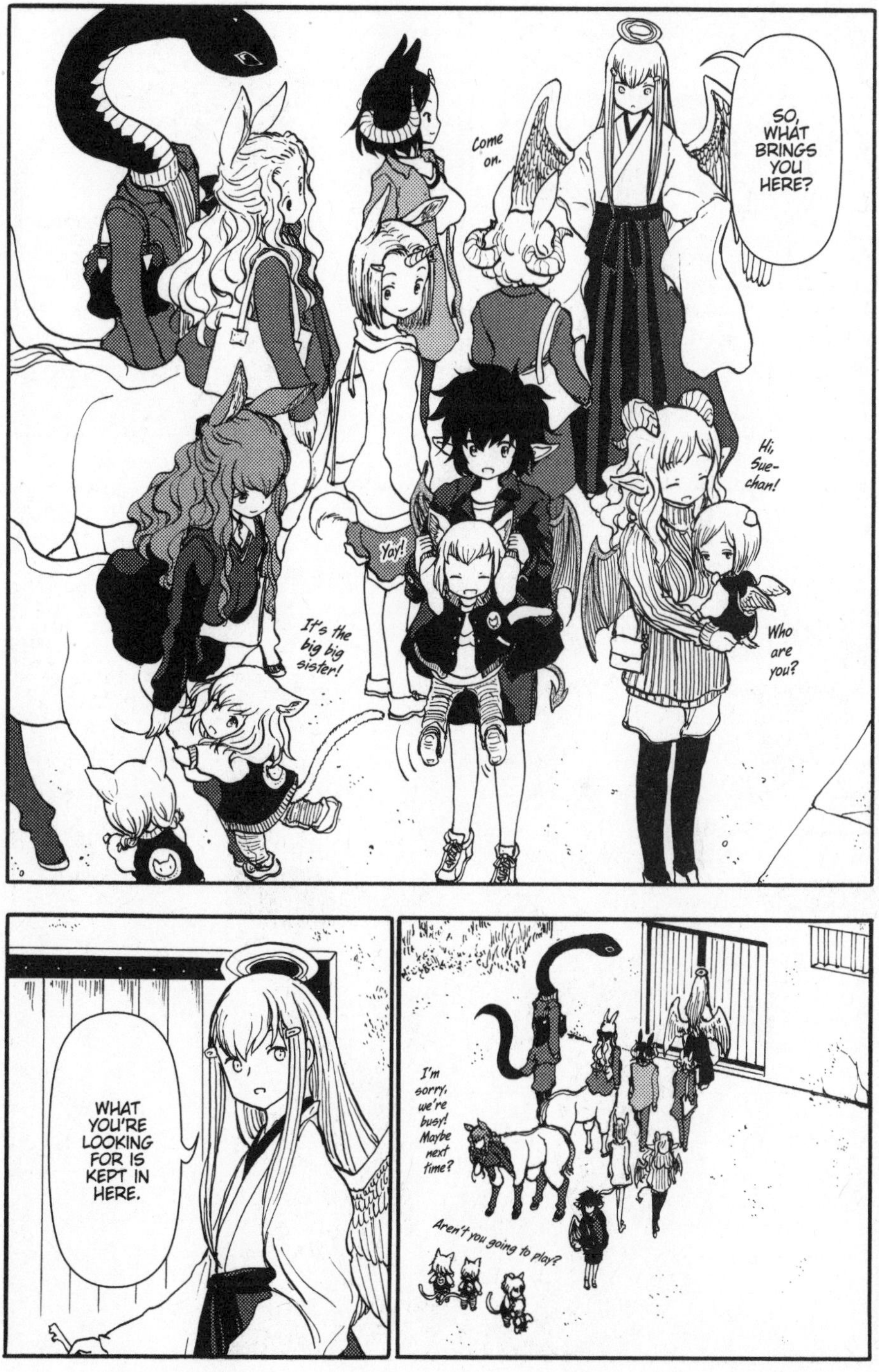
SO, WHAT BRINGS YOU HERE?
Come on.
Hi, Sue-chan!
Who are you?
Yay!
It's the big big sister!
I'm sorry, we're busy! Maybe next time?
Aren't you going to play?
WHAT YOU'RE LOOKING FOR IS KEPT IN HERE.

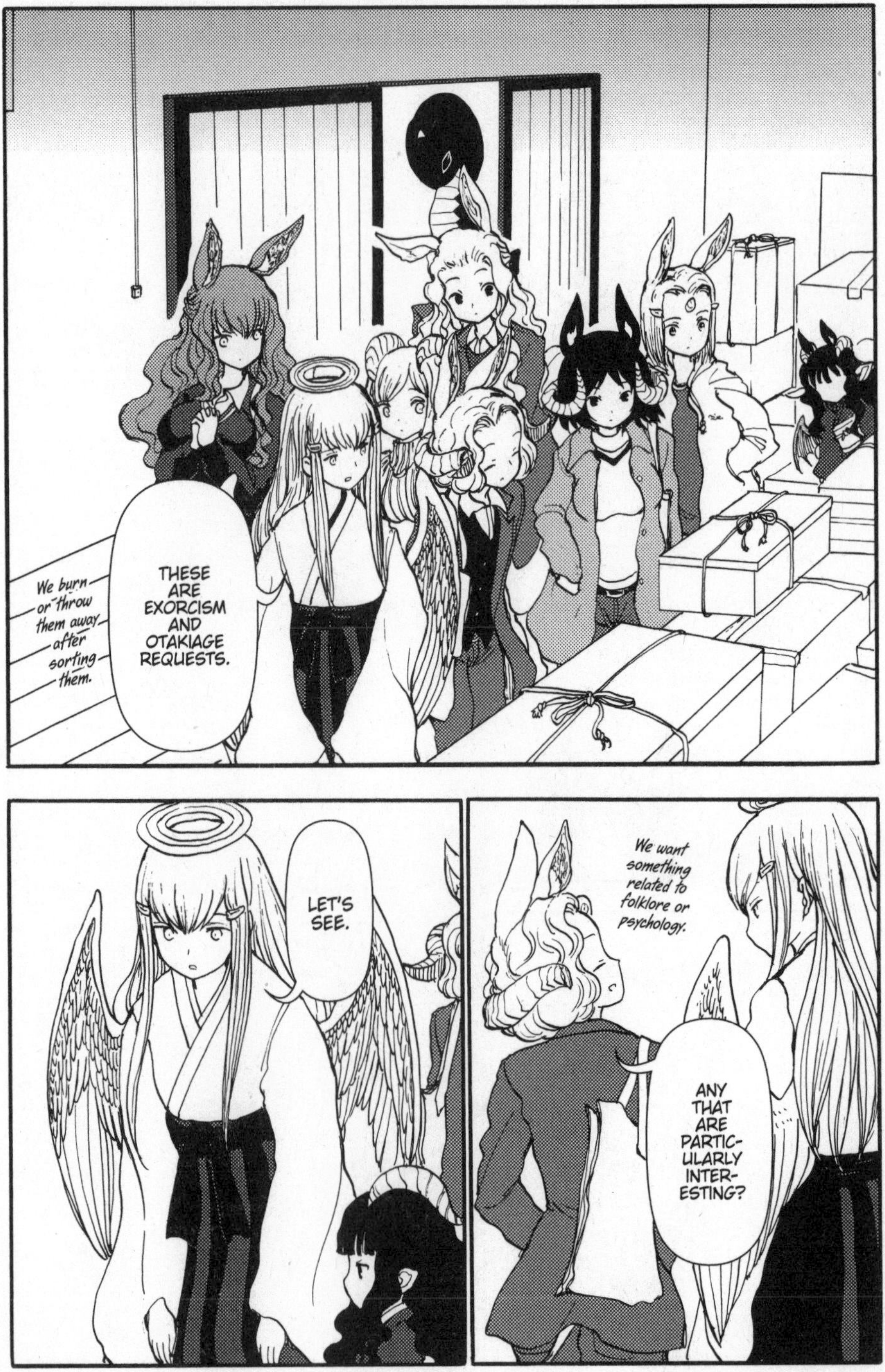
THESE ARE EXORCISM AND OTAKIAGE REQUESTS.
We burn or throw them away after sorting them.
We want something related to folklore or psychology.
ANY THAT ARE PARTICULARLY INTERESTING?
LET'S SEE.

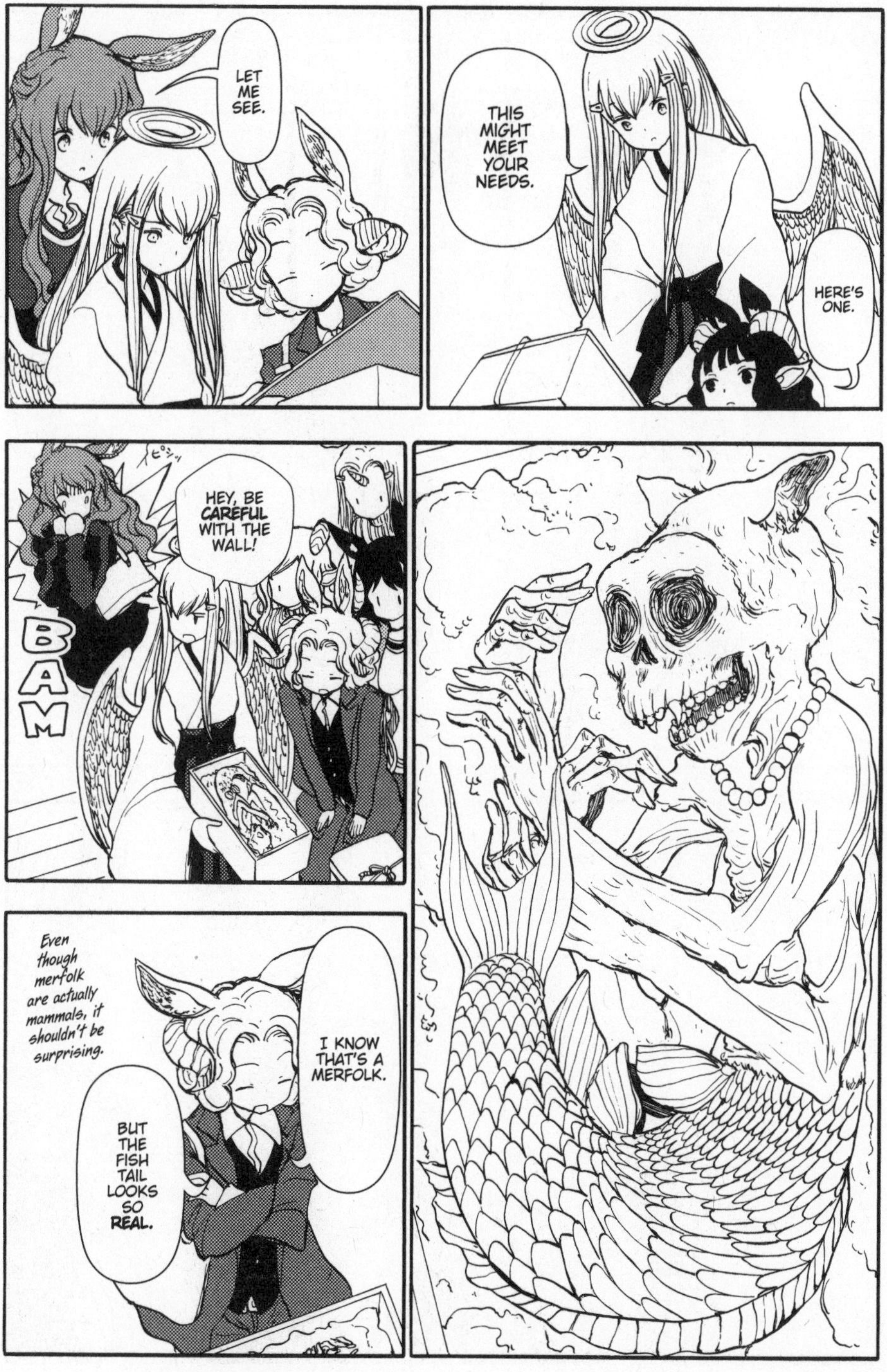
THIS MIGHT MEET YOUR NEEDS.
HERE'S ONE.
LET ME SEE.
HEY, BE **CAREFUL** WITH THE WALL!
BAM
I KNOW THAT'S A MERFOLK.
Even though merfolk are actually mammals, it shouldn't be surprising.
BUT THE FISH TAIL LOOKS SO **REAL.**

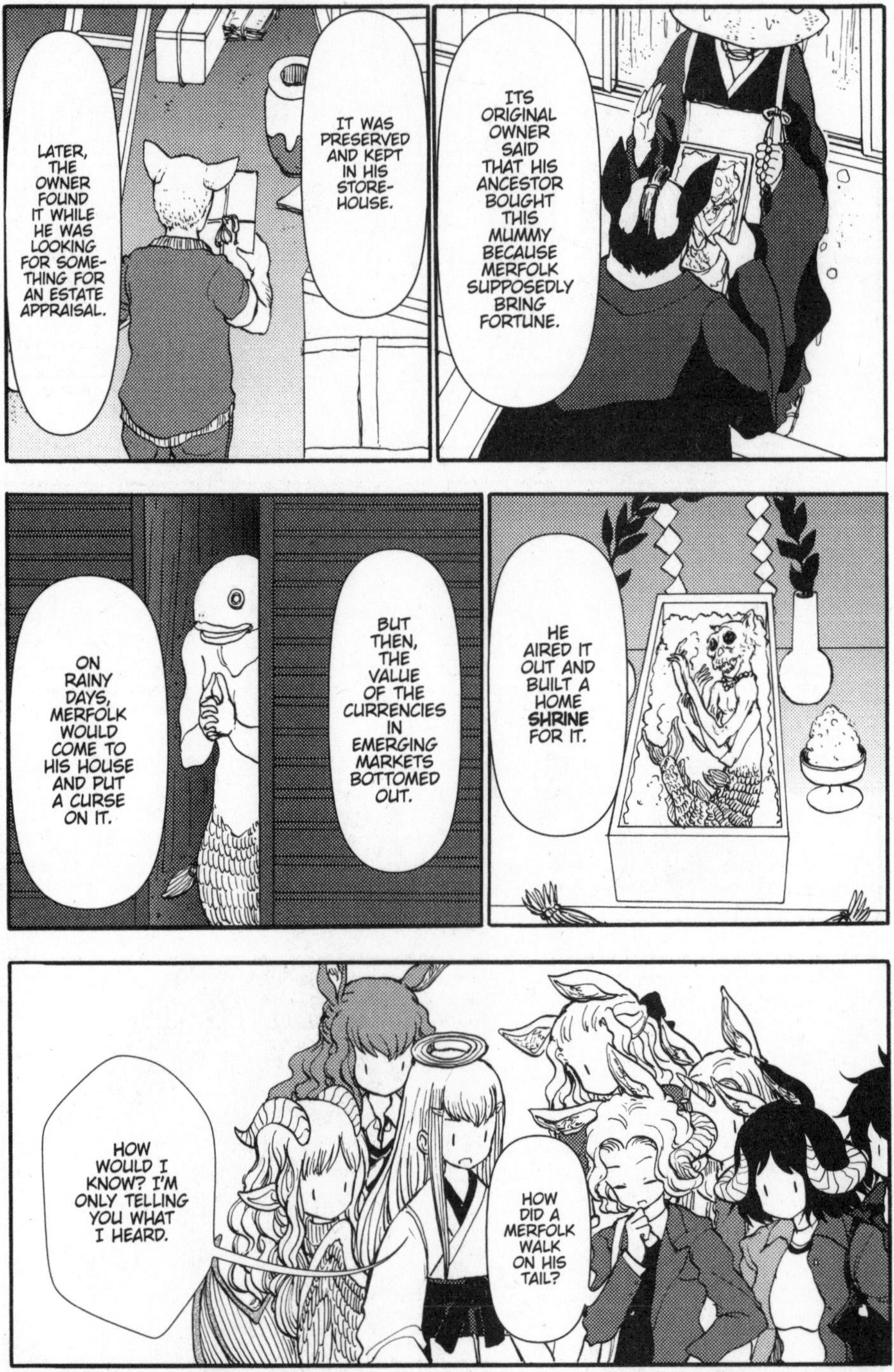
ITS ORIGINAL OWNER SAID THAT HIS ANCESTOR BOUGHT THIS MUMMY BECAUSE MERFOLK SUPPOSEDLY BRING FORTUNE.
IT WAS PRESERVED AND KEPT IN HIS STORE-HOUSE.
LATER, THE OWNER FOUND IT WHILE HE WAS LOOKING FOR SOME-THING FOR AN ESTATE APPRAISAL.
HE AIRED IT OUT AND BUILT A HOME **SHRINE** FOR IT.
BUT THEN, THE VALUE OF THE CURRENCIES IN EMERGING MARKETS BOTTOMED OUT.
ON RAINY DAYS, MERFOLK WOULD COME TO HIS HOUSE AND PUT A CURSE ON IT.
HOW DID A MERFOLK WALK ON HIS TAIL?
HOW WOULD I KNOW? I'M ONLY TELLING YOU WHAT I HEARD.

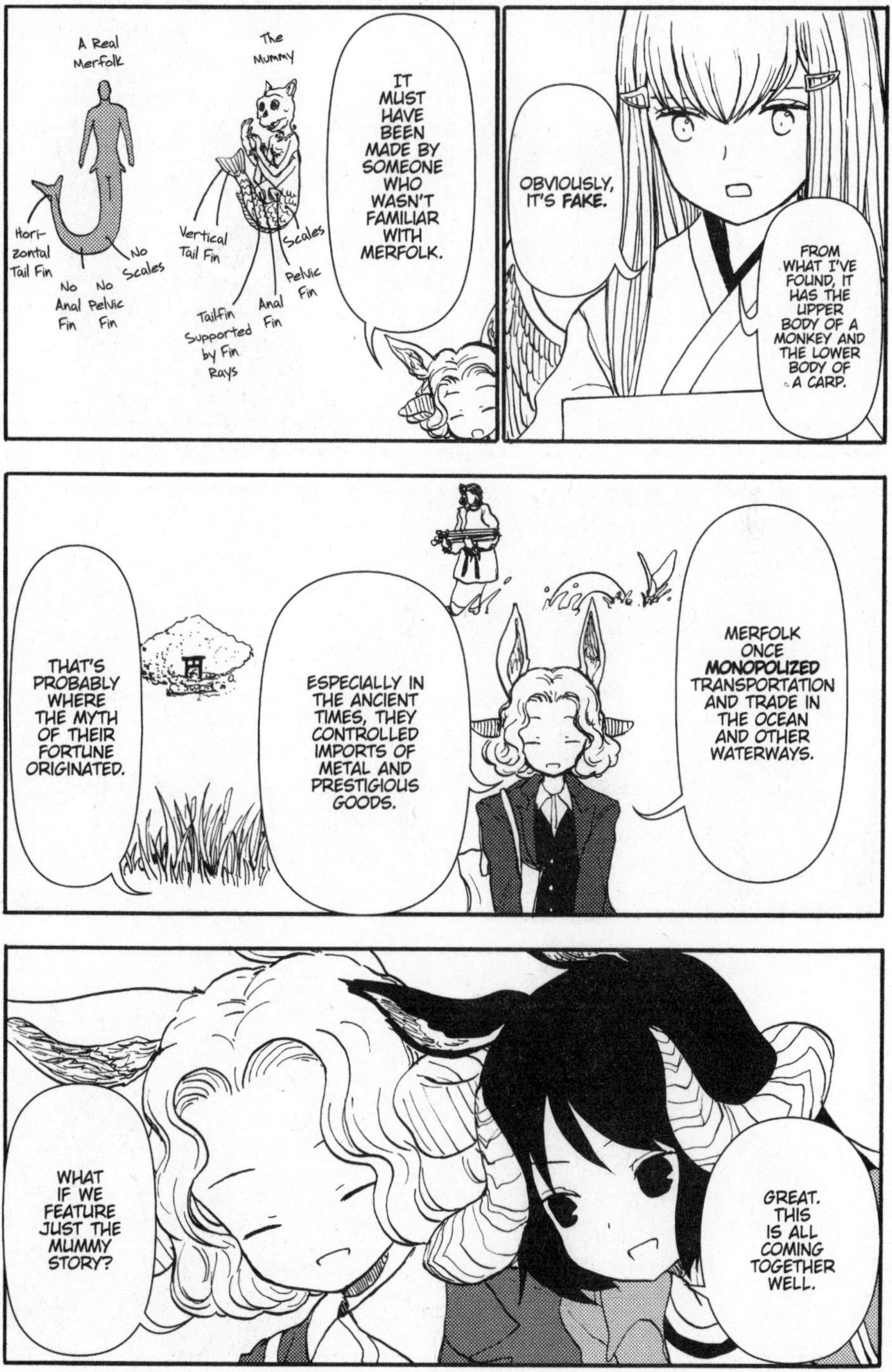
FROM WHAT I'VE FOUND, IT HAS THE UPPER BODY OF A MONKEY AND THE LOWER BODY OF A CARP.
OBVIOUSLY, IT'S **FAKE**.
IT MUST HAVE BEEN MADE BY SOMEONE WHO WASN'T FAMILIAR WITH MERFOLK.
The Mummy
Vertical Tail Fin
Scales
Pelvic Fin
Anal Fin
TailFin Supported by Fin Rays
A Real Merfolk
Hori-zontal Tail Fin
No Scales
No Anal Fin
No Pelvic Fin
MERFOLK ONCE **MONOPOLIZED** TRANSPORTATION AND TRADE IN THE OCEAN AND OTHER WATERWAYS.
ESPECIALLY IN THE ANCIENT TIMES, THEY CONTROLLED IMPORTS OF METAL AND PRESTIGIOUS GOODS.
THAT'S PROBABLY WHERE THE MYTH OF THEIR FORTUNE ORIGINATED.
GREAT. THIS IS ALL COMING TOGETHER WELL.
WHAT IF WE FEATURE JUST THE MUMMY STORY?

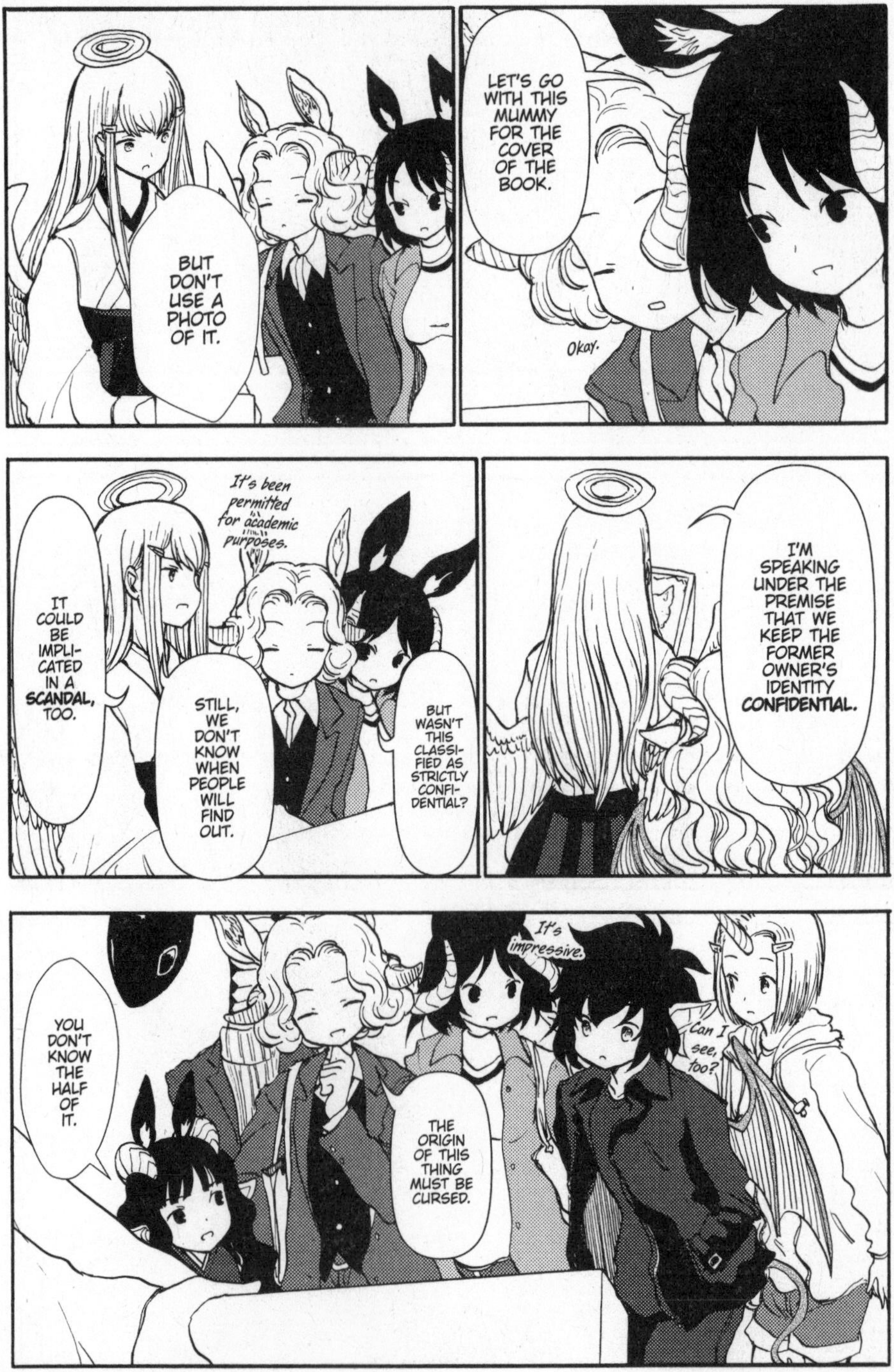
LET'S GO WITH THIS MUMMY FOR THE COVER OF THE BOOK.
Okay.
BUT DON'T USE A PHOTO OF IT.
I'M SPEAKING UNDER THE PREMISE THAT WE KEEP THE FORMER OWNER'S IDENTITY **CONFIDENTIAL.**
BUT WASN'T THIS CLASSIFIED AS STRICTLY CONFIDENTIAL?
It's been permitted for academic purposes.
STILL, WE DON'T KNOW WHEN PEOPLE WILL FIND OUT.
IT COULD BE IMPLICATED IN A **SCANDAL,** TOO.
Can I see, too?
It's impressive.
THE ORIGIN OF THIS THING MUST BE CURSED.
YOU DON'T KNOW THE HALF OF IT.

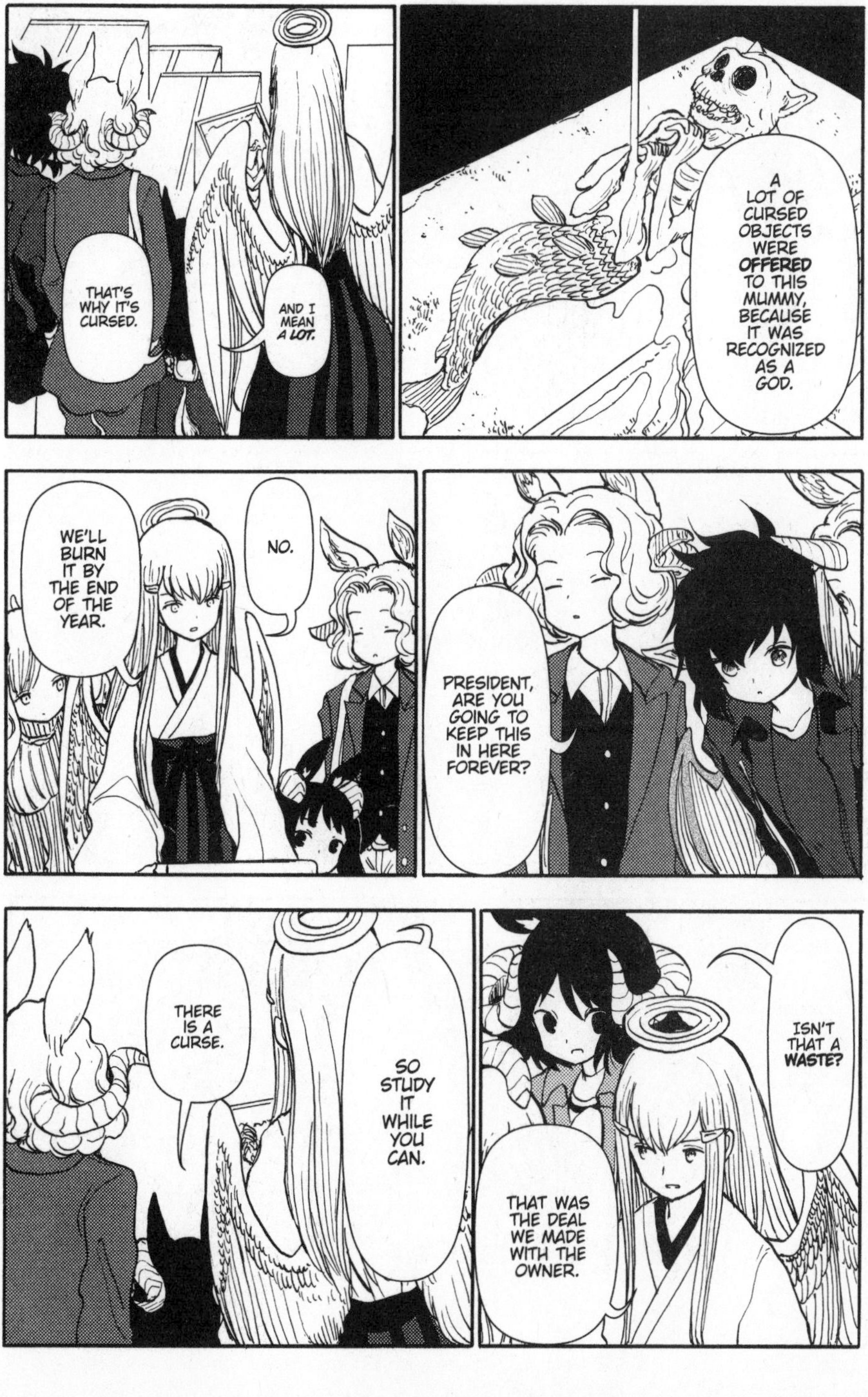
A LOT OF CURSED OBJECTS WERE **OFFERED** TO THIS MUMMY, BECAUSE IT WAS RECOGNIZED AS A GOD.
AND I MEAN ***A LOT.***
THAT'S WHY IT'S CURSED.
PRESIDENT, ARE YOU GOING TO KEEP THIS IN HERE FOREVER?
NO.
WE'LL BURN IT BY THE END OF THE YEAR.
ISN'T THAT A **WASTE?**
THAT WAS THE DEAL WE MADE WITH THE OWNER.
SO STUDY IT WHILE YOU CAN.
THERE IS A CURSE.

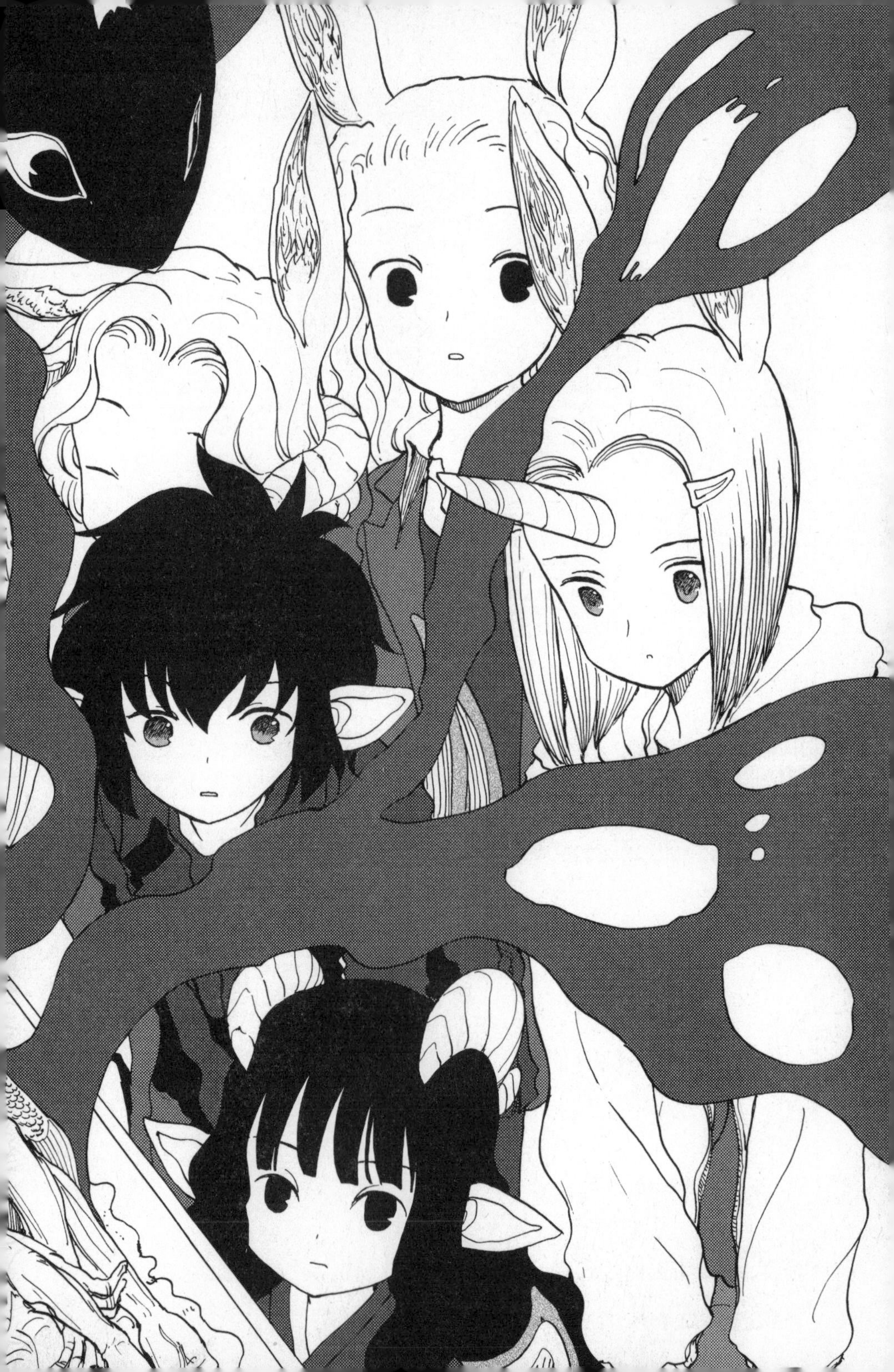

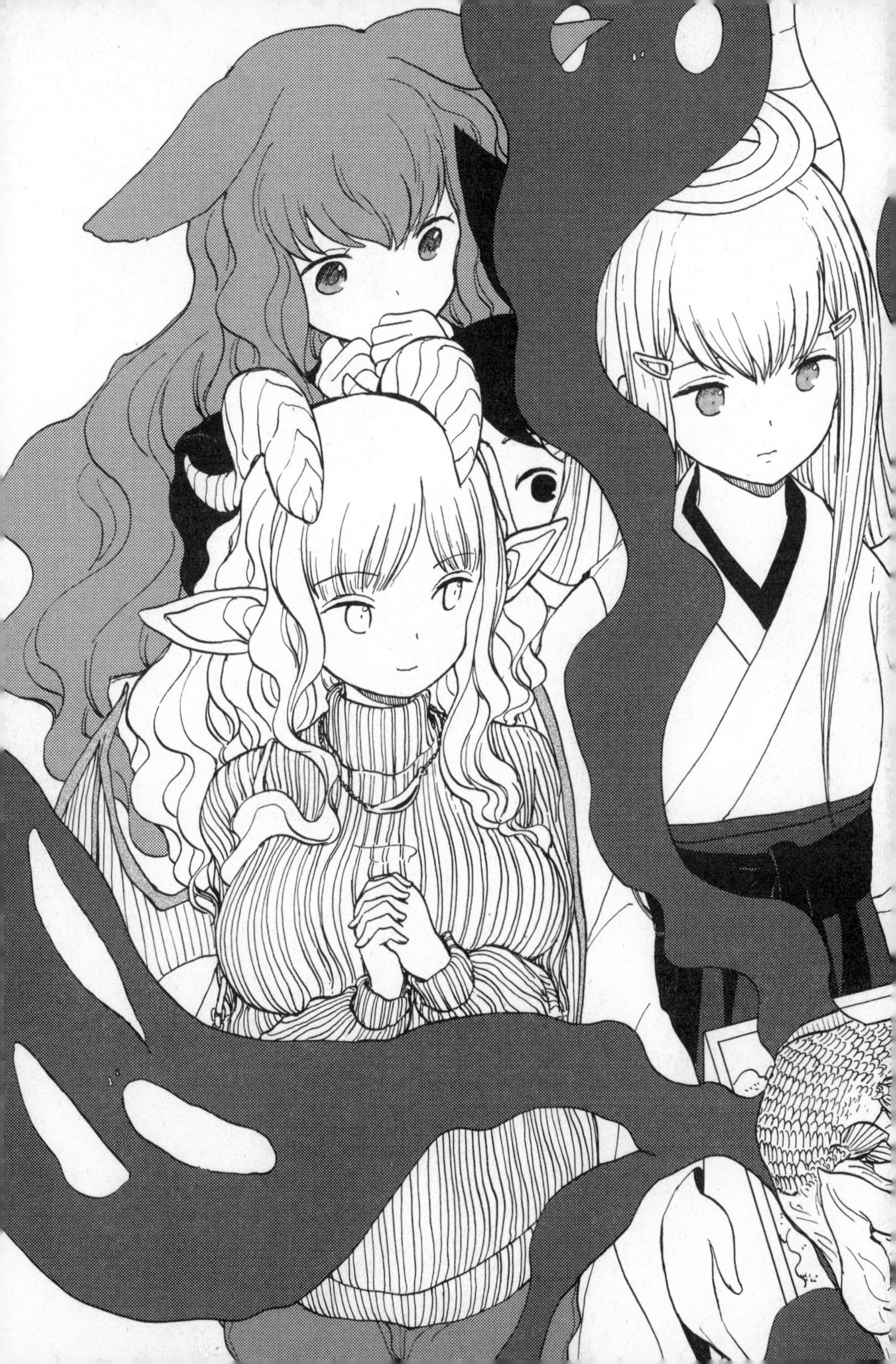

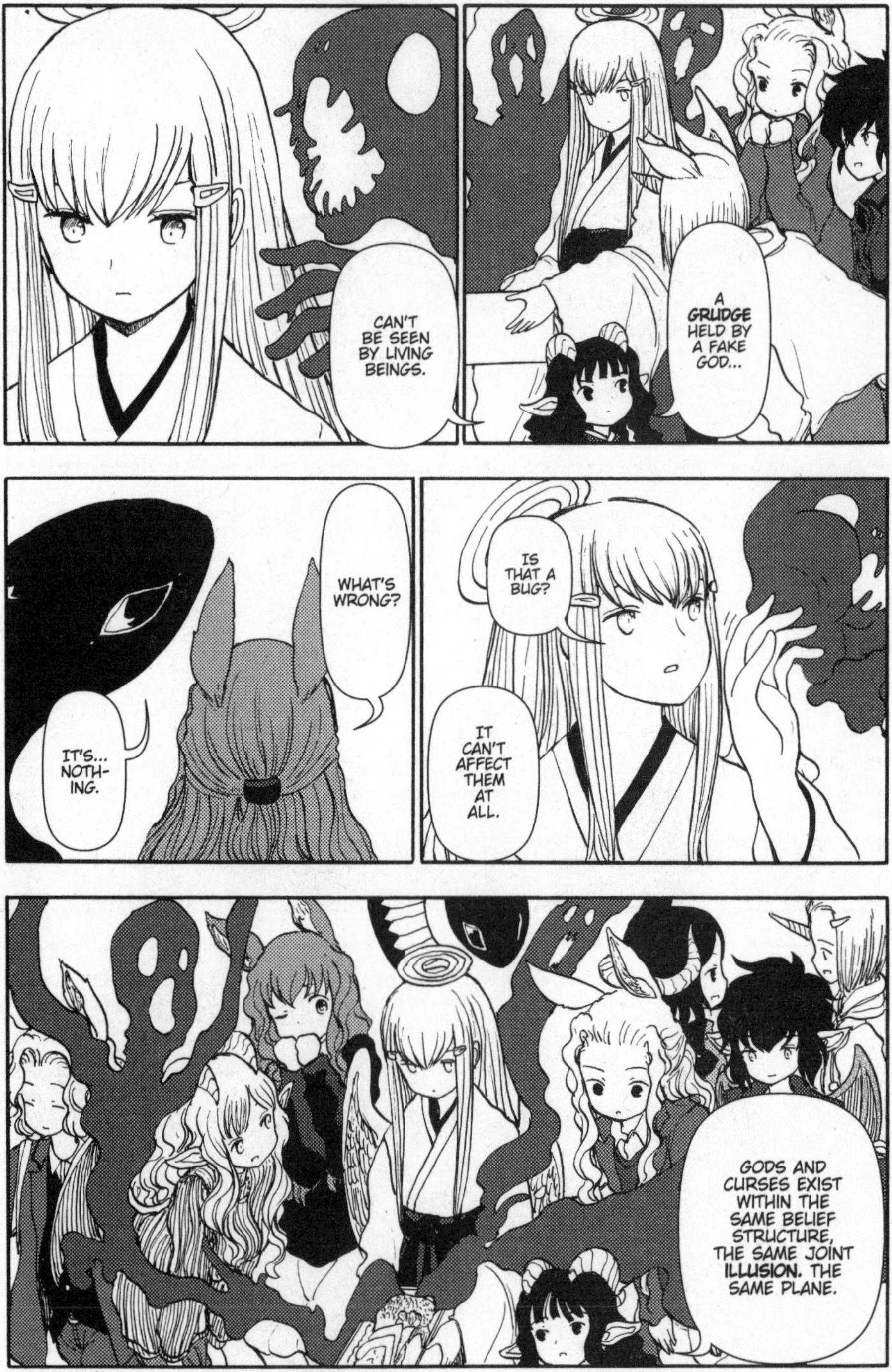
A GRUDGE HELD BY A FAKE GOD...
CAN'T BE SEEN BY LIVING BEINGS.
IS THAT A BUG?
IT CAN'T AFFECT THEM AT ALL.
WHAT'S WRONG?
IT'S... NOTH-ING.
GODS AND CURSES EXIST WITHIN THE SAME BELIEF STRUCTURE, THE SAME JOINT ILLUSION. THE SAME PLANE.

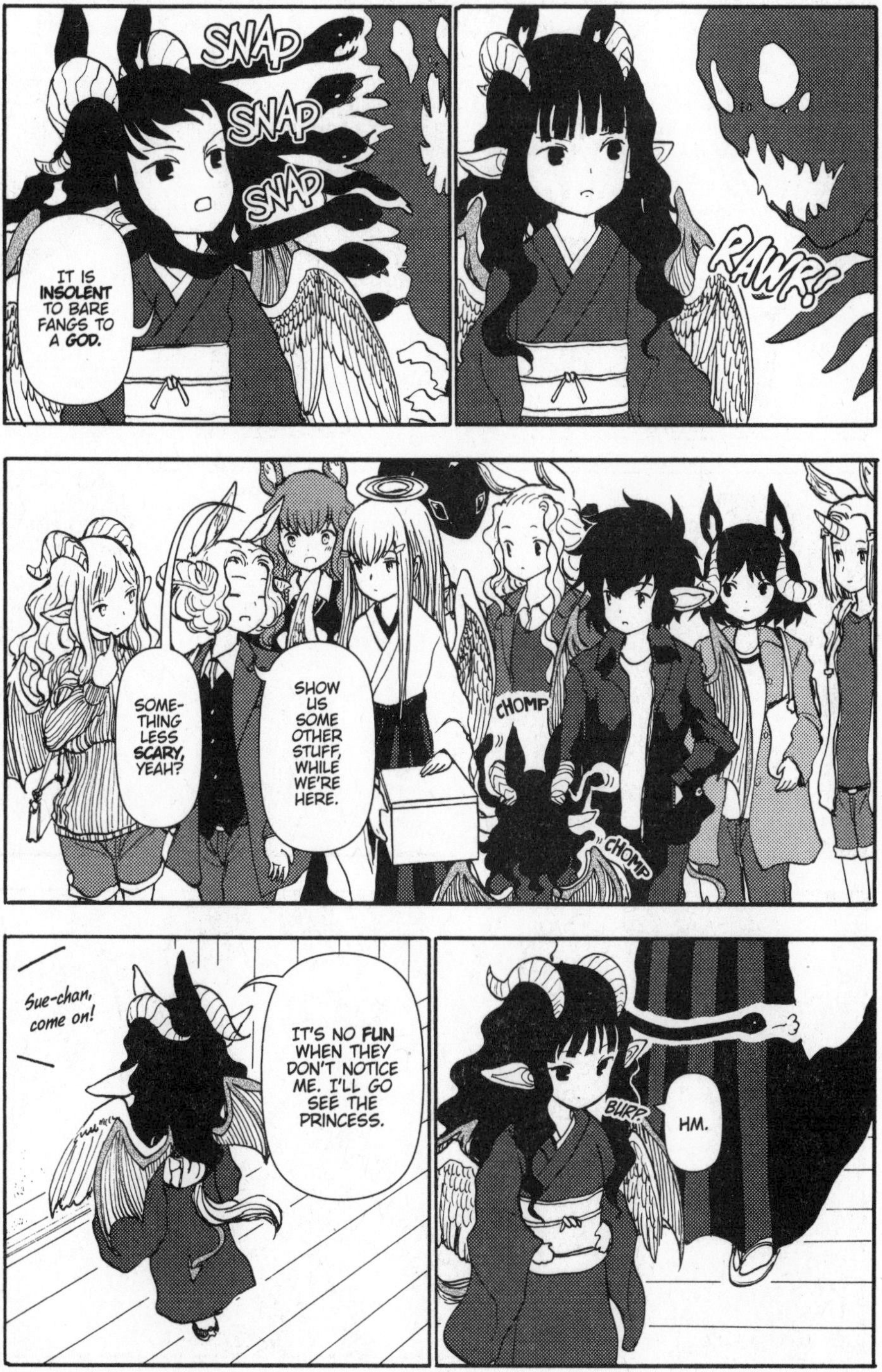
RAWR!
SNAP
SNAP
SNAP
IT IS INSOLENT TO BARE FANGS TO A GOD.
CHOMP
SHOW US SOME OTHER STUFF, WHILE WE'RE HERE.
SOME-THING LESS SCARY, YEAH?
CHOMP
BURP
HM.
IT'S NO FUN WHEN THEY DON'T NOTICE ME. I'LL GO SEE THE PRINCESS.
Sue-chan, come on!

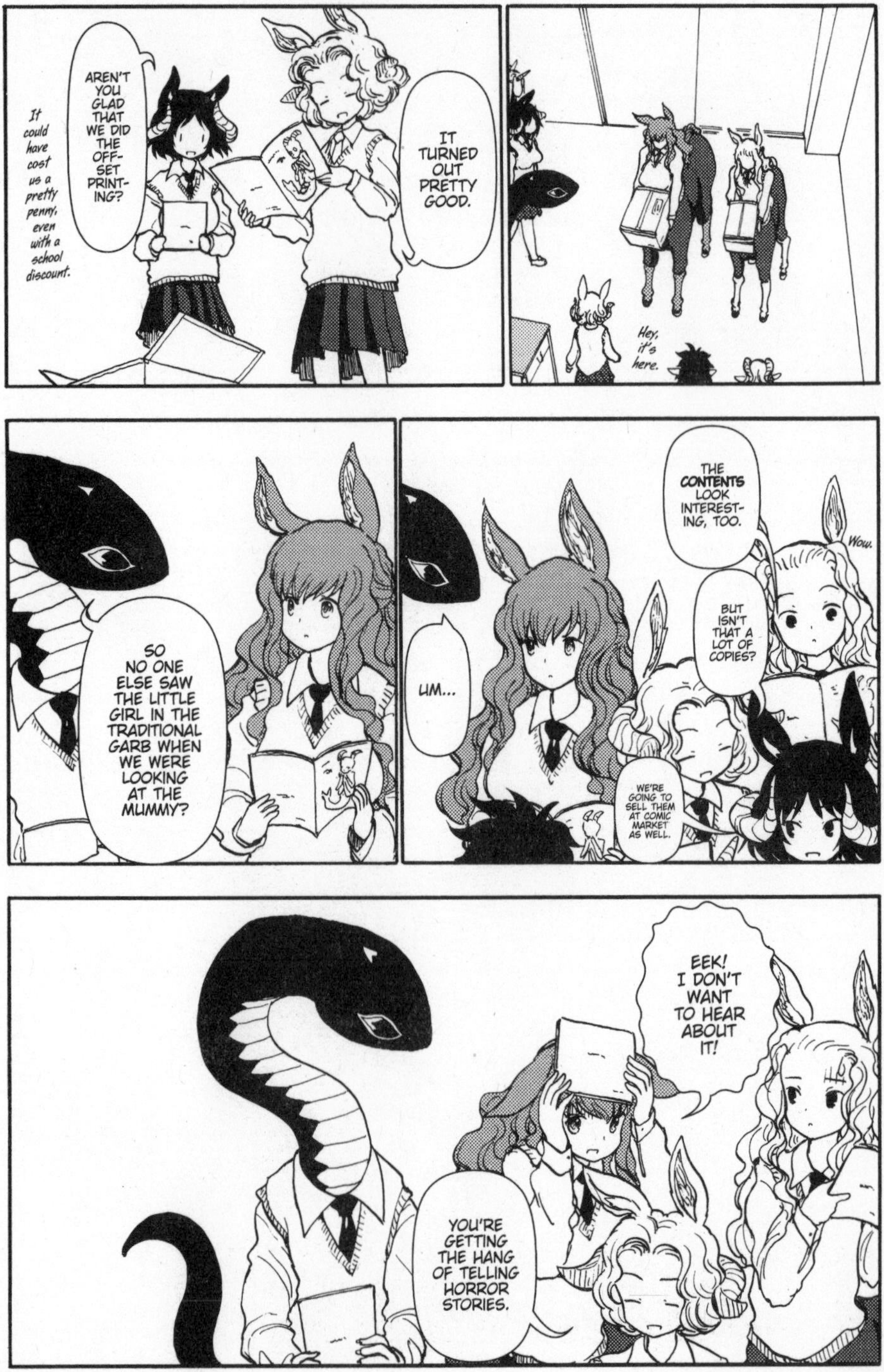
Hey, it's here.
IT TURNED OUT PRETTY GOOD.
AREN'T YOU GLAD THAT WE DID THE OFF-SET PRINTING?
It could have cost us a pretty penny, even with a school discount.
Wow.
THE CONTENTS LOOK INTERESTING, TOO.
BUT ISN'T THAT A LOT OF COPIES?
WE'RE GOING TO SELL THEM AT COMIC MARKET AS WELL.
UM...
SO NO ONE ELSE SAW THE LITTLE GIRL IN THE TRADITIONAL GARB WHEN WE WERE LOOKING AT THE MUMMY?
EEK! I DON'T WANT TO HEAR ABOUT IT!
YOU'RE GETTING THE HANG OF TELLING HORROR STORIES.

A Centaur's Life

UNDERSTANDING AMPHIBIANFOLK PART 8: THE ANTI-GOVERNMENT MILITIA GROUP, CTHULCTHUL

CTHULCTHUL IS AN ANTI-GOVERNMENT MILITIA, FORMED BY AMPHIBIANFOLK, WHOSE MISSION IS TO PROTECT THE CIVIL RIGHTS OF THEIR PEOPLE AND TO ACQUIRE AUTONOMOUS GOVERNMENT. BUT THE EXISTENCE OF THIS GROUP RAISES IMPORTANT QUESTIONS: HOW WERE THE DIVIDED AMPHIBIANFOLK TRIBES, WHO HAVE MAINTAINED A PALEOLITHIC LIFE-STYLE DESPITE THEIR RAPID MODERNIZATION, ABLE TO FORM A UNIFIED ORGANIZATION AND OBTAIN MODERN MILITARY-GRADE WEAPONS AND EQUIPMENT?

ONE THEORY IS THAT THEY ACQUIRED THE WEAPONRY WHEN THEY CHASED MAMMALIAN HUMANS OUT OF THEIR OCCUPATION ZONE, WHICH HAPPENED TO BE AN EXCELLENT HIDING PLACE FOR MAMMALIAN DRUG CARTELS AND ANTI-GOVERNMENT GUERRILLAS. THE FACT THAT CTHULCTHUL'S EQUIPMENT VARIED FROM PERSON TO PERSON IN THE BEGINNING MAY LEND CREDENCE TO THIS THEORY. OTHERS SEE THIS AS A PROXY WAR BETWEEN TRADITIONAL NATIONS, INCLUDING TAWANTINSUYU, AND A RISING AGGRESSOR NATION ESTABLISHED BY CONQUISTADORS IN SOUTH AMERICA. YET ANOTHER THEORY IS THAT A PROMINENT AMPHIBIANFOLK ENTREPRENEUR, JEAN ROUSSEAU, ORGANIZED THE GROUP AND SECURED BACKING FROM WESTERN COUNTRIES. WHATEVER THE CASE, JAPAN HOPES ONLY FOR PEACE. PARTICIPATION IN A MILITIA GROUP THAT AGGRAVATES THE SITUATION SHOULD BE PROHIBITED BY LAW.

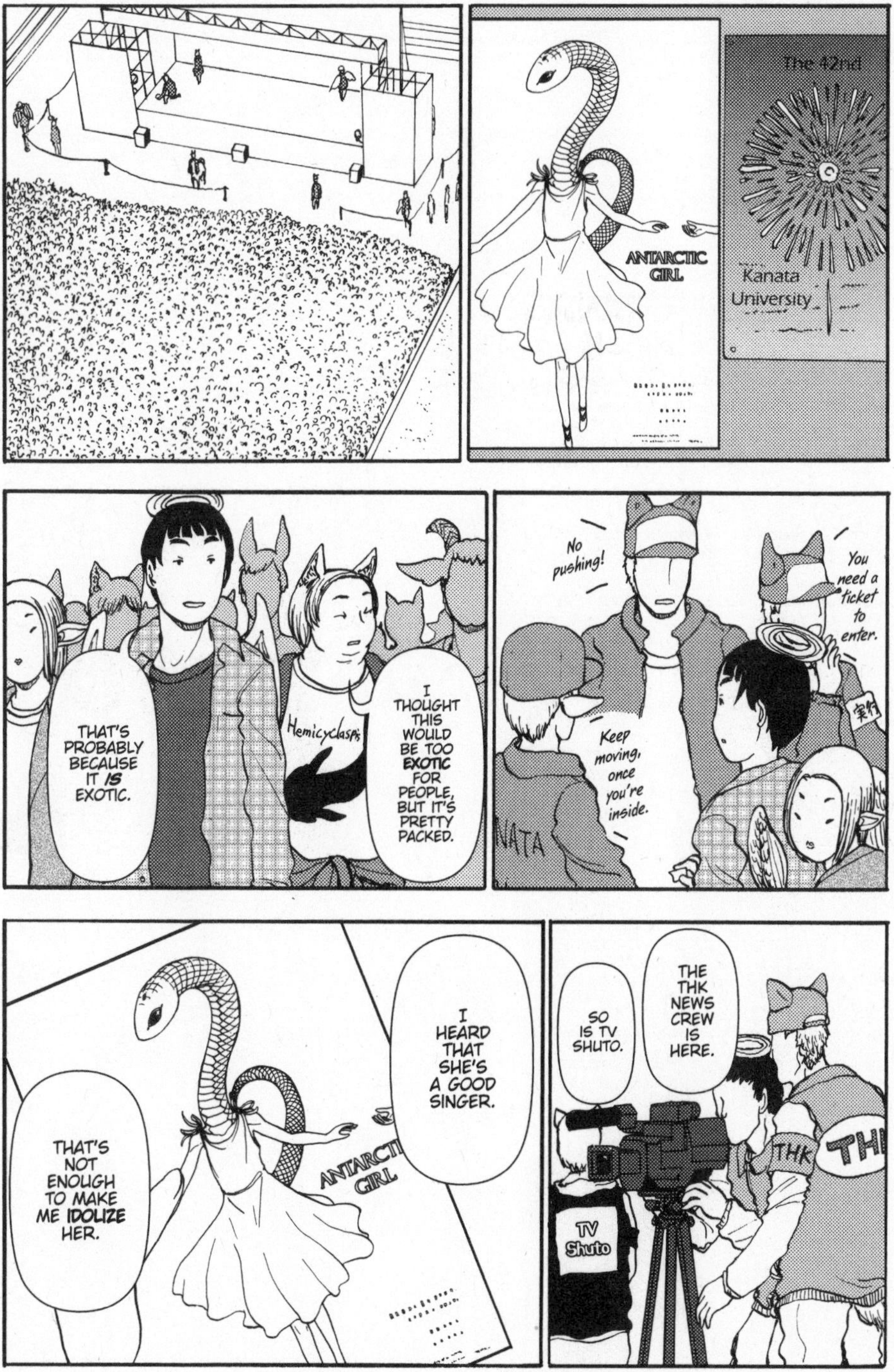

The 42nd
Kanata University
ANTARCTIC GIRL
You need a ticket to enter.
No pushing!
実行
Keep moving, once you're inside.
NATA
I THOUGHT THIS WOULD BE TOO **EXOTIC** FOR PEOPLE, BUT IT'S PRETTY PACKED.
Hemicyclaspis
THAT'S PROBABLY BECAUSE IT *IS* EXOTIC.
THE THK NEWS CREW IS HERE.
SO IS TV SHUTO.
THK
THK
TV Shuto
I HEARD THAT SHE'S A GOOD SINGER.
ANTARCTIC GIRL
THAT'S NOT ENOUGH TO MAKE ME **IDOLIZE** HER.

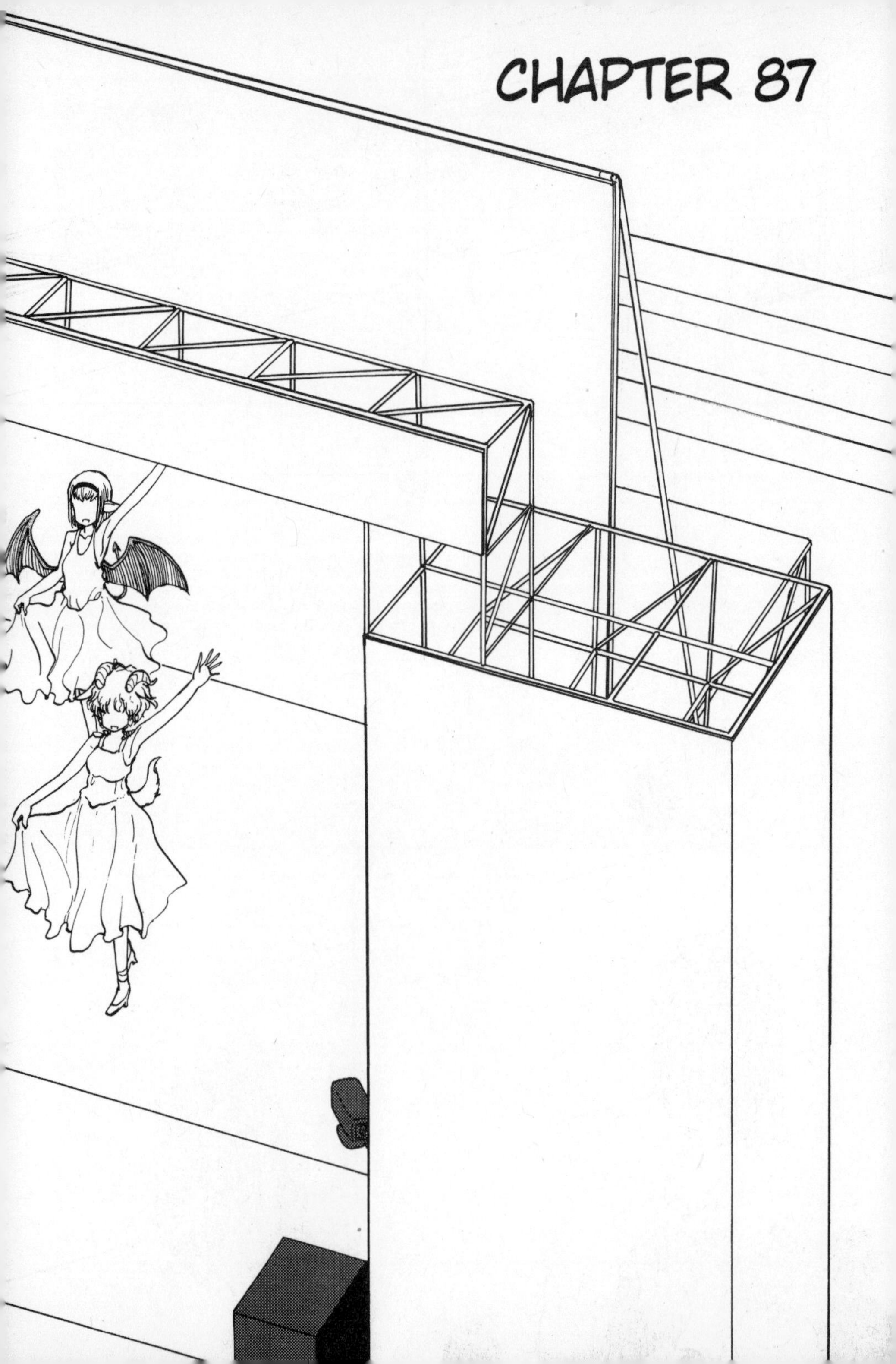
CHAPTER 87

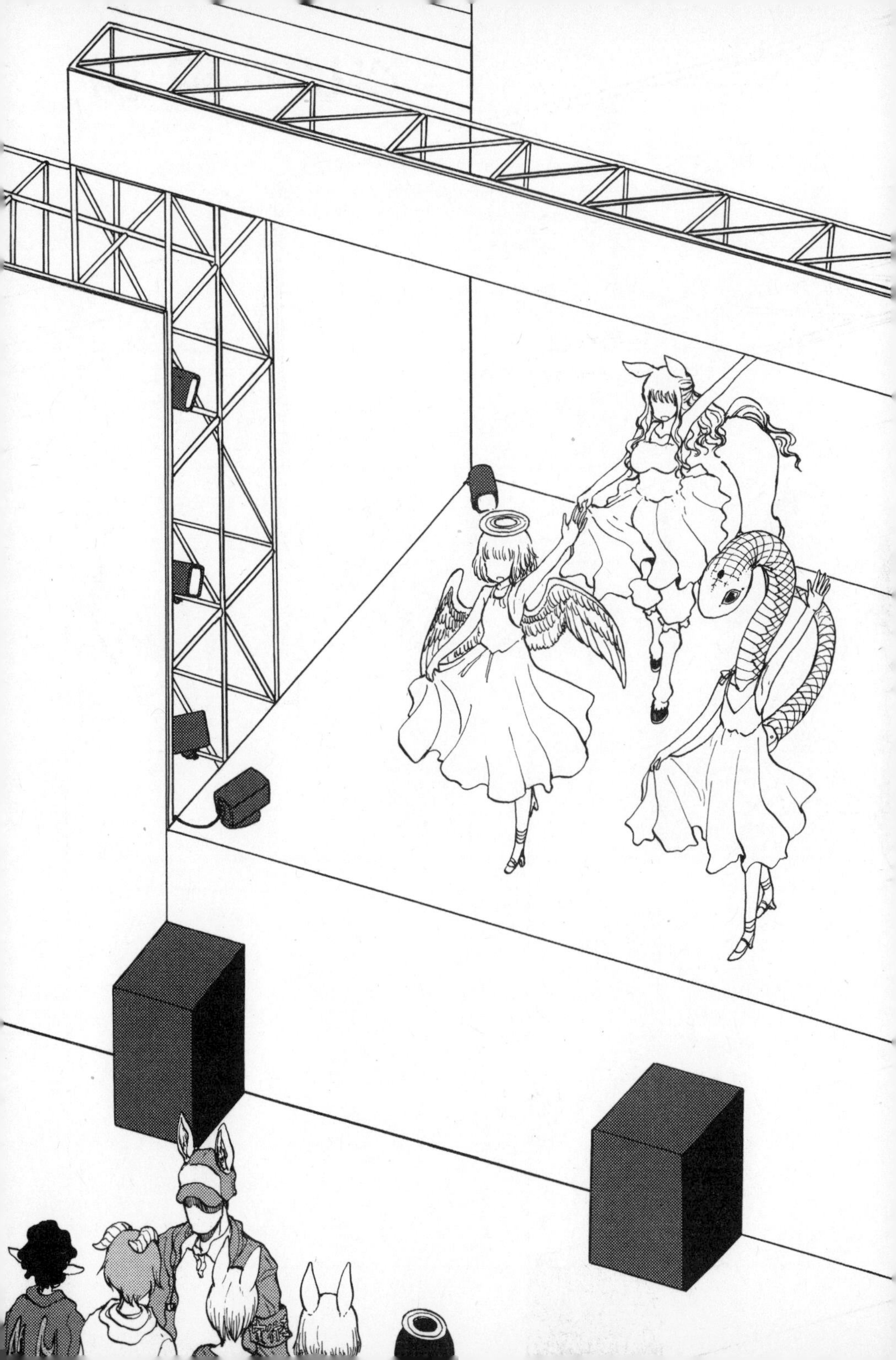

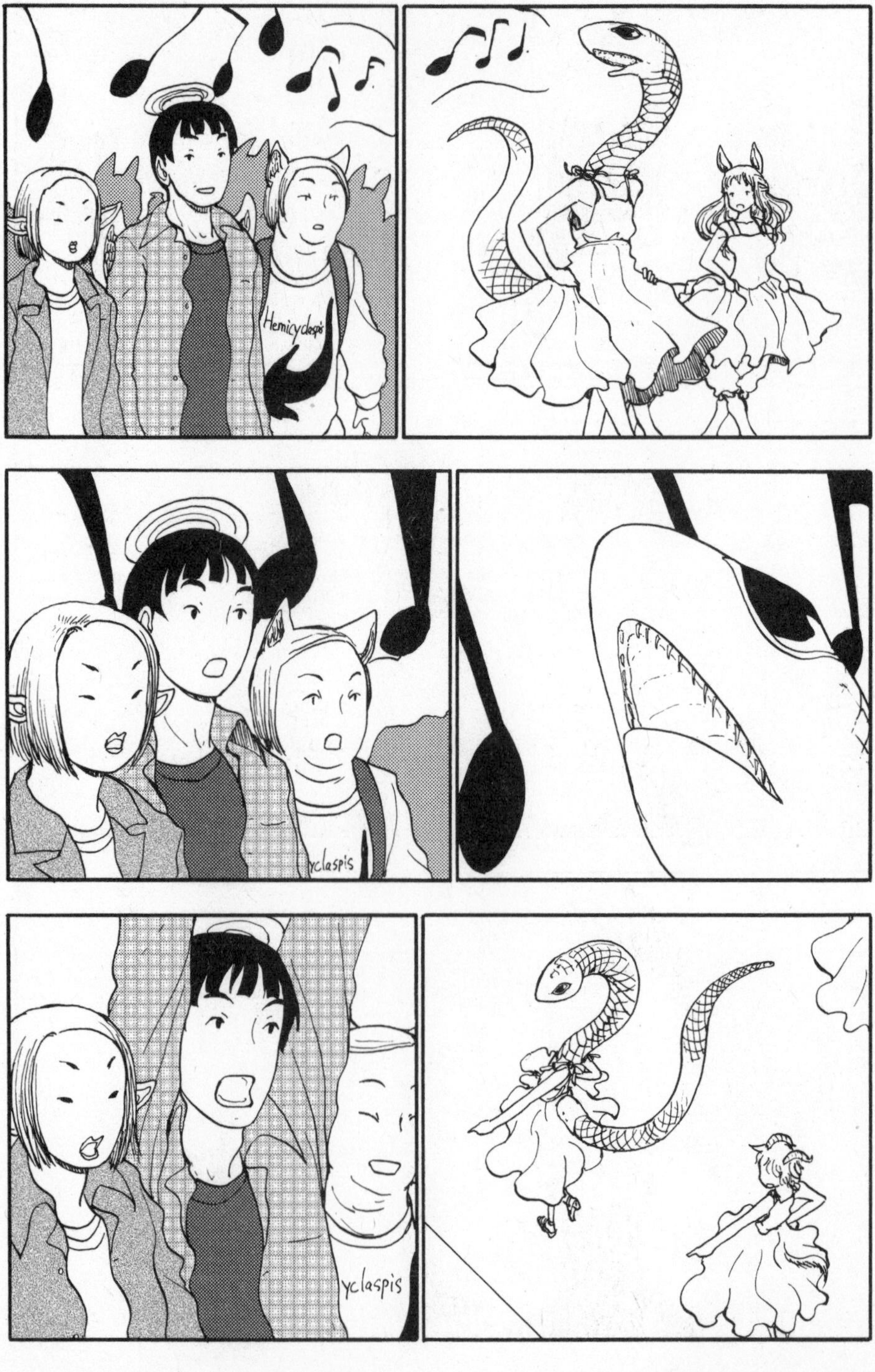
Hemicyclaspis
yclaspis
yclaspis

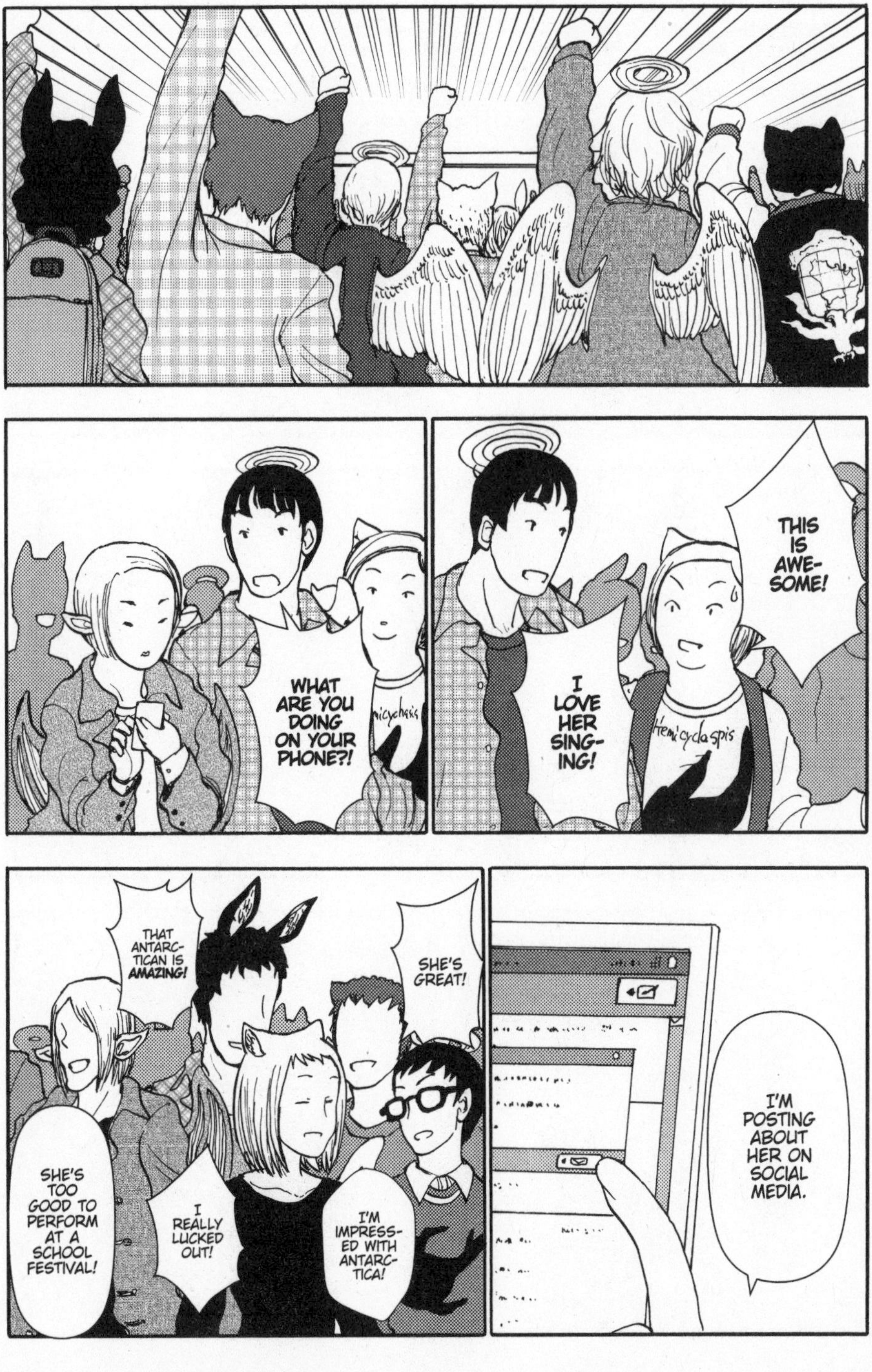
THIS IS AWESOME!
I LOVE HER SINGING!
Hemicyclaspis
WHAT ARE YOU DOING ON YOUR PHONE?!
I'M POSTING ABOUT HER ON SOCIAL MEDIA.
SHE'S GREAT!
THAT ANTARCTICAN IS **AMAZING!**
I'M IMPRESSED WITH ANTARCTICA!
I REALLY LUCKED OUT!
SHE'S TOO GOOD TO PERFORM AT A SCHOOL FESTIVAL!

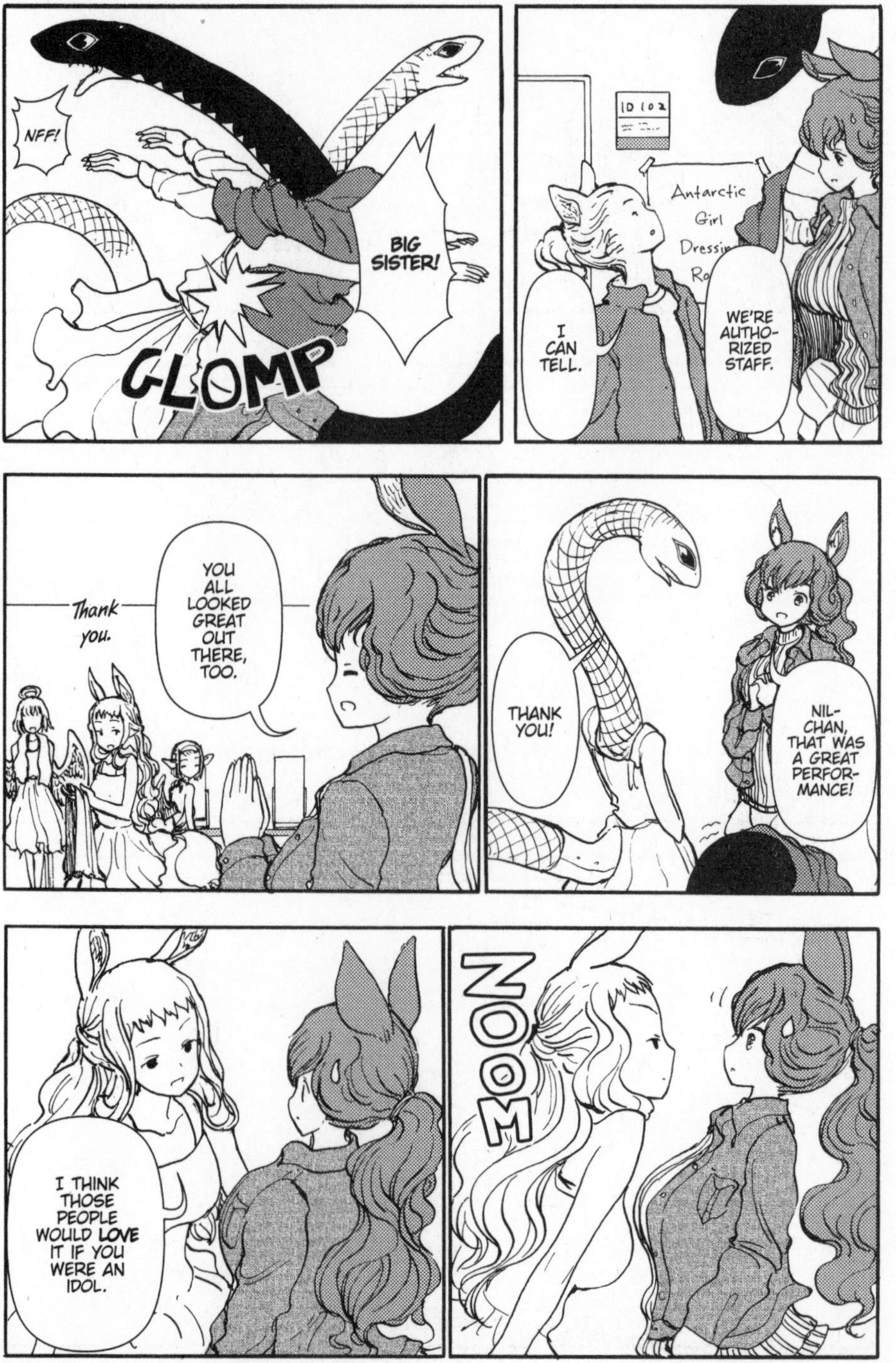
ID 102
Antarctic
Girl
WE'RE AUTHORIZED STAFF.
I CAN TELL.
BIG SISTER!
NFF!
GLOMP
NIL-CHAN, THAT WAS A GREAT PERFORMANCE!
THANK YOU!
YOU ALL LOOKED GREAT OUT THERE, TOO.
Thank you.
ZOOM
I THINK THOSE PEOPLE WOULD **LOVE** IT IF YOU WERE AN IDOL.

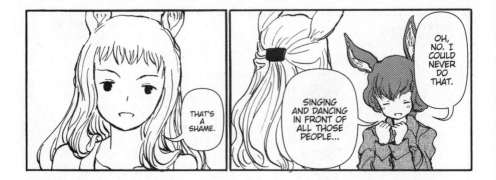

OH, NO. I COULD NEVER DO THAT.
SINGING AND DANCING IN FRONT OF ALL THOSE PEOPLE...
THAT'S A SHAME.
OH, MAN. THIS IS SO COOL.
WHAT'S UP?
MY MOM SAW ME ON TV.
Here
SHE WAS IMPRESSED THAT I WAS DOING MY WORK.

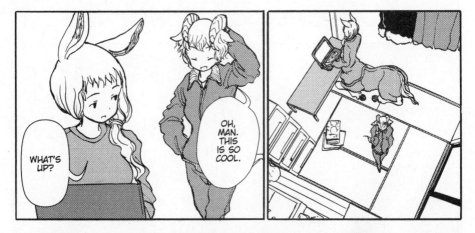

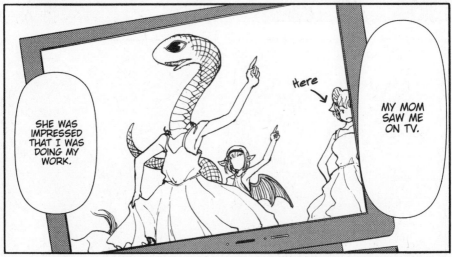

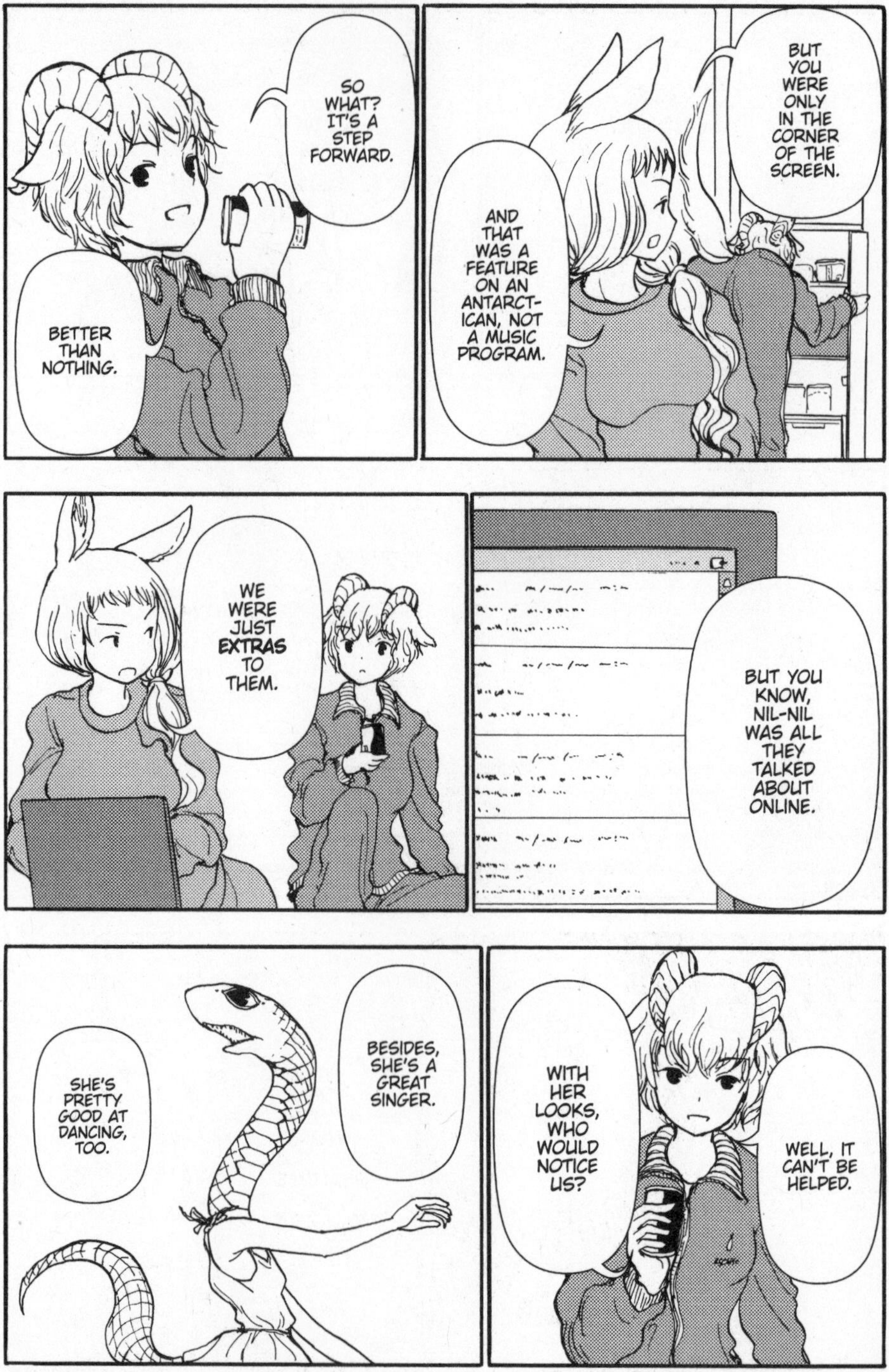
BUT YOU WERE ONLY IN THE CORNER OF THE SCREEN.
AND THAT WAS A FEATURE ON AN ANTARCTICAN, NOT A MUSIC PROGRAM.
SO WHAT? IT'S A STEP FORWARD.
BETTER THAN NOTHING.
BUT YOU KNOW, NIL-NIL WAS ALL THEY TALKED ABOUT ONLINE.
WE WERE JUST **EXTRAS** TO THEM.
WELL, IT CAN'T BE HELPED.
WITH HER LOOKS, WHO WOULD NOTICE US?
BESIDES, SHE'S A GREAT SINGER.
SHE'S PRETTY GOOD AT DANCING, TOO.

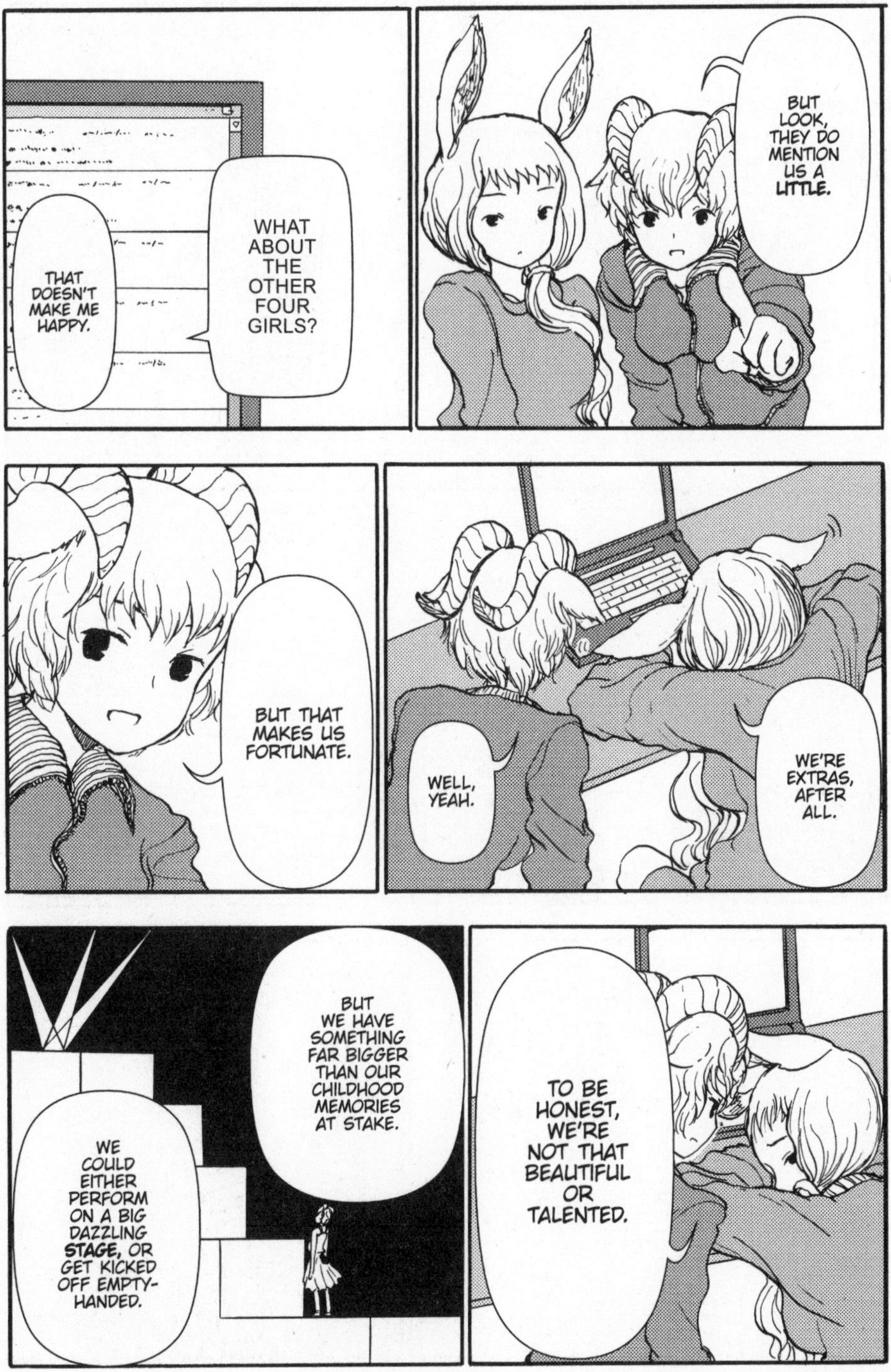
BUT LOOK, THEY DO MENTION US A LITTLE.
WHAT ABOUT THE OTHER FOUR GIRLS?
THAT DOESN'T MAKE ME HAPPY.
WE'RE EXTRAS, AFTER ALL.
WELL, YEAH.
BUT THAT MAKES US FORTUNATE.
TO BE HONEST, WE'RE NOT THAT BEAUTIFUL OR TALENTED.
BUT WE HAVE SOMETHING FAR BIGGER THAN OUR CHILDHOOD MEMORIES AT STAKE.
WE COULD EITHER PERFORM ON A BIG DAZZLING STAGE, OR GET KICKED OFF EMPTY-HANDED.

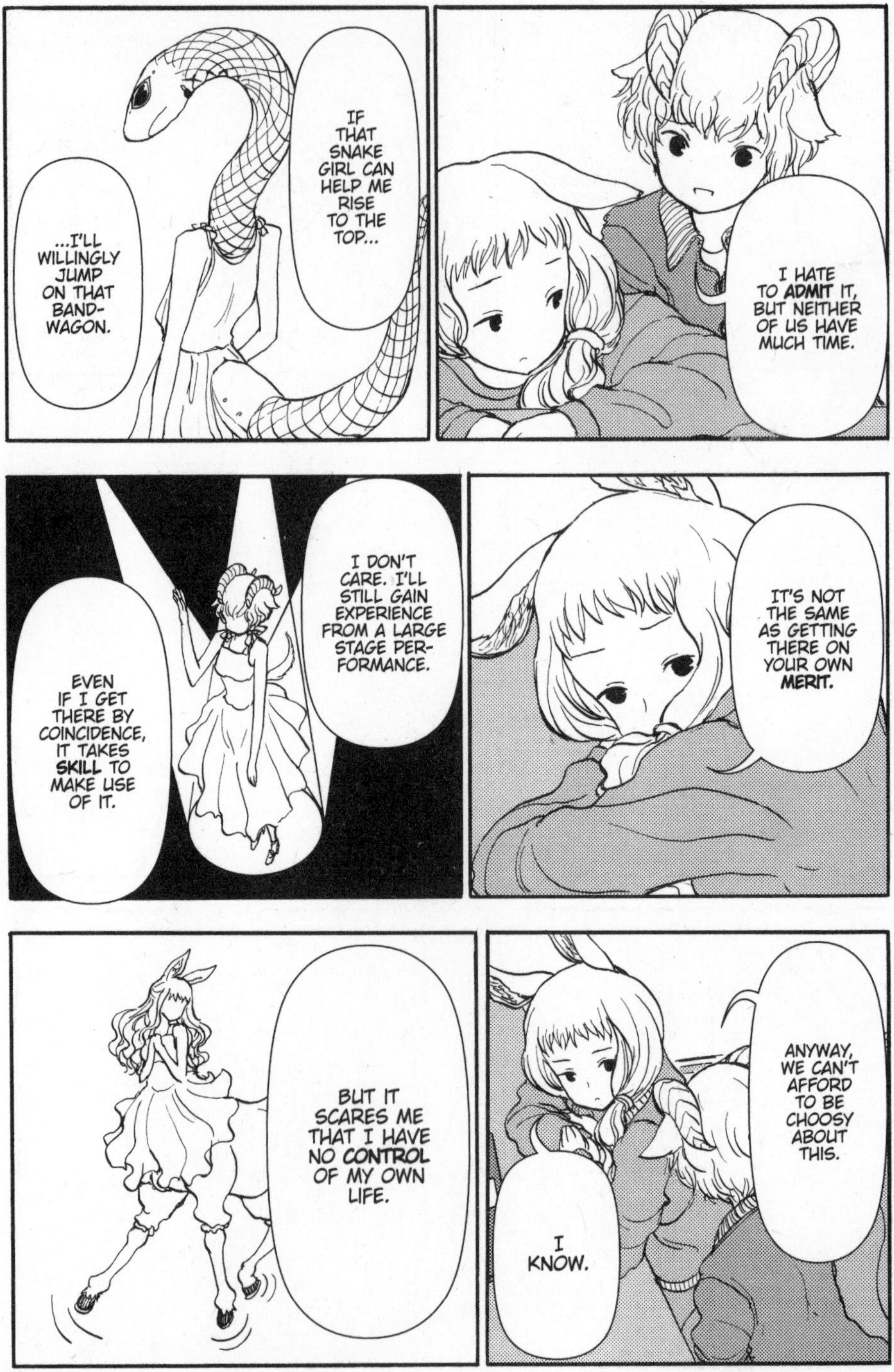
I HATE TO ADMIT IT, BUT NEITHER OF US HAVE MUCH TIME.
IF THAT SNAKE GIRL CAN HELP ME RISE TO THE TOP...
...I'LL WILLINGLY JUMP ON THAT BAND-WAGON.
IT'S NOT THE SAME AS GETTING THERE ON YOUR OWN MERIT.
I DON'T CARE. I'LL STILL GAIN EXPERIENCE FROM A LARGE STAGE PERFORMANCE.
EVEN IF I GET THERE BY COINCIDENCE, IT TAKES SKILL TO MAKE USE OF IT.
ANYWAY, WE CAN'T AFFORD TO BE CHOOSY ABOUT THIS.
I KNOW.
BUT IT SCARES ME THAT I HAVE NO CONTROL OF MY OWN LIFE.

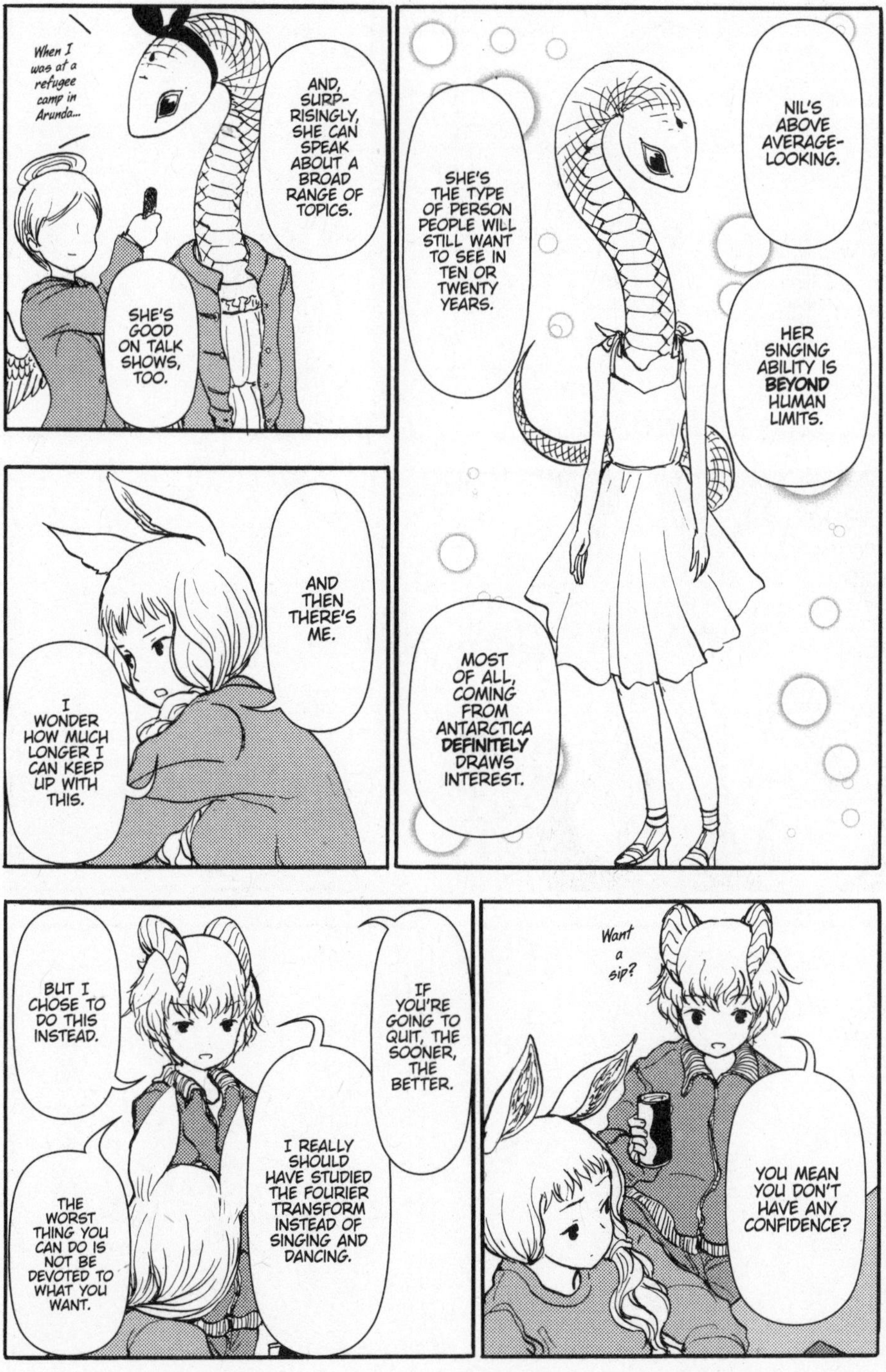
NIL'S ABOVE AVERAGE-LOOKING.
SHE'S THE TYPE OF PERSON PEOPLE WILL STILL WANT TO SEE IN TEN OR TWENTY YEARS.
HER SINGING ABILITY IS **BEYOND** HUMAN LIMITS.
MOST OF ALL, COMING FROM ANTARCTICA **DEFINITELY** DRAWS INTEREST.
AND, SURP-RISINGLY, SHE CAN SPEAK ABOUT A BROAD RANGE OF TOPICS.
When I was at a refugee camp in Arunda...
SHE'S GOOD ON TALK SHOWS, TOO.
AND THEN THERE'S ME.
I WONDER HOW MUCH LONGER I CAN KEEP UP WITH THIS.
Want a sip?
YOU MEAN YOU DON'T HAVE ANY CONFIDENCE?
IF YOU'RE GOING TO QUIT, THE SOONER, THE BETTER.
BUT I CHOSE TO DO THIS INSTEAD.
I REALLY SHOULD HAVE STUDIED THE FOURIER TRANSFORM INSTEAD OF SINGING AND DANCING.
THE WORST THING YOU CAN DO IS NOT BE DEVOTED TO WHAT YOU WANT.

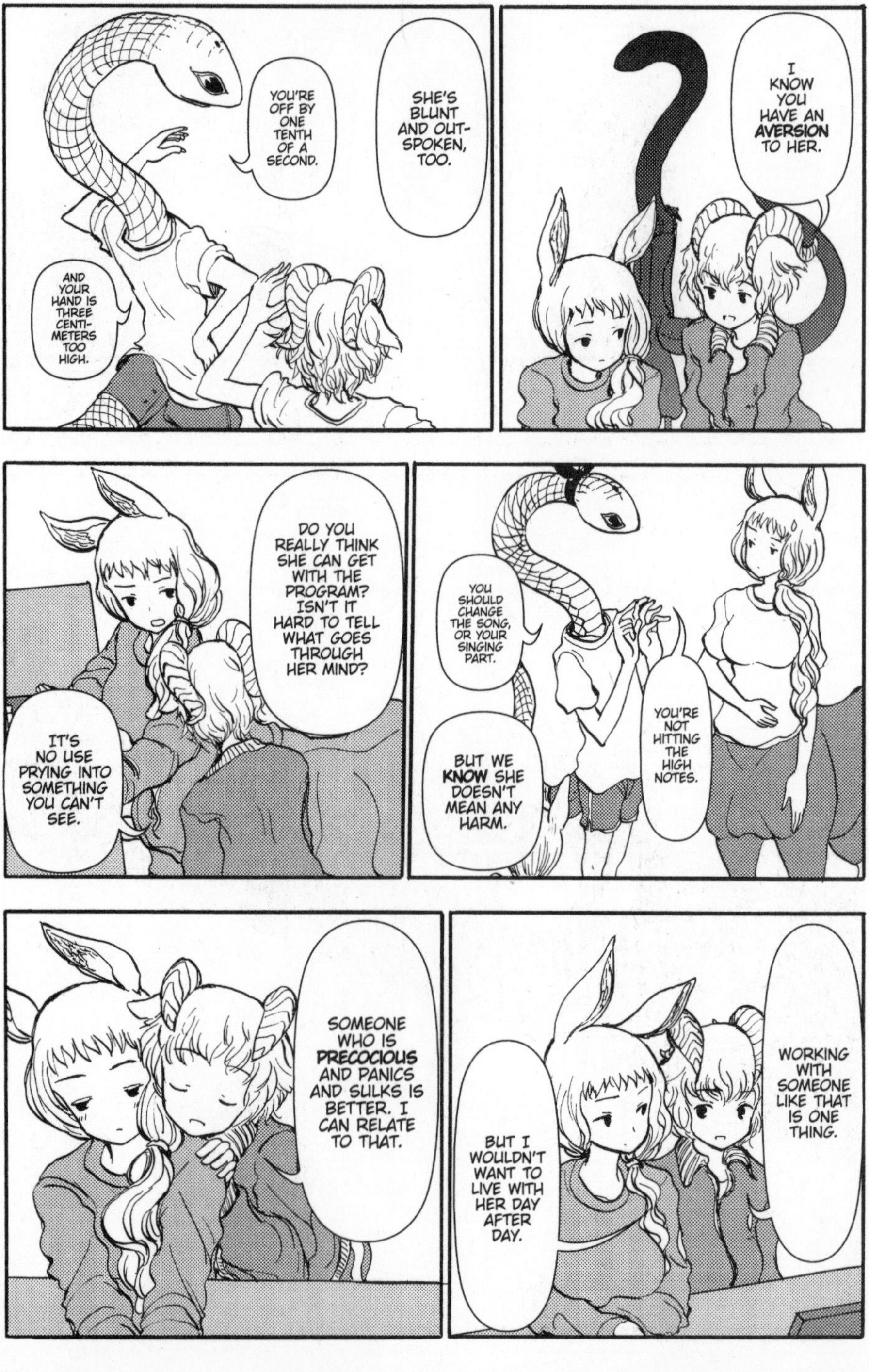
I KNOW YOU HAVE AN AVERSION TO HER.
SHE'S BLUNT AND OUT-SPOKEN, TOO.
YOU'RE OFF BY ONE TENTH OF A SECOND.
AND YOUR HAND IS THREE CENTI-METERS TOO HIGH.
YOU SHOULD CHANGE THE SONG, OR YOUR SINGING PART.
YOU'RE NOT HITTING THE HIGH NOTES.
BUT WE KNOW SHE DOESN'T MEAN ANY HARM.
DO YOU REALLY THINK SHE CAN GET WITH THE PROGRAM? ISN'T IT HARD TO TELL WHAT GOES THROUGH HER MIND?
IT'S NO USE PRYING INTO SOMETHING YOU CAN'T SEE.
WORKING WITH SOMEONE LIKE THAT IS ONE THING.
BUT I WOULDN'T WANT TO LIVE WITH HER DAY AFTER DAY.
SOMEONE WHO IS PRECOCIOUS AND PANICS AND SULKS IS BETTER. I CAN RELATE TO THAT.

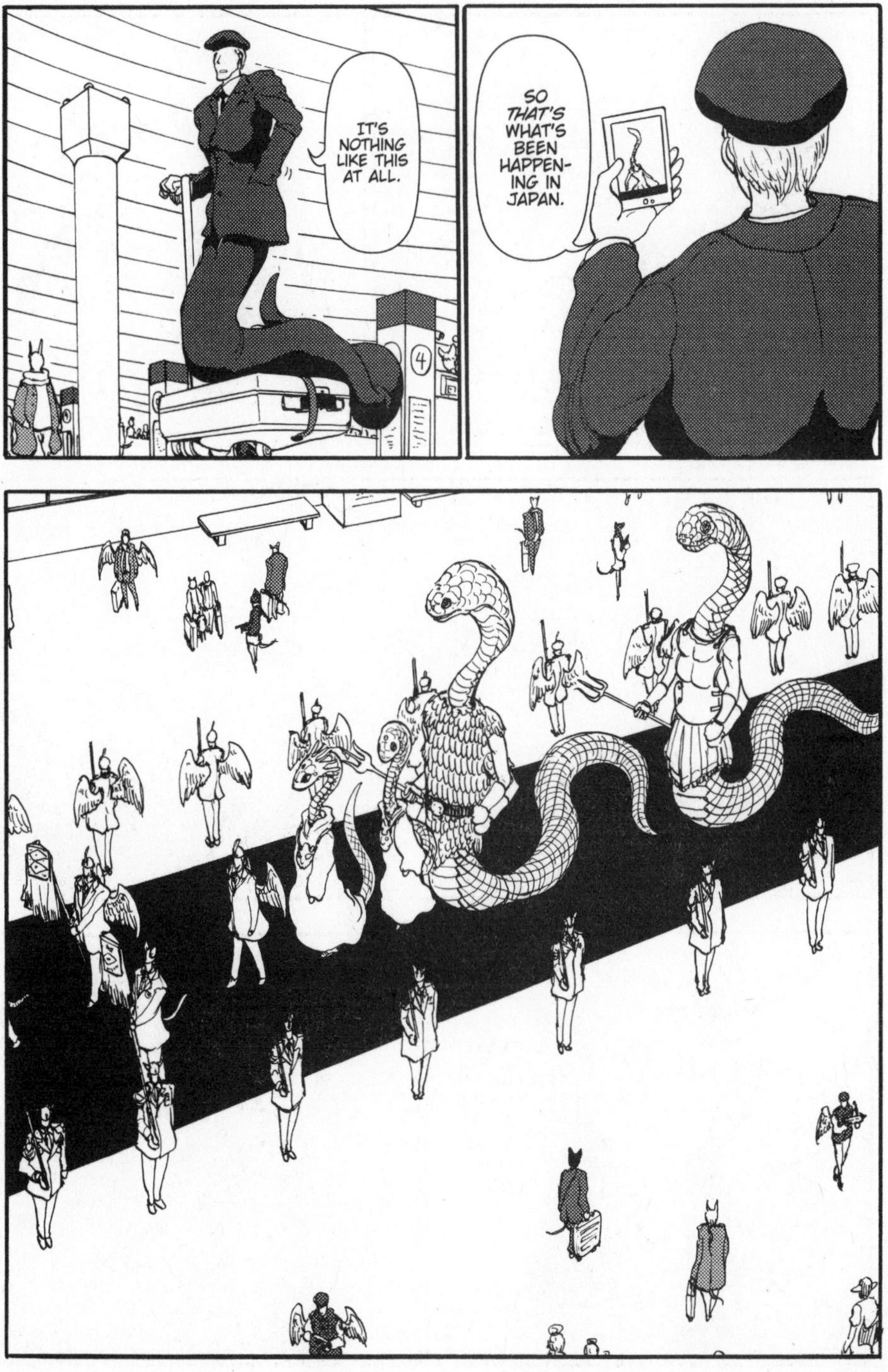
SO *THAT'S* WHAT'S BEEN HAPPENING IN JAPAN.
IT'S NOTHING LIKE THIS AT ALL.

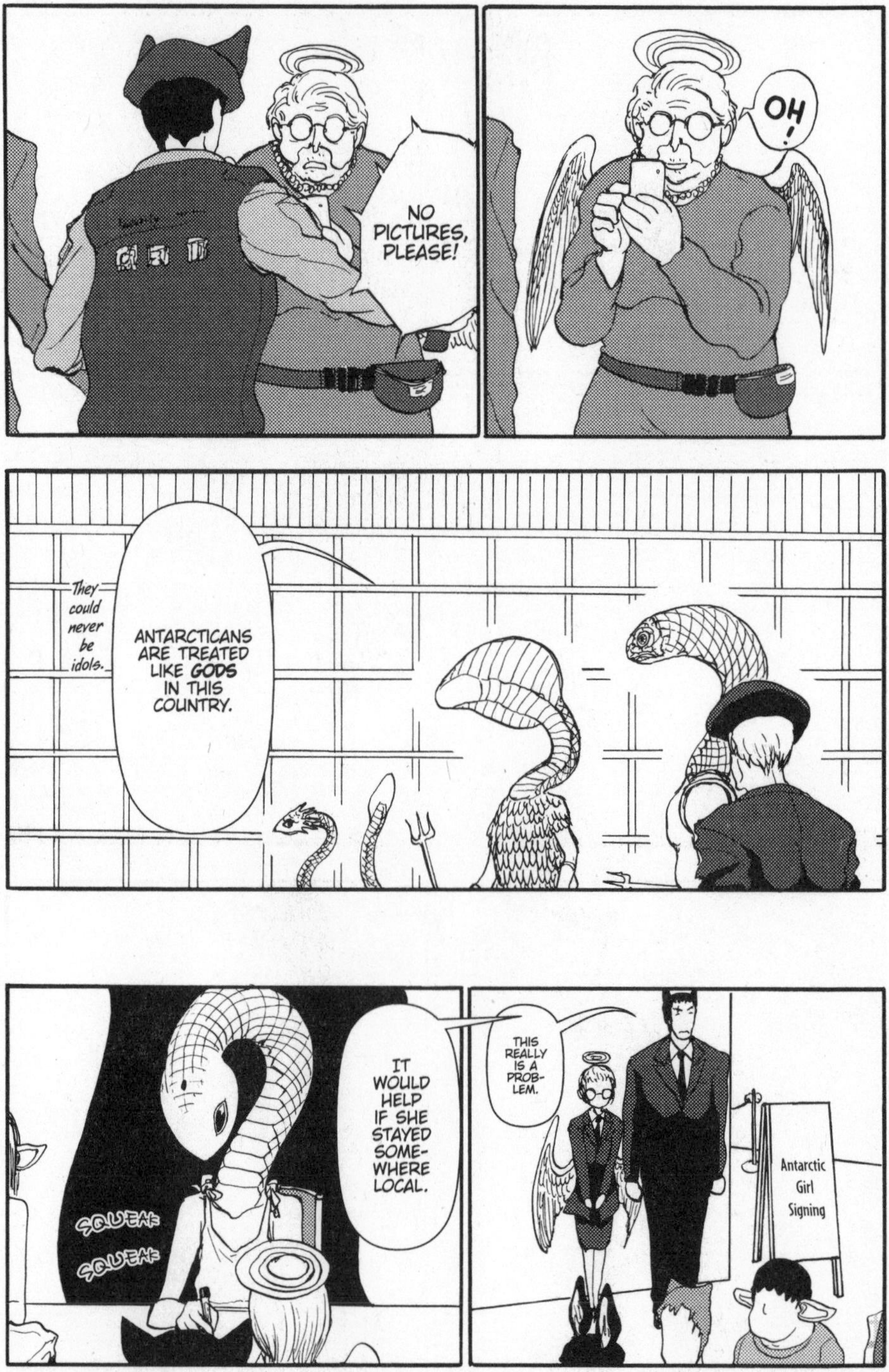
OH!
NO PICTURES, PLEASE!
ANTARCTICANS ARE TREATED LIKE **GODS** IN THIS COUNTRY.
They could never be idols.
THIS REALLY IS A PROBLEM.
Antarctic Girl Signing
IT WOULD HELP IF SHE STAYED SOMEWHERE LOCAL.
SQUEAK
SQUEAK

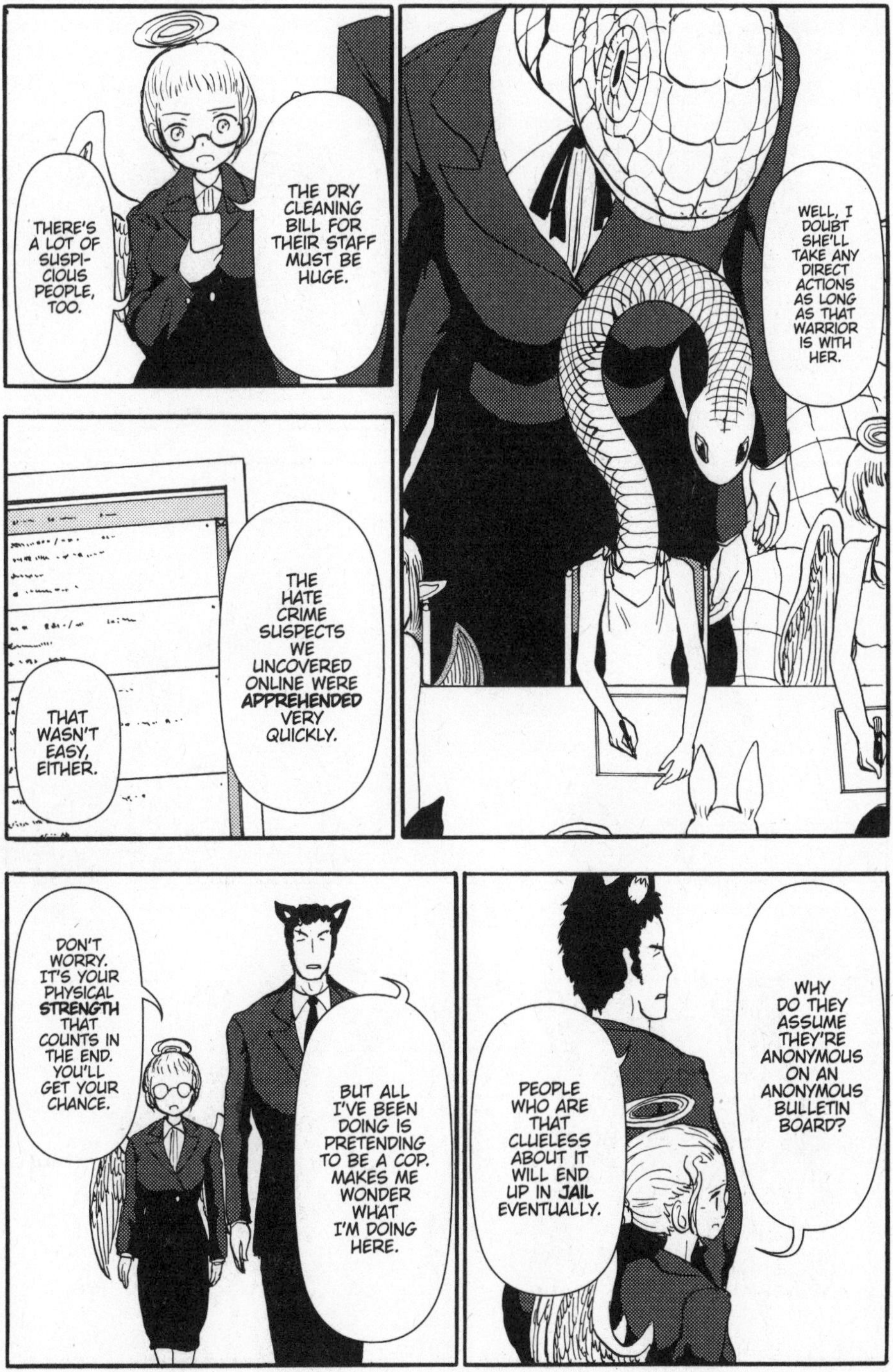
WELL, I DOUBT SHE'LL TAKE ANY DIRECT ACTIONS AS LONG AS THAT WARRIOR IS WITH HER.
THE DRY CLEANING BILL FOR THEIR STAFF MUST BE HUGE.
THERE'S A LOT OF SUSPI-CIOUS PEOPLE, TOO.
THE HATE CRIME SUSPECTS WE UNCOVERED ONLINE WERE **APPREHENDED** VERY QUICKLY.
THAT WASN'T EASY, EITHER.
WHY DO THEY ASSUME THEY'RE ANONYMOUS ON AN ANONYMOUS BULLETIN BOARD?
PEOPLE WHO ARE THAT CLUELESS ABOUT IT WILL END UP IN **JAIL** EVENTUALLY.
BUT ALL I'VE BEEN DOING IS PRETENDING TO BE A COP. MAKES ME WONDER WHAT I'M DOING HERE.
DON'T WORRY. IT'S YOUR PHYSICAL **STRENGTH** THAT COUNTS IN THE END. YOU'LL GET YOUR CHANCE.

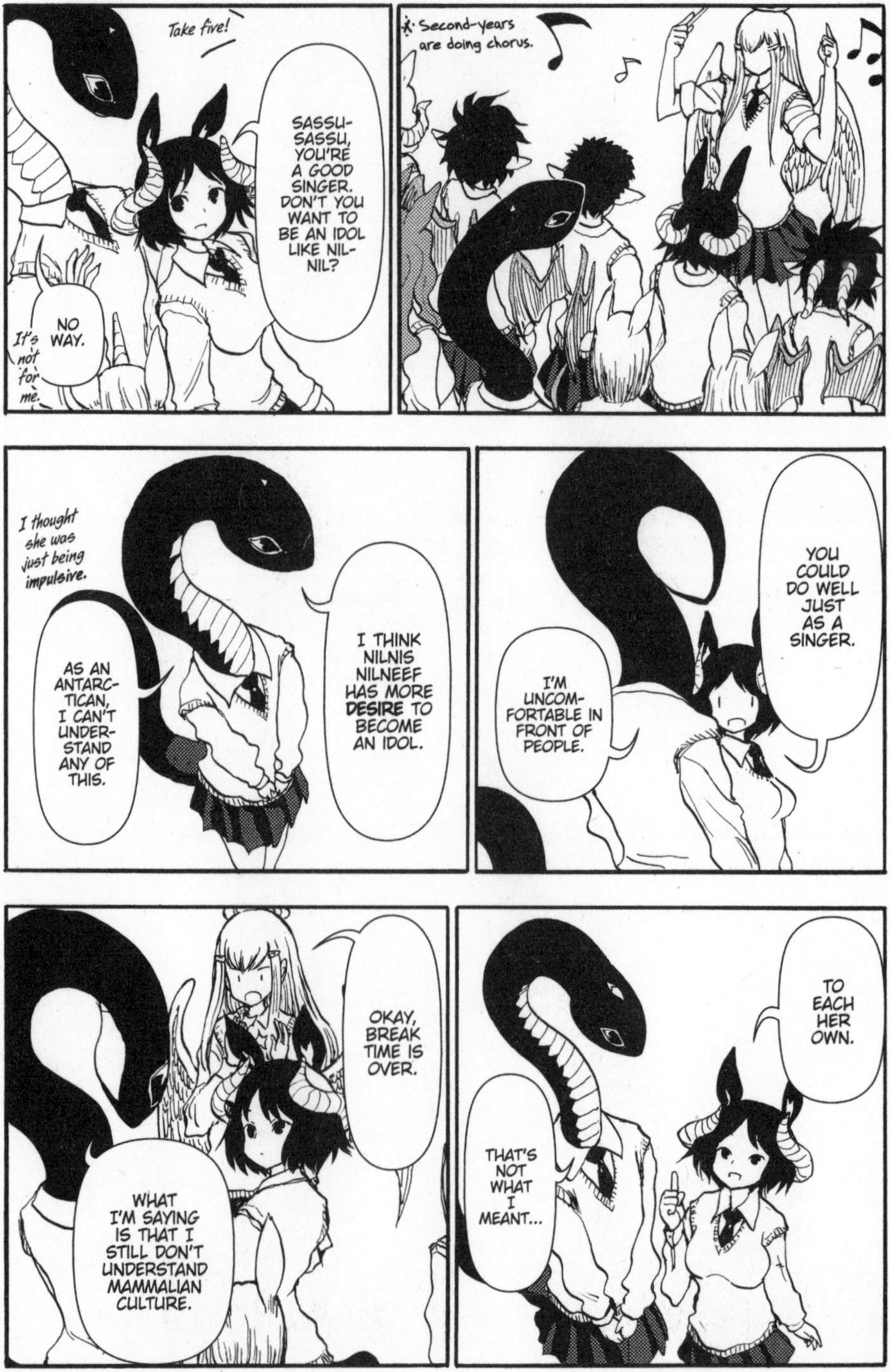
※ Second-years are doing chorus.
Take five!
SASSU-SASSU, YOU'RE A GOOD SINGER. DON'T YOU WANT TO BE AN IDOL LIKE NIL-NIL?
NO WAY.
It's not for me.
YOU COULD DO WELL JUST AS A SINGER.
I'M UNCOM-FORTABLE IN FRONT OF PEOPLE.
I THINK NILNIS NILNEEF HAS MORE **DESIRE** TO BECOME AN IDOL.
I thought she was just being *impulsive*.
AS AN ANTARC-TICAN, I CAN'T UNDER-STAND ANY OF THIS.
TO EACH HER OWN.
THAT'S NOT WHAT I MEANT...
OKAY, BREAK TIME IS OVER.
WHAT I'M SAYING IS THAT I STILL DON'T UNDERSTAND MAMMALIAN CULTURE.

A CentaUr's Life

UNDERSTANDING AMPHIBIANFOLK PART 9: MULTIRACIAL SYMBIOSIS

DESPITE BEING AN INTELLIGENT SPECIES, AMPHIBIANFOLK WERE FREQUENTLY TREATED AS BEASTS AND WERE THE TARGET OF GENOCIDE, ESPECIALLY BY THE RISING AGGRESSOR NATION. THIS TREATMENT OF INDIGENOUS PEOPLES IS UNFORTUNATELY HISTORICALLY COMMON, AND MAY NOT BE CONSIDERED RACIAL DISCRIMINATION. THIS PERCEPTION CHANGED WHEN IT CAME TO LIGHT THAT PAST DISCRIMINATION AGAINST AMPHIBIANFOLK BASED UPON APPEARANCE, ETHNICITY AND RACE WAS LARGELY AN EXCUSE TO JUSTIFY STEALING RESOURCES AND USING AMPHIBIANFOLK AS SCAPEGOATS TO DISGUISE MISMANAGEMENT.

REGARDLESS OF WHETHER THEY ARE MAMMALIAN, ALL INTELLIGENT RACES SHOULD BE ENTITLED TO CIVIL RIGHTS. JAPAN, WITH ITS ANCIENT HISTORY OF COEXISTENCE--CLEARLY DEMONSTRATED BY THE FACT THAT MERFOLK, WHO ONCE LIVED IN COASTAL AREAS WORLDWIDE, CURRENTLY ONLY EXIST IN JAPAN--WAS REMISS IN NOT GRANTING RIGHTS TO AMPHIBIANFOLK EARLY ON. DISCRIMINATION MUST BE AVOIDED BY ANY MEANS AVAILABLE TO A PEACEFUL AND IDEAL NATION. TO BE SPECIFIC: A STRICTLY DEFENSIVE SECURITY POLICY AGAINST AMPHIBIANFOLK IS UNNECESSARY AND INAPPROPRIATE.

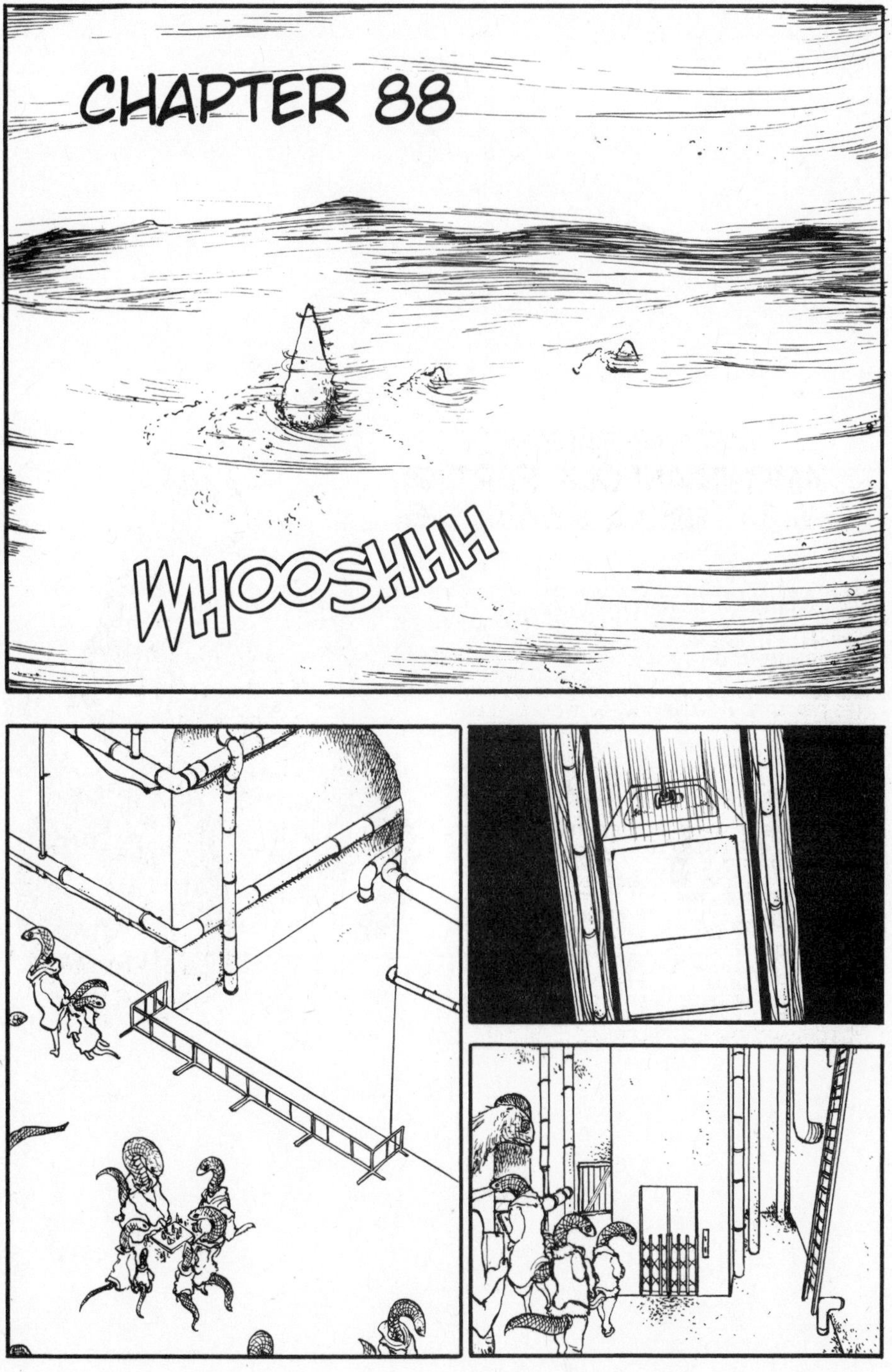
CHAPTER 88
WHOOSHHH

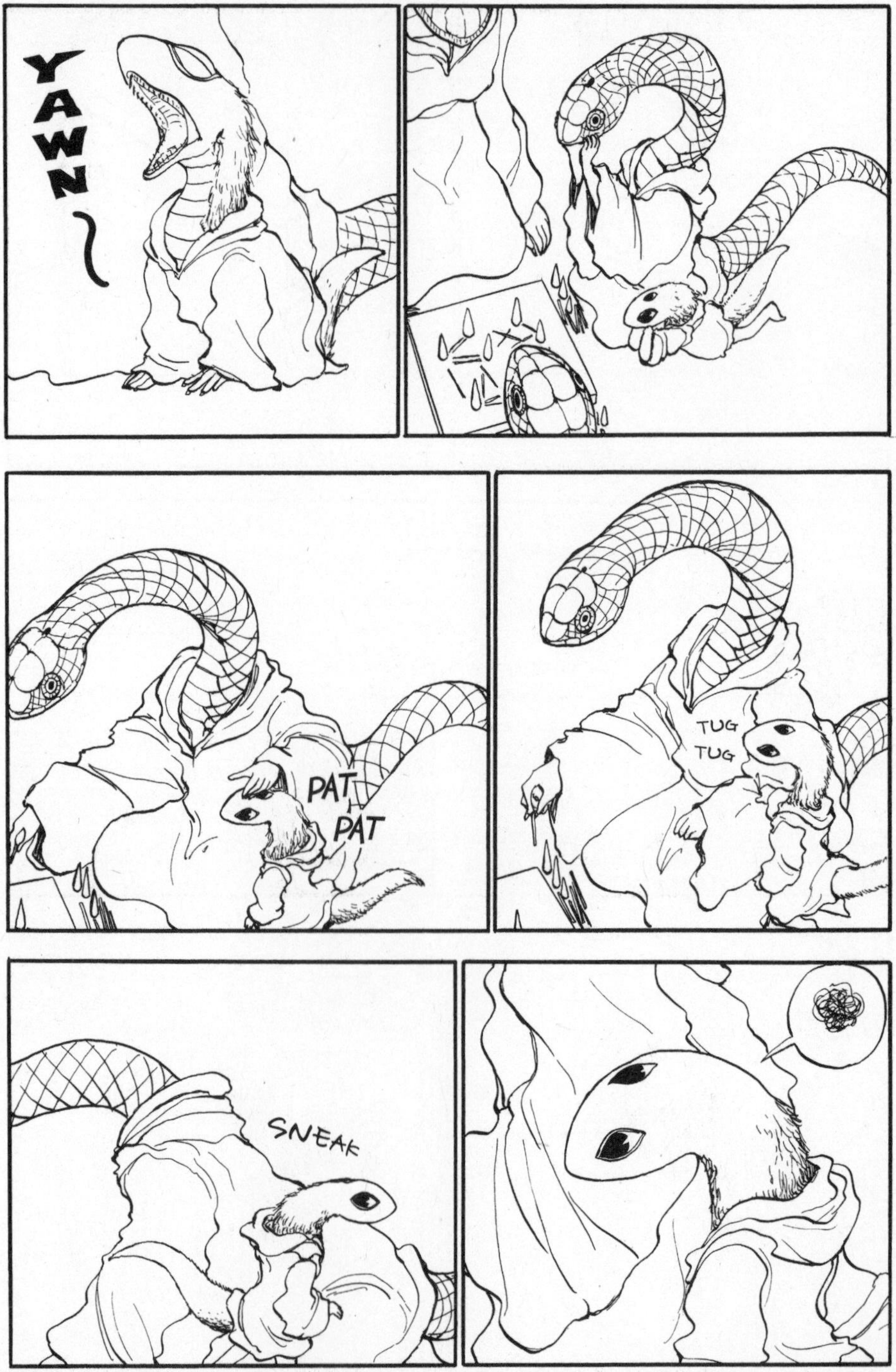
YAWN
TUG TUG
PAT PAT
SNEAK

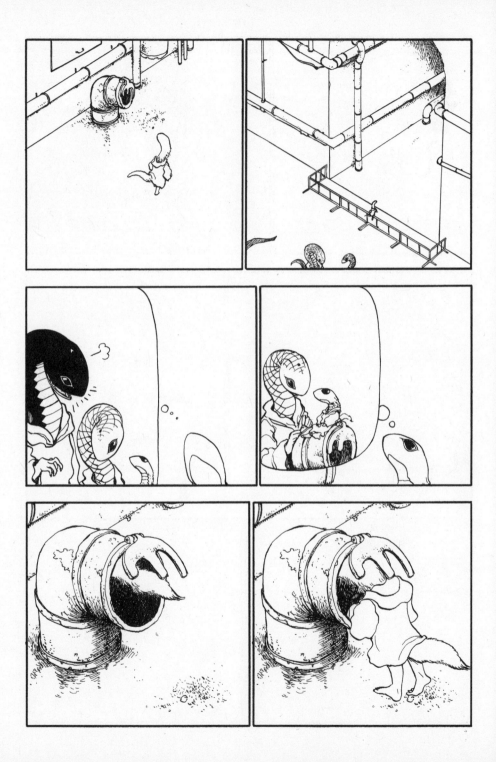

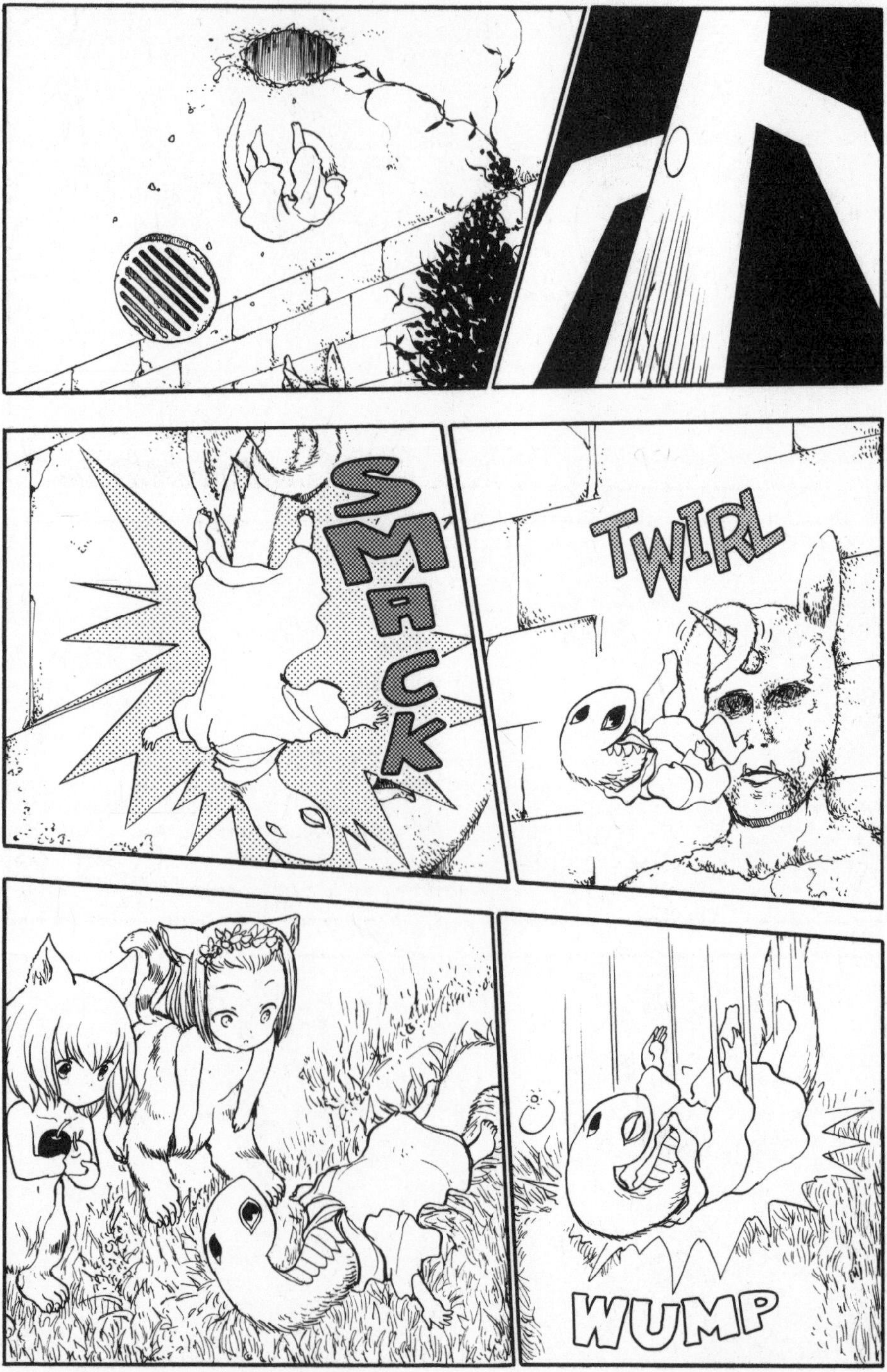
TWIRL
SMACK
WUMP

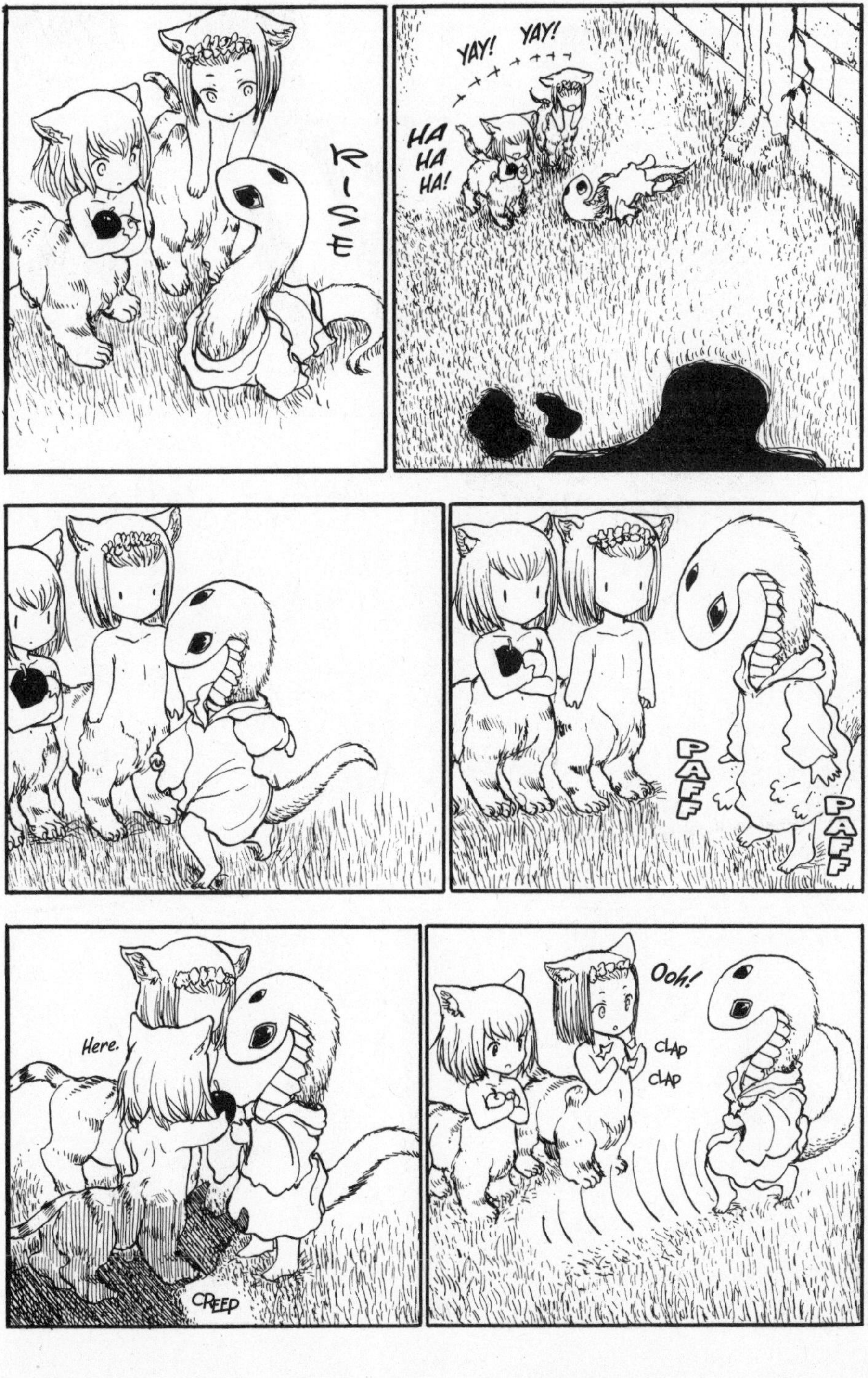
YAY!
YAY!
HA HA HA!
RISE
PAFF
PAFF
Ooh!
CLAP
CLAP
Here.
CREEP

RAWR!!
Came for the girl
HISS!

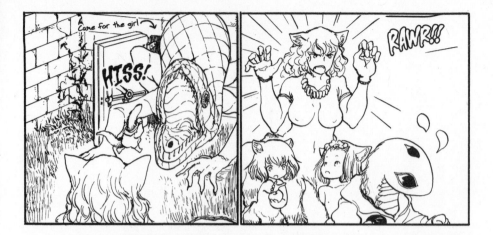

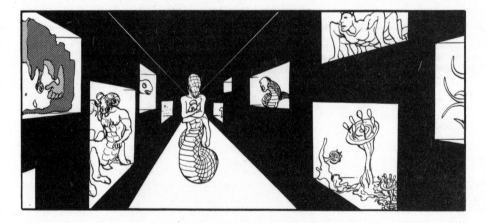

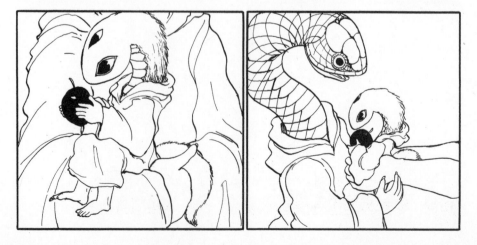

A CentaUr's Life

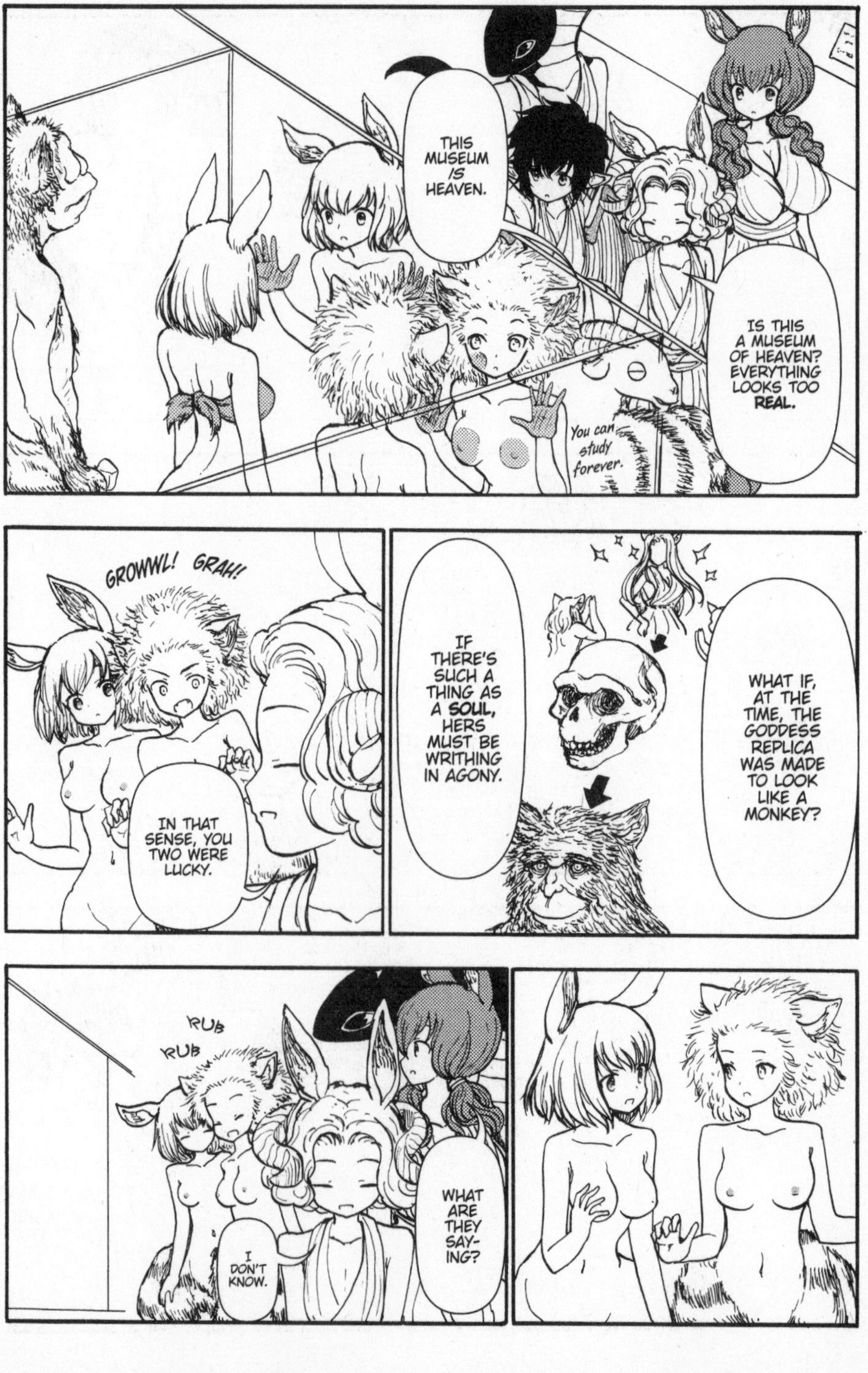
THIS MUSEUM IS HEAVEN.
IS THIS A MUSEUM OF HEAVEN? EVERYTHING LOOKS TOO **REAL.**
You can study forever.
WHAT IF, AT THE TIME, THE GODDESS REPLICA WAS MADE TO LOOK LIKE A MONKEY?
IF THERE'S SUCH A THING AS A **SOUL,** HERS MUST BE WRITHING IN AGONY.
GROWWL! GRAH!
IN THAT SENSE, YOU TWO WERE LUCKY.
WHAT ARE THEY SAYING?
I DON'T KNOW.
RUB
RUB

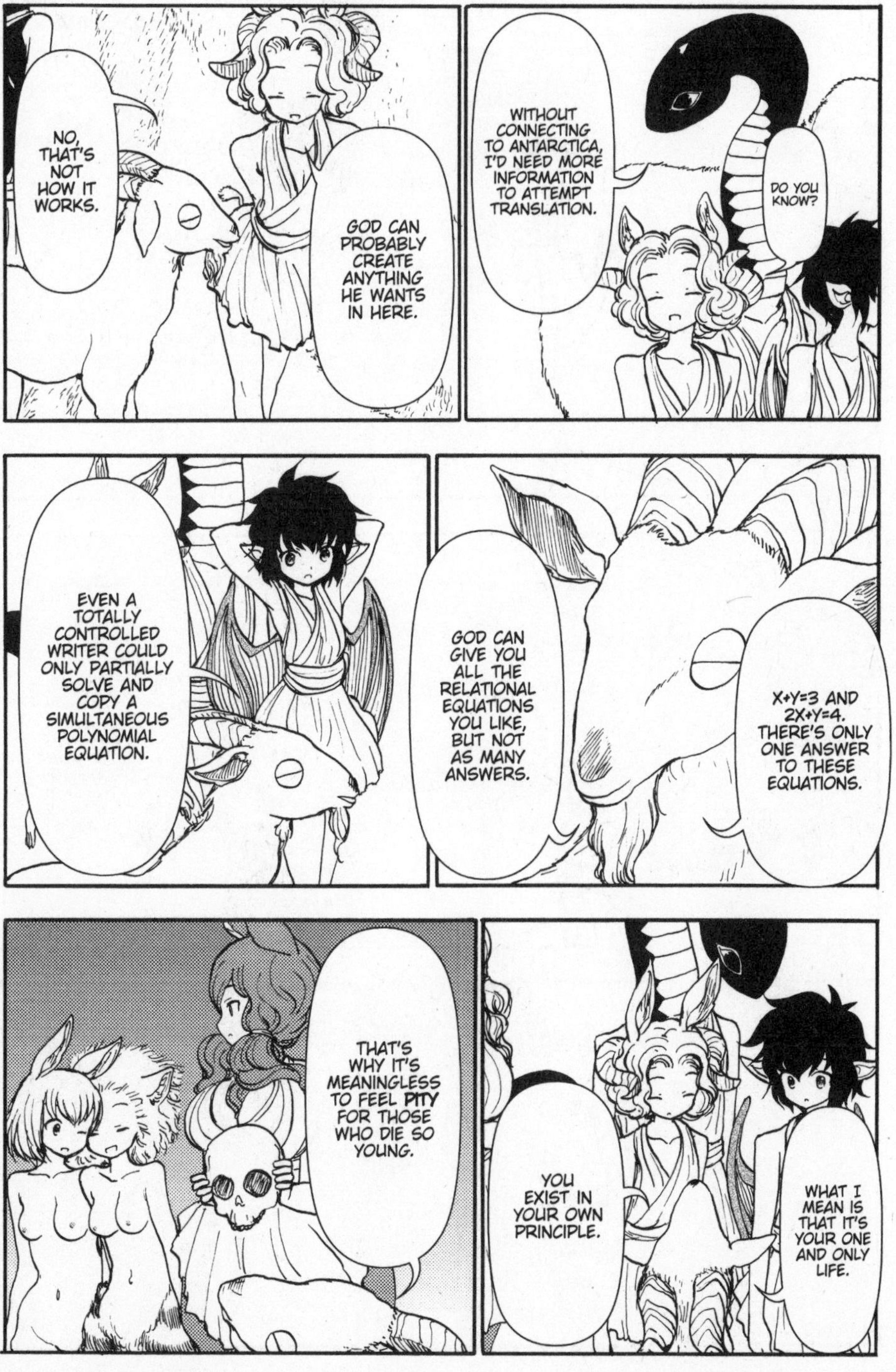
WITHOUT CONNECTING TO ANTARCTICA, I'D NEED MORE INFORMATION TO ATTEMPT TRANSLATION.
DO YOU KNOW?
GOD CAN PROBABLY CREATE ANYTHING HE WANTS IN HERE.
NO, THAT'S NOT HOW IT WORKS.
X+Y=3 AND 2X+Y=4. THERE'S ONLY ONE ANSWER TO THESE EQUATIONS.
GOD CAN GIVE YOU ALL THE RELATIONAL EQUATIONS YOU LIKE, BUT NOT AS MANY ANSWERS.
EVEN A TOTALLY CONTROLLED WRITER COULD ONLY PARTIALLY SOLVE AND COPY A SIMULTANEOUS POLYNOMIAL EQUATION.
WHAT I MEAN IS THAT IT'S YOUR ONE AND ONLY LIFE.
YOU EXIST IN YOUR OWN PRINCIPLE.
THAT'S WHY IT'S MEANINGLESS TO FEEL PITY FOR THOSE WHO DIE SO YOUNG.

SEVEN SEAS ENTERTAINMENT PRESENTS

A Centaur's Life

story and art by KEI MURAYAMA

VOLUME 12

TRANSLATION
Elina Ishikawa

ADAPTATION
Holly Kolodziejczak

LETTERING AND RETOUCH
Jennifer Skarupa

LOGO DESIGN
Courtney Williams

COVER DESIGN
Nicky Lim

PROOFREADER
Patrick King

ASSISTANT EDITOR
Jenn Grunigen

PRODUCTION ASSISTANT
CK Russell

PRODUCTION MANAGER
Lissa Pattillo

EDITOR-IN-CHIEF
Adam Arnold

PUBLISHER
Jason DeAngelis

CENTAUR NO NAYAMI VOLUME 12
© KEI MURAYAMA 2016
Originally published in Japan in 2016 by TOKUMA SHOTEN PUBLISHING
CO., LTD., Tokyo. English translation rights arranged with TOKUMA SHOTEN
PUBLISHING CO., LTD., Tokyo, through TOHAN CORPORATION, Tokyo.

Seven Seas books may be purchased in bulk for promotional, educational, or
business use. Please contact your local bookseller or the Macmillan Corporate
and Premium Sales Department at 1-800-221-7945, extension 5442, or by
e-mail at MacmillanSpecialMarkets@macmillan.com.

Seven Seas and the Seven Seas logo are trademarks of
Seven Seas Entertainment, LLC. All rights reserved.

ISBN: 978-1-626925-09-0

Printed in Canada

First Printing: August 2017

10 9 8 7 6 5 4 3 2 1

FOLLOW US ONLINE: www.gomanga.com

READING DIRECTIONS

This book reads from *right to left*, Japanese style. If
this is your first time reading manga, you start
reading from the top right panel on each page and
take it from there. If you get lost, just follow the
numbered diagram here. It may seem backwards at
first, but you'll get the hang of it! Have fun!!

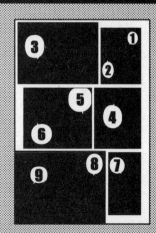